# FAITH STEPS

*Moving toward God
through personal choice
and public policy*

## JONATHAN IMBODY

**LOGION PUBLISHING**
WASHINGTON, DC

**LOGION PUBLISHING**
P.O. Box 16351
Washington, DC 20041
Printed in the United States of America

# Table of Contents

Acknowledgements   v

Introduction   vii

PART ONE: The principle of faith steps   1

Chapter 1: Prodigals or prophets? Christians engaged in public policy   2

Chapter 2: How worldview impacts public policy   15

Chapter 3: Faith steps – Moving toward God   27

PART TWO: How Faith Steps work   33

Chapter 4: A personal journey   34

Chapter 5: How individuals take faith steps   45

Chapter 6: How a nation takes faith steps   57

Chapter 7: How to encourage faith steps toward God   66

PART THREE: Faith Steps in vital issues   74

Chapter 8: Euthanasia and assisted suicide   75

Chapter 9: Sexual risk avoidance   82

Chapter 10: Abortion   93

Chapter 11: Stem cells and human cloning   110

Chapter 12: Human trafficking   121

Chapter 13: Freedom of faith, conscience and speech   141

**PART FOUR:  Government and faith**                                   **163**

**Chapter 14:  Toward a Christian view of government**                 **165**

**Chapter 15:  The "free exercise" of religion**                       **176**

**Chapter 16:  The role of Christians in government**                  **185**

**Chapter 17:  Christ-like in controversy**                            **201**

**Chapter 18:  Reaching a secular culture**                            **211**

**Chapter 19:  Is America too far gone?**                              **223**

**Chapter 20:  Our challenge and opportunity**                         **242**

Index                                                                  252

# *Acknowledgements*

With deep appreciation for the example and encouragement of many intrepid colleagues and friends who daily traipse up and down the halls of power along Pennsylvania Avenue in a vital effort to ensure that our nation lives up to its noble ideals.

Men and women such as Claude Allen, Matt Bowman, Ashley Brannon, Rhett Butler, Stanley Carlson-Thies, Sam Casey, Autumn Christensen, David Christiansen, Kim Colby, Richard Doerflinger, Katie Doherty, Chuck Donovan, Will Estrada, Leslie Ford, Joxel Garcia, Tim Goeglein, Arina Grossu, Jacqueline Halbig Schleppenbach, Cherie Harder, Matthew Hawkins, Katherine Hayley, Valerie Huber, Douglas Johnson, Laura Lederer, Natalie Maki, Nick Manetto, Jennifer Marshall, Connie Marshner, Casey Mattox, Tom McClusky Sr., Lauren McCormack, Steve McFarland, Jeanne Monahan-Mancini, Michael Moses, Mike O'Dea, David Prentice, Anita Smith, Shepherd Smith, Lisa Thompson, Sarah Torre, P. George Tryfiates, Vince Ventimiglia Jr., Brian Walsh, Bill Wichterman, Wendy Wright, Jack and Charmaine Yoest and many others serve on your behalf on the front lines of the culture-shaping battles that determine our future as a nation. May God bless each one of these faithful men and women and equip them with power and love to advance His Kingdom by encouraging individuals and our nation to take Faith Steps.

Special thanks to Erica Reiter, for insights and encouragements during the writing process.

With deepest appreciation for the partnership and encouragement of my wife Amy and our children Bethany, Daniel, Jeanne and David; and with great love and affection for our grandchildren Levi, Vienna and Lia (and any others yet to come).

*God bless you all.*

To **Athanasius** of Alexandria

and all who likewise
dare to stand for Truth,

*contra mundum.*

# Introduction

*F* *aith Steps* begins with the precept that God reveals Himself to each of us–through the created world and through our conscience.

The Scriptures teach that rejecting this revelation darkens our minds (as we reject the truth about ourselves and our world) and hardens our hearts (as we reject the living God who reaches out to us).

The *good* news is that *receiving* and *responding* to God's revelation–by taking moral steps aligned with God's principles–keeps our minds open to His enlightenment and our hearts softened toward Him.

Ultimately these steps in God's direction, this spiritual preparation of our minds and our hearts through the decisions we make, can lead us toward a real relationship with God by His grace, through faith in Jesus Christ.

*Faith Steps* offers guidance in lovingly sharing God's principles, through personal discussions and public policy, by helping others consider how certain choices and behaviors will *harm* them or *help* them.

*Faith Steps* calls followers of Christ to examine, from a biblical and practical viewpoint, God's plan for government and the opportunity and responsibility of His people to reach their neighbors through public policy. This book offers a faith perspective on a host of vital issues from abortion and assisted suicide to stem cell research and human trafficking and more. It also encourages each of us to examine not only how we are presenting our perspectives publicly, but also how consistently we personally mirror the example and commands of Jesus Christ.

God creates every human being in His image. From a public policy standpoint, this means that we honor and protect human life at every stage of development, especially when individuals cannot protect themselves. From a personal standpoint, it means that as God's image-bearers, we need to walk consistently with His principles if the image we reflect is to help others better understand Him.

May God open our eyes, soften our hearts and enlighten our minds so that we may reflect His image and glorify Him in all we are and in all we do.

Jonathan Imbody
Ashburn, Virginia
May 2015

# PART ONE:
## *The principle of faith steps*

# Chapter 1:
# *Prodigals or prophets? Christians engaged in public policy*

*"What therefore you worship as unknown, this I proclaim to you. [God] made from one man every nation of mankind to live on all the face of the earth, having determined allotted periods and the boundaries of their dwelling place, that they should seek God, and perhaps feel their way toward him and find him. Yet he is actually not far from each one of us...."*
–Acts 17:23, 26-27

On a typically sweltering summer day[1] in the nation's capital, a small group of us huddled together quietly at a Starbucks shop a block from the White House. We plotted last-minute strategy for our meeting within the hour in the West Wing.

We would be meeting with President Bush's Domestic Policy Advisor and a fellow believer, Claude Allen. Our topic: human trafficking, an insidious and lucrative form of modern-day slavery that inflicts horrors on millions worldwide, including women and young children trafficked for sex and labor.

What we did not know yet was that earlier that morning, President George W. Bush had called Claude from the president's ranch in Crawford, Texas. The president had charged Claude with heading a White House task force to help address the ravages inflicted by Hurricane Katrina.

The hurricane had ripped through New Orleans with a vengeance the previous day. No one yet knew the full impact of the devastation the hurricane had wrought on the region. It would prove to be the costliest natural disaster in U.S. history. The controversial rebuilding effort would

---

[1] August 30, 2005.

amount to one of the costliest public relations disasters for the Bush administration.

Both President Bush and Claude cared with deep Christian compassion for the people of New Orleans and for all the hurricane's victims. Still, political enemies seized upon perceptions of the president's aloofness as he flew over the city rather than landing there. They accused him of hard-heartedness, even racism.

Some political opponents simply disliked the president's policies; still others hated him intensely for what they perceived as imposing Christian values on a secular nation.

### God and country

A few days later, I attended a service at the National Cathedral, held for victims of the hurricane and featuring an address by the president.

"And in our search we're reminded that God's purposes," President Bush offered, "are sometimes impossible to know here on earth. Yet even as we are humbled by forces we cannot explain, we take comfort in the knowledge that no one is ever stranded beyond God's care. The creator of wind and water is also the source of even a greater power: a love that can redeem the worst tragedy, a love that is stronger than death."[2]

As so often in our nation's history, a U.S. president offered a spiritual perspective to help the country cope in a crisis. Behind the scenes, Christian speechwriters such as Michael Gerson helped craft such messages that comforted a nation from the perspective of the Christian worldview that echoes through our history.

But even the deeply moving, spiritually powerful speeches and hymns that day could not adequately convey the ravaging heartache and misery felt by the battered people of New Orleans. That was something that could only be experienced on the ground.

Scores of Christian relief organizations, churches and ordinary citizen volunteers did just that.

They waded in the muck, they labored and sweated in the sweltering heat and humidity and they put their loving arms around the soul-shocked residents.

A Christian president leading a secular government. Christian organizations fighting human trafficking. Christian volunteers delivering aid

---

[2] "National Day of Prayer: Service at Washington's National Cathedral," CNN transcript, September 16, 2005, http://archives.cnn.com/TRANSCRIPTS/0509/16/se.01.html, accessed January 17, 2014.

for flood victims. What role, if any, did each have in fulfilling what evangelicals refer to as the Great Commission–Jesus' departing command to make disciples of all nations?

> "Go therefore and make disciples of all the nations, baptizing them in the name of the Father and the Son and the Holy Spirit, teaching them to observe all that I commanded you...[3]

Is Christian relief work and public policy involvement a distraction to the Church's evangelistic mission? Should Christians instead focus solely on presenting the *words* of the Gospel as the best way to evangelize and fulfill the Great Commission?

After all, some might argue, when the New Testament lists offices to which God calls Christians–offices such as apostles, prophets, evangelists, pastors and teachers[4]–the list does not include politicians, public policy activists, pro-life advocates, and relief workers.

What about the so-called "separation of Church and state"? Didn't our founders deliberately design a secular state free from religious coddling and meddling?

### Freeing the slaves

Our small group gathered at Starbucks that day might have triggered such objections. But we were not trying to create a theocracy; we were trying to free the slaves. That effort seemed the most natural expression of our Christian faith and a meaningful and worthy use of our positions in the public policy arena.

At our Starbucks huddle, Dr. Joe McIlhaney, a tall and affable Texan, stretched out his long frame under our tiny table. President Bush liked and respected Dr. Joe personally yet had passed him over for Surgeon General, perhaps because of his organization's lightning rod stance on sexual health issues.

Next to Joe sat my friend Dr. Jeff Barrows, a sincere, middle-aged Obstetrician-Gynecologist from a small town in Ohio. Jeff had risen at four that morning from his sleepy little town to start the trek to Capitol Hill, the maniacally paced, cutthroat political center of the nation. Jeff could not have guessed that day that within a few years he would sense God's call to leave his practice, sell his quiet 140-acre homestead, launch a nonprofit ministry and open a group home to shelter prostituted girls.

---

[3] Matthew 28:19-20.

[4] Ephesians 4:11.

Sometimes it's best we don't know God's plans in advance. We might be tempted to do our utmost to avoid them.

Dr. Laura Lederer, a tall, auburn-haired State Department political appointee and veteran combatant of the wars against human trafficking, prostitution and violence against women, rounded out our group. Laura had invited me to the U.S. Department of State months earlier to meet privately, under the radar screen. She wanted to strategize about how the Christian Medical Association, the 16,000-member nonprofit professional medical organization for which I worked, might begin to help address the critical medical issues related to human trafficking.

Studies of rescued sex trafficking victims–mostly women and children who had been prostituted for profit through force, fraud or coercion–had revealed that a high percentage of victims during their captivity had actually visited a healthcare professional for care. Normally captors and pimps keep victims secreted away in the dark and slimy underground world that sex-sick johns frequent. But if a captive sex slave gets sick or injured, the pimp's profits decline.

At that point, the captor likely will take the prostituted woman or child to a health clinic or emergency room. His goal: to repair the human "merchandise" and get her back on the "shelf" where she will be violated and degraded up to dozens of times daily.

Incredibly, the contacts with healthcare professionals cited in the studies had not resulted in the reporting of a single victim.

### Master plan

The medical community's ignorance of human trafficking presented at the same time both a huge deficit and a significant opportunity. The problem was that because many healthcare professionals had never even heard about human trafficking, few knew how to recognize the telltale signs that the patient they were seeing might be a victim. The insistent presence of an unrelated man who spoke for the patient ... bruises or other signs of sexual trauma or battering ... fear or depression ... inability to speak English ... lack of a passport, immigration or identification documentation–the more signs, the more likely the patient was a victim of human trafficking.

The opportunity lay in the fact that if we could educate healthcare professionals and train them to recognize and report victims, authorities could significantly increase rescues and rehabilitation of victims. Besides benefiting victims, an upsurge in numbers rescued could also increase awareness and resources devoted to fighting the scourge.

5

For our West Wing meeting, I had worked up a single-page agenda. Top government officials, I had found after years in government relations, are disinclined to read much more than a single page memo on any single topic. They make big decisions based on big ideas and rely on aides for the details.

The big ideas in our agenda included developing a strategy to conduct medical research to establish the links between human trafficking and prostitution, AIDS, tuberculosis and other communicable diseases. Common sense indicates that when disease-ridden, unprotected sex trafficking victims are forced to have dozens of sexual encounters daily with travelers, such diseases will spread like wildfire. Nevertheless, the medical community does not gives as much credence to common sense as to peer-reviewed, published randomized controlled trials. So generating published studies would prove key to convincing the medical community to engage in human trafficking.

To engage and educate healthcare professionals, I also had developed a plan for the president and the surgeon general to host a White House summit of medical specialty group leaders. At the summit, medical experts would review the data, government agency officials would provide the resources and the president would charge them with the task of developing awareness campaigns to educate their medical members. Hundreds of thousands of physicians and nurses could learn about identifying, reporting and treating human trafficking victims, and at very little cost to the taxpayer.

For the long term, our plan called for establishing a national human trafficking center to provide treatment, research and education, serving as a best practice for others to replicate worldwide.

### Curbing abuses

We also needed a comprehensive anti-prostitution, anti-human trafficking policy across U.S. government agencies. Government officials needed to monitor grant recipients to insure compliance with the anti-prostitution policy and to enforce mandated reporting of victims.

Unfortunately, nongovernment organizations sometimes spend federal grant funds in ways that actually undermine the purpose of the grant. I had learned while serving on federal government grant review panels how organizations can hire high-priced grant writers who know all the buzz words and frequent the Washington watering holes where they conspire with their drinking buddy grant officials. Meanwhile, thousands of smaller, often faith-based organizations that devote their resources to on-the-ground care rather than paying grant writers and lobbyists, come up empty in seeking federal funds to supplement their lifesaving work.

Incredibly, some organizations working in other countries would actually leave sex-trafficked victims enslaved in order to avoid alienating the captors and pimps who had granted them access to the victims for research and health interventions, such as condom distribution and education. We needed to counter the strategy known as "harm reduction," a pervasive view within the medical culture that called for simply treating victims' health symptoms rather than rescuing them.

All that agenda to fit into a one-hour meeting with a man now submerged in a national emergency hurricane relief effort.

### Inside the West Wing

The time came and we strode over to the White House grounds, where the black, wrought-iron gates buzzed opened for us to check in and proceed through Secret Service security checks. Identification badges now slung around our necks, we walked by the bank of network and cable television cameras constantly posted outside the West Wing entrance. Passing under the portico framed by white columns, we turned the brass knob on the familiar, white double doors above which rests the seal of the President of the United States of America.

Through those doors have strode scores of political leaders, foreign dignitaries, news anchors and, thanks to the "We the people" cornerstone of our democratic republic, simple citizens like us.

Although serving as the command center of the most power-laden building in the world, the West Wing actually feels like an old house. The original artwork, of course, sets it off from most houses. But it's not at all difficult to imagine Teddy Roosevelt's or John F. Kennedy's children gleefully romping through the building.

Just inside the West Wing entry, a pair of blue and white alabaster vases sit on tables in the small, cream-colored foyer, which is carpeted in brown. Two small brass sconces and a simple ceiling lamp supplement the natural light from the transom above the double doors, but the room is still dimly lit.

Through an open set of interior double doors into the small, dark reception room, pastoral paintings in golden frames and dark wood doors bespeak the White House's nineteenth-century roots. A sober receptionist greets us, then calls up to the Domestic Policy Council office suite for our escort. The escort leads us through a narrow hallway, up a wooden staircase and past small rooms.

The West Wing houses the Oval Office where the president works, and in many cases, where the president prays. It also houses the Cabinet Room, where President Richard Nixon had installed one of the secret tape recording systems that both symbolized his secretive, scheming tenure in office and helped end it. Those tapes revealed President Nixon telling top aide Charles Colson that the Watergate break-in was "going to be forgotten."

As the scandal unfolded and the prosecution bore down on both him and the president, Colson surrendered his life to Christ. After pleading guilty to obstruction of justice and doing time in prison, where he exchanged advising the president for doing inmates' laundry, Colson launched a worldwide prison ministry.

Chuck Colson impacted politics and culture from a Christian perspective, heading a center for Christian worldview education and the Wilberforce Forum, named after the nineteenth-century Christian abolitionist. Having paid the price for falling prey to the trappings of political power, Colson spoke truth to power, seeing his evangelistic mission as a Christian inextricably intertwined with a biblical mandate to impact culture.

## Political nobody

Unlike Chuck Colson, I was a political nobody, an unlikely visitor to the West Wing. I represented a small nonprofit faith-based organization that had only begun a few years prior to speak out on public policy issues. Yet our organization seemed providentially designed to fill a crucial gap within the pro-life community, providing credible medical evidence and physicians to speak from a scientific and ethical platform on abortion, assisted suicide and other bioethical issues.

After a few years of dangling our organizational toes in the public policy waters, I had sensed a compelling call to move to Washington, DC. I told our CEO, Dr. David Stevens, that I was prepared to move my family there and commute on weekends to and from our Bristol, TN headquarters, six hours south. I knew that I had to be in Washington one way or another, even though I had little idea what lay in store for me in the nation's capital.

Ironically, unlike the call I sensed to engage in public policy, during my years in seminary I had never sensed the more traditional call to enter church ministry. I had thought that seminary would help me determine whether to serve the Lord either on the mission field or in the local church.

Instead, my time in seminary helped me determine to do neither. I had figured that no one in his right mind should pursue the pastorate or missionary service *apart* from God's call, since both careers pose enough people problems and spiritual attacks to drive a sane man loopy.

### Sacred v. secular?

Prior to attending seminary, our pastor's wife had remarked upon learning of our interest in attending seminary and perhaps serving on the mission field, "Ah–that's the highest calling."

This pastor's wife probably believed that axiom in large part because the culture of our denomination at the time–the Christian & Missionary Alliance–had elevated "sacred" missionary service so far beyond "secular" professions that a missionary's work seemed immensely superior. Sometimes lost in the adulation of "official" ministers is God's calling of the rest of us to ambassadorial roles in our families, communities and country.

In fact, I had given my life to Christ while a sophomore at Penn State University, after hearing a Bible study lesson delivered by a football player, about how God calls us all to serve as ambassadors for Christ:

> Therefore, we are ambassadors for Christ, as though God were entreating through us; we beg you on behalf of Christ, be reconciled to God.[5]

For years after seminary, instead of serving as a pastor or missionary, I advanced the evangelistic mission of the Church in a supportive role, promoting Christian colleges and other ministries through public relations, marketing and fundraising. I served on the faculty and in the administration of a Christian college. I operated a business providing marketing services to Christian ministries.

I also spent a couple years writing for evangelist and Samaritan's Purse relief organization leader Franklin Graham. I highly valued the relief work ministry and liked and respected Franklin, but I finally realized that he didn't so much need a writer as a stenographer. He dictated newsletters and, for that matter, most of what happened in the organization.

So I jumped at the chance to help advance the Christian Medical Association with a colleague, a physician who had left Graham's ministry to lead the then 7,000-member Christian Medical Association (CMA).

### Ambassador to Washington, DC

Within a few years, membership in the CMA doubled. Speaking out publicly on public policy and life issues may have driven away a few members who disdained public policy engagement as a distraction, but Christian physicians who welcomed a voice for their values joined the organization in droves.

---

[5] 2 Corinthians 5:20

With doors opening wide in the media and political arenas, God seemed to be clearly calling the organization to articulate life-affirming public policies–a mission best advanced by establishing a presence in the nation's capital. That led to my reassignment to Washington, DC. Within a week after moving to Washington in August 2000, I found myself in Senate Majority Leader Don Nickles' ornate office in the U.S. Capitol, plotting strategy to pass a bill outlawing assisted suicide. God was opening doors.

After the election of November 2000, the doors to high-level public policy officials swung open even wider, as pro-life President George W. Bush set about using the political process to rebuild a culture of life. President Bush seemed to understand that while politics alone cannot long override a culture, public policy can help encourage a culture in a certain direction. And at least for the present in our democratic republic, Christians enjoy the privilege of impacting public policy and consequently, encouraging our culture to make good choices.

## For such a time as this

As my human trafficking issue colleagues and I climbed the West Wing stairs to President Bush's Domestic Policy Advisor's office, I keenly appreciated the fact that the God of Moses, Daniel and Esther had called us, for such a time as this, to advance His kingdom in the halls of power. I find that an awareness of His providence actually takes the pressure off high-level meetings. The God who called you is the God who will enable you to accomplish whatever purpose He has determined.

It also helps to remember that people at the highest levels of power, men and women with exceptional talents and character, are still just people. Presidents, senators, cabinet members and ambassadors all share the same needs, frailties and humanity that you and I do. That realization can facilitate focusing not just on achieving political objectives but also on opportunities to minister to others, as would occur this morning in our meeting with Claude Allen.

We entered the Domestic Policy Council office area and passed by aides working at desks in the hallway. Every inch of space in the White House is premium real estate, and no one serves there for the sake of spacious or luxurious offices.

Some staff quietly watched a television, tuned to Fox News, that showed the devastation and stunned victims of Hurricane Katrina in New Orleans. Soon those staff would be engaging those victims virtually, by facilitating the federal rescue and resources the victims needed to begin rebuilding their lives.

Our host, Claude Allen, greeted us with his typical warmth and graciousness. As an African-American with blue collar roots, Claude transcended tacit boundaries of race and class with uncommon initiative and industry. Attracted to the Republic Party's stance on individual responsibility and individual rights, Claude served as an aide to the iconic conservative southern senator Jesse Helms of North Carolina, who earlier in his career had opposed busing, the Civil Rights Act and the Voting Rights Act. After obtaining a law degree from the Duke University School of Law, Claude met up with a mentor in Clarence Thomas, a person of faith who had wended his way to the top of American public policy as a Supreme Court justice.

As Secretary of Health and Human Resources for the Commonwealth of Virginia and later as Deputy Secretary of the U.S. Department of Health and Human Services, Claude did not shy away from controversy. He promoted teen abstinence education programs, an approach recognized by Christians as biblical and by a few intrepid researchers–those who dared to challenge their politically correct colleagues–as the most medically effective strategy for the prevention of sexually transmitted infections and diseases.

After President Bush appointed Claude to head his Domestic Policy Council at the White House, I connected with Claude in the fight against human trafficking. I coordinated a letter, signed by over 100 organizations and experts, to support the administration's stance that recipients of federal anti-trafficking funds could not promote or condone prostitution.

That stance may seem a no-brainer to most Americans, but a slew of radical leftist groups opposed the policy and even launched a lawsuit to stop it. The Bush administration stood firm on the policy, which would prevail until the Obama administration later sided with the radicals.

### *Mapping anti-slavery strategy*

As we sat down in Claude's office to begin our meeting, after an exchange of pleasantries, he explained the President's call and his new assignment to head the White House task force on the hurricane relief efforts. We launched into our topic.

Claude immediately took up on the idea of a White House summit to engage the medical community in building awareness of human trafficking, saying the event should take place soon. The summit would include a surgeon general's call to action. Events involving the president often required what aides refer to as a "deliverable"–the announcement of a notable new action, policy or funding venture. At our summit, the deliverable would be the announcement of the new national center for victims, research and education.

We discussed the need for much more data from medical studies of victims. The paucity of peer-reviewed articles threatened to inhibit the medical community's responsiveness. We agreed that Drs. Barrows and McIlhaney would oversee a review of existing data with an eye to developing new studies on the linkage between human trafficking, prostitution and HIV-AIDS. The studies would document evidence to back up common sense–that prostitution through sex trafficking fuels AIDS and other sexually transmitted infections and diseases, and thus poses a public health threat as well as harm to the victims.

Potential funding sources for contractors to do the research would include federal agencies such as USAID's Global Health, headed by fellow believer Dr. Kent Hill; the Office of the Global AIDS Coordinator, headed by our friend Dr. Mark Dybul, a homosexual physician who braved his community's ire for promoting the health benefits of sexual risk avoidance (abstinence) education; and the Global Fund to Fight AIDS, Tuberculosis and Malaria, where Bill Steiger of the US Department of Health and Human Services was working hard to ensure fairer consideration of faith-based organizations for grants.

We identified several researchers who could get the ball rolling in documenting the evidence. Claude checked off a list of agency leaders he would enlist in the effort, including Centers for Disease Control and Prevention (CDC) director Dr. Julie Gerberding.

How God directs decisions and knits together events for His purposes, I thought.

### Bucking the brethren

Some evangelical leaders at Focus on the Family and other groups had unsuccessfully leaned heavily on me to get our organization to publicly oppose Dr. Gerberding's presidential nomination to head the CDC. I had considered the evidence of Dr. Gerberding's ideological leanings inconclusive, and stopping the nomination seemed unrealistic. I also didn't see much benefit in publicly undermining a president who had taken abuse from our mutual opponents for advancing our shared goal of building a culture of life.

There are times to oppose a friendly administration's policies and nominees, but this didn't seem one of them. In politics you want to choose your battles carefully. Such public opposition can also make evangelical leaders seem perpetually angry and combative, known more for what we oppose than for what we support.

Preparing now for a meeting in which we hoped to prevail upon Dr. Gerberding to take up our cause in fighting human trafficking, the decision to withhold our organization's public censure of her appointment certainly seemed prudential–perhaps providential.

Claude and our group agreed that I would draft a detailed plan and invitation list for the White House summit. I would also draft the agenda for our meeting with CDC Director Gerberding.

We agreed to continue developing plans for the national center, possibly involving a partnership between the government and faith-based organizations. Our plan envisioned a holistic, multi-disciplinary approach to victims that addressed their medical, psychological, financial, occupational and even spiritual needs. Medical doctors, psychologists and social workers would staff the center. If run by faith-based organizations, programs could include opportunities for victims to choose whether to voluntarily participate in spiritual counseling and ministry.

As we drew our meeting to a close, I asked Claude if we could pray for him. I knew from previous discussions with Claude that he and his family attended the vibrant Covenant Life Church in Gaithersburg, Md., pastored for 27 years by C.J. Mahaney. CJ's mind-renewing guest preaching and teaching ministry at Penn State University in 1976 had helped establish my own new walk of faith.

I prayed not only for God to enable and empower Claude's public policy work and his new task of coordinating the White House's hurricane relief task force, but also for God's protection and blessing on his family. We concluded our prayer and left the White House energized and with plans in hand, eager to fulfill our "great commission."

I prayed for Claude specifically for his family because I knew that the incredible demands of White House service can chew up the best family man, and our spiritual enemy loves few things better than to destroy Christian marriages and families. In fact, a number of the high-profile officials and politician believers for whom I prayed at private meetings– including Claude–subsequently watched their careers crash and burn in the heat of ethical scandals of their own making.

One of these friends confided to me later that the aura of power in high places can intoxicate one with a sense of invincibility, providing the enemy with ample opportunity for temptations and swift tumbles from heights of pride. Thankfully, God can use such fiery falls from grace to disabuse us of deception and replace pride and self with humility and divine power.

## Questions

The leadership of Christian believers during the Bush presidency, our efforts to combat human trafficking through faith-based organizations, and Christian volunteers and ministries responding in the wake of Hurricane Katrina serve to illustrate Christians' engagement in the public square. The examples also help frame important questions about the biblical and prudential role of believers and the Church in politics and society:

*What role, if any, should Christians play in influencing our government and our culture?*

*Does God call Christians to separate from the world for the sake of spiritual purity, or does He call us to engage the world for the sake of others?*

*Does shunning engagement in the public square preserve the Church's resources for the Great Commission, or is cultural isolationism a Great Omission?*

*Is America too far gone in the direction of secularism for Christian influence to turn her toward godly principles?*

*Since God is in control of history and we know how it all ends, does public policy really even matter?*

To begin to answer these questions, we first must understand how our worldview drives our moral values, our laws and our lives–and how to take faith steps toward God and His kingdom.

# Chapter 2:
# *How worldview impacts public policy*

*"I have set before you life and death, the blessing and the curse.
So choose life in order that you may live, you and your descendants,
by loving the LORD your God, by obeying His voice,
and by holding fast to Him...."*
–Deuteronomy 30:19-20

Comity seldom graces Washington. Polls show that many Americans see partisanship escalating rather than mellowing.[1]

Why does partisanship so dominate American politics? Americans no longer share the same *worldview*–the way we understand the world and our role in it.

As my friend Nancy Pearcey explains in her book, *Total Truth,*

A worldview is like a mental map that tells us how to navigate the world effectively. It is the imprint of God's objective truth on our inner life. We might say that each of us carries a model of the universe inside our heads that tells us what the world is like and how we should live in it.

German Romanticism developed the idea that cultures are complex wholes, where a certain outlook on life, or spirit of the age, is expressed across the board-in art, literature, and social institutions as well as in formal philosophy. The best way to understand the products of any culture, then, is to grasp the underlying worldview being expressed.[2]

While secular worldviews change with time, Nancy explains that Christian thinkers such as the Dutch theologian Abraham Kuyper articulated

---

[1] "Partisan Politics: "Voters Don't See Much Bipartisanship in Washington, D.C.,"
Rasmussen, October 17, 2013,
http://www.rasmussenreports.com/public_content/politics/mood_of_america/partisan_politics,
accessed January 18, 2014.
[2] Nancy Pearcey, *Total Truth,* (Wheaton, IL: Crossway Books, 2004), 23.

the concept of a constant, unchanging Christian worldview based on Scripture:

> They argued that Christians cannot counter the spirit of the age in which they live unless they develop an equally comprehensive biblical worldview-an outlook on life that gives rise to distinctively Christian forms of culture-with the important qualification that it is not merely the relativistic belief of a particular culture but is based on the very Word of God, true for all times and all places.[3]

A worldview holds a set of internal values and responses to questions about what's right, what's wrong, and if there even is a right and a wrong. Christians hold a worldview based on the truth that God exists and that He created us in His image.

Just imagine how your perspective would change without those assumptions. Welcome to the modern mindset.

The Christian worldview is based on the fact that God reveals Himself and His principles to us–through His natural creation and our consciences; through His written Word, the Scriptures; and through the incarnate Word, Jesus Christ.

God in His perfection does not change; He is *immutable*. His truth does not change–it remains constant and absolute.

Orthodox Christians understand that God's truth is objective. The Merriam-Webster Dictionary defines "objective" as "expressing or dealing with facts or conditions as perceived without distortion by personal feelings, prejudices, or interpretations." God's truth remains outside of ourselves and remains true no matter what we feel or think about it. It applies equally to everyone.

We did not create God's truth and we cannot change it. We have no right to make up alternatives to His truth. We do not stand in judgment of His truth. In fact, God's truth, His principles, stand in judgment of us.

This fundamental understanding of absolute truth and universally applicable, self-evident moral standards drove the development of Western law and the American Constitution. Our founders expressed this worldview in the Declaration of Independence:

> We hold these Truths to be self-evident, that all Men are created equal, that they are endowed by their Creator with certain unalienable Rights….

---

[3] Pearcey, *Total Truth*, 24.

## "The times, they are a'changin'"

Over the past several decades, however, the influence of the formerly consensus Judeo-Christian worldview on American values and public policy has been declining. When a democratic country lacks consensus, politics form a battlefield for competing worldviews.

The "Greatest Generation" that won World War II largely subscribed to religious morals and orthodoxy, homogeneity, and institutions. The American Way paralleled Christian teaching in significant respects–such as the value placed on personal virtue, justice, hard work and compassion. Children praying in school or singing Christmas carols seemed consistent with a society that blended the Christian faith with American culture as "one nation under God."

In the sixties, however, Baby Boomers revolted against such traditions by experimenting spiritually and sexually and also by accentuating individuality. Ideas expressed in catchphrases like "Turn on, tune in, drop out," "Make love–not war," and "Power to the people" permeated the hip new culture.

Folk singer Bob Dylan captured the revolutionary spirit in a song:
```
The line it is drawn,
The curse it is cast.
The slow one now
Will later be fast,
As the present now
Will later be past.
The order is rapidly fadin'
And the first one now will later be last,
For the times they are a-changin'.⁴
```
Successive generations, taking cues from a culture "liberated" of restraints, trended even more radically toward antinomianism, hedonism and narcissism, as personified in pop culture headliners such as Eminem, Madonna and Paris Hilton.

The driving cultural forces within our country–education, science, the arts, philosophy, the news and entertainment industry and social media– accelerated these successive shifts away from traditional and Judeo-Christian values. Educators adopted supposedly "values-free" curricula that replaced absolute truth with relativistic assumptions. Creation-denying scientists advanced a randomistic, evolutionary dogma that drained life of spiritual and moral meaning.

---

[4] Bob Dylan, "The Times They Are A-Changin'," copyright 1963, 1964 by Warner Bros. Inc.; renewed 1991, 1992 by Special Rider Music. All Rights Reserved. Used by permission.

17

Artists likewise continued to move away from God and His creation and toward meaninglessness, replacing realism and beauty with abstract expressionism dripping with despair. Philosophers, rejecting the theism of their philosophical forebears, despaired of the search for truth and espoused nihilism.

The news media exchanged the traditional ideal of objectivity for advocacy and entertainment, joining Hollywood's campaign for liberal social policies and the assault on Christian morality. The Internet and social media like Facebook, YouTube and blogs opened doors for literally everyone to espouse an opinion without the institutional intermediaries that had tended to preserve the status quo.

A lot changes when a worldview shifts.

The Gallup polling firm notes that "one major trend that is clear from Gallup's and other organizations' surveys is the increase in the percentage of Americans who do not have a formal religious identity."[5]

A Barna poll found that half of American adults "agreed that Christianity is no longer the faith that Americans automatically accept as their personal faith."[6]

For some, this has meant simply relief from putting on the pretense of faith for purposes of social acceptability. But others have left the church because their Christian worldview has been swept away by the tsunami of secular attacks on Christian assumptions and values.

The bottom line is that more and more Americans today are eschewing the American religious institutions that in the past inculcated a consensus faith-based worldview. That shift has profound implications for public policy as well as personal living.

## When worldviews clash

If someone has deserted the Christian worldview—namely, that God created us and reveals Himself and His truth through nature and His Word— then that person is not left with much to go on. If we do not receive truth from God, the only option remaining is to *make up our own worldview*.

---

[5] "Christianity Remains Dominant Religion in the United States," Gallup, December 23, 2011, http://www.gallup.com/poll/151760/Christianity-Remains-Dominant-Religion-United-States.aspx, accessed January 18, 2014.
[6] "Christianity Is No Longer Americans' Default Faith," Barna, https://www.barna.org/barna-update/article/12-faithspirituality/15-christianity-is-no-longer-americans-default-faith#.UtrahyMo5aQ, accessed January 18, 2014.

If we are each making up our own truth, each arriving at different conclusions, what do we do when our individually made-up worldviews conflict?

One of two things can happen: *coexistence* or *domination*.

Conflicting worldviews may coexist in tension for a time, especially if the holders of the worldview are willing to compromise with holders of conflicting worldviews. Key to such coexistence is the assumption, aggressively enforced if necessary, that all worldviews are *equally valid*.

After all–the unspoken assumption goes–if we each are making up our own worldviews, who is anyone to say that their worldview is superior to another's? On what basis could anyone possibly make such a claim?

If we claim our worldview is superior on the basis of logic and reason, then someone who sees life as random and meaningless will say, "What are logic and reason but your own vain constructions?"

If we say our worldview is superior because it is based on respect for others, then someone will say, "Fine–while you respect others, I will conquer and subjugate you to my will, for my worldview boils down to this: survival of the fittest."

Who will referee this dizzying mix of vastly differing worldviews?

No one. Since there are no objective rules in our self-made worlds, there can be no referee. How can you referee without a rulebook?

When everyone makes up his or her own worldview, only one alternative universal ethic remains: *autonomy*. Literally, self-law. A society based on autonomy boils down to, "If you let me do my thing, I will let you do yours." Sound familiar?

Unfortunately for modern America, autonomy–self-rule–is a grossly ineffective foundation for a society.

The trouble with adopting *autonomy* as the only guiding "rule" is that while compromise and avoidance may work for a while, conflicting worldviews inevitably produce an *irreconcilable conflict*. By definition, autonomy is utterly incapable of resolving an irreconcilable conflict. The rule of autonomy can only avoid judgment; it cannot make a judgment.

For example, let's say that my worldview uncompromisingly values trees as possessing the same inherent value as humans, as such worthy of protection. (Like many modern worldviews, this post-Christian manufactured worldview still hangs on to vestiges of the Christian worldview, such as the notion that human beings have inherent worth.) On the other hand, you see trees as just one more meaningless organism in a closed system of meaningless molecules. You just want to cut them down to use the wood to build houses.

19

Obviously, both of these worldviews cannot occupy the same space and each achieve their aims. Apart from compromise–which our stubbornly held made-up worldviews and self-centered personal nature will not allow–one of us will lose and the other will win. In such a case, the worldview held by the strongest and most dominant group or individual will prevail over competitors. You will end up either with dense forests or dense suburbs.

## How worldview impacts human trafficking policy

One issue in our fight against human trafficking provides a case study illustrating the contrast and clash of secular versus Christian worldviews.

As my good friend Lisa Thompson, an expert on sex trafficking and pornography, has explained, "Sex trafficking is a battle of ideas. The Church in America too often does not do enough to address the ideology upon which sex trafficking is based–an ideology that disassociates sex from love, responsibility and children."[7]

Although the fight against human trafficking generally is marked by bipartisan cooperation, the concord breaks down and the conflict of worldviews comes into focus as soon as the notions of "choice" and "autonomy" arise.

Some even within the human trafficking-battling community have come to believe that many prostituted women and girls are not victims but that they have actually *chosen* prostitution as a legitimate career. They find it difficult if not impossible to condemn prostitution as morally wrong. On what basis could they do so? Without objective moral standards, such as the Judeo-Christian Scriptures, who really can say what is right or wrong for someone else?

Debbie Nathan, writing in the liberal magazine, *The Nation*, advocates for the choice view of prostitution, insisting that "most immigrants who work as prostitutes do so voluntarily."

As proof, she offers a quote from a San Francisco AIDS worker who asserts, "I've never met a Thai woman smuggled in for sex work who didn't know that's what she'd be coming here to do."[8] By this theory, all those women voluntarily placed themselves as slaves under the control of violent criminals, for the very purpose of subjecting themselves to a lifestyle of daily rape, degradation and abuse.

---

[7] "To Fight Sex Trafficking, Fight the Ideology That Creates It, Expert Says," *Christian Post*, Feb. 25, 2015, http://www.christianpost.com/news/to-fight-sex-trafficking-fight-the-ideology-that-creates-it-expert-says-90694/ accessed Feb. 8, 2014.

[8] Debbie Nathan, "Oversexed," *The Nation*, Aug. 29, 2005, http://www.thenation.com/article/oversexed?page=ful, accessed Feb. 8, 2014.

Nathan also attempts to minimize research and statistics related to sex trafficking in her quest to undermine the focus on fighting the trade. Why would someone want to do that? One can only guess, but one explanation is that her worldview cannot accommodate the traditional view of sex as a sacred gift from God reserved for marriage. If sex has no moral implications, then neither does selling sex.

Such a worldview casts us not as created beings dependent upon and answerable to God but instead as autonomous, self-determining beings free to do whatever we want. If sex feels good, I do it. If I have to walk over you to reach my goal, I do it. When we make up our own rules with no referee, the ethic most likely to ensue boils down to "doing whatever it takes to get what I want."

To insist, then, that sex is not merely a natural instinct but a moral issue threatens the entire way such a person sees the world–their whole foundation for their beliefs and behavior.

Small wonder that Nathan seems especially antagonistic toward Christians and anyone else who dares to challenge her apparently Darwinian view of sex. Writing about groups that lobbied for the passage of the landmark Trafficking Victims Protection Act, she fumes,

> "On one side were evangelical Christians, with their typical fears of foreigners, leftists and sex-and their morbid fascination with forced prostitution, even though more people may be forced to pick broccoli than to rent out their genitals. Then there were feminists whose concern about the exploitation of women-like the evangelicals'-also fixated on commercial sex."[9]

I suppose one could say worse things about the faith community than that we focus on fighting sex trafficking.

## Who would choose subjection to rape and violence?

Many Christians fight sex trafficking not because of a "morbid fascination" but because of a worldview that any form of prostitution is an inherently evil, abusive scourge that exploits, enslaves and robs precious individuals of their God-given value. Prostitution wrongly rips sex away from the marriage relationship, where God designed it to provide cementing bonds of love and to create children.

No one willingly chooses a lifestyle of rape, violence, death and disease except under coercion by individuals or circumstances, under deceit or fraud,

---

[9] Ibid.

or out of sheer ignorance of the horrific consequences of prostitution. Even in the absence of direct force, fraud or coercion, many individuals end up prostituted as an indirect result of causes they had no control over, such as sexual abuse and extreme poverty. Others, such as runaway teens, sell sex for money, food or drugs, thinking of it as a casual pragmatic proposition and not realizing the grip and terrible toll it will take on them.

As prostitution researcher Melissa Farley has noted,

"Survivors of prostitution have described it as 'volunteer slavery' and as 'the choice made by those who have no choice.' No other 'employment' has comparable rates of physical assault, rape, and homicide except for war combat."[10]

Not surprisingly, these vastly different worldviews make huge differences regarding public policy on sex trafficking and prostitution.

Those who hold a "choice and autonomy" view of prostitution–which they legitimize by relabeling it as "sex work"–do so because they consider the ultimate ethic to be *autonomy*.

Absent God and His revealed truth and morality, what else is left?

As with all worldviews, the "choice and "autonomy" stance yields practical consequences. It becomes difficult, if not impossible, to justify *rescuing* prostituted girls and women who may have "chosen" the sex work profession. So instead, individuals and groups driven by the "choice and autonomy" worldview focus instead on simply mitigating the physical dangers incurred through sex trafficking and other forms of prostitution.

Melissa Farley nails the coffin on the dangerous fallacy of this misguided approach:

Health organizations can be lethally complicit with pimps and johns when they promote safe sex negotiation but at the same time fail to see that when she asks a john to use a condom she can get killed.[11]

---

[10] Melissa Farley, "Unequal," personal paper, © Melissa Farley, August 30, 2005, Prostitution Research & Education, San Francisco California, www.prostitutionresearch.com used with permission. See also Melissa Farley PhD, Ann Cotton PsyD, Jacqueline Lynne MSW, Sybille Zumbeck PhD, Frida Spiwak PhD, Maria E. Reyes PhD, Dinorah Alvarez BA and Ufuk Sezgin PhD, "Prostitution and Trafficking in Nine Countries: An Update on Violence and Posttraumatic Stress Disorder," *Journal of Trauma Practice*, Volume 2, Issue 3-4, 2004, pp. 33-74.
[11] Ibid.

## "Choice and autonomy" worldview cannot confront evil

As noted, the "choice and autonomy" godless worldview spawns a harm reduction approach to sex trafficking–handing out condoms, negotiating with pimps, lobbying for better working conditions. This effete approach parallels that taken by choice and autonomy believers in educating teens about sex. If sex outside marriage is not *wrong* (without Truth, who can say what is right or wrong?), then it becomes simply a matter of choice and autonomy. Totally bereft of any reason to convince teens to wait, sex education focuses on trying to merely reduce rather than *avoid* the harm.

A worldview based on the flimsy ethic of choice and autonomy permits nothing more than such a hands-off approach. Even a harm reduction approach skirts the boundaries of violating absolute individual autonomy–by potentially pushing harm reduction on someone who doesn't ask for it.

A severe problem that arises trying to implement an "autonomy and choice" worldview is that it cannot draw a bright line between choice and compulsion. While harm reduction model advocates might publicly condemn human trafficking, such a condemnation may prove practically ineffectual.

How can they effectively distinguish sex trafficking victims enslaved in brothels from those they would consider voluntary "sex workers? Coerced and tortured human trafficking victims have been trained through intimidation and violence to say whatever they are told to say, in order to protect their captors. Additionally, the Stockholm Syndrome–a psychological condition that can cause captives to actually come to see their captors as benefactors–will even cause some rescued victims to "choose" to run right back to their pimps.

Are they all "choosing" prostitution?

Contrast this confusing dilemma with the clear vision and mission of those with an unobscured worldview of prostitution as a moral injustice and inherently evil. They can focus on rescuing victims, prosecuting captors and pimps as criminals and unapologetically pursuing absolute abolition.

While contrasting the practical effects of worldviews, I do not suggest that harm reduction advocates care little for victims, but rather that their strategy, however well-intentioned, is fundamentally inappropriate and ineffective.

The harm reduction strategy arising from the choice and autonomy worldview just doesn't pass what I call the "daughter test."

The "daughter test" is simple. If your daughter were being prostituted, raped, infected and abused to the point of violence or death, would you supply condoms and negotiate with her pimp for better working conditions, or would you focus on rescuing her and bringing her captors to justice?

23

## Judicial worldviews: Rule of law or reign of power?

The impact of worldview extends far beyond the realm of human trafficking. Worldview potentially impacts virtually every law, regulation and policy. Whether one begins with God and His revealed truth or with autonomous man impacts the *rule of law* on which our society rests–and now totters.

The rule of law, as contrasted with the rule of a sovereign, traces back to the ancient Greeks. In his last book, *Laws,* Plato wrote,

> And when I call the rulers servants or ministers of the law, I give them this name not for the sake of novelty, but because I certainly believe that upon such service or ministry depends the well- or ill-being of the state. For that state in which the law is subject and has no authority, I perceive to be on the highway to ruin; but I see that the state in which the law is above the rulers, and the rulers are the inferiors of the law, has salvation, and every blessing which the Gods can confer."[12]

Aristotle emphasized,

> It is more proper that law should govern than any one of the citizens: upon the same principle, if it is advantageous to place the supreme power in some particular persons, they should be appointed to be only guardians, and the servants of the laws.[13]

An alarming number of American judges today, however, are undermining the rule of law by viewing the U.S. Constitution as a flexible, "living" document, bendable by successive generations to suit changing values and preferences. Such a view is patently inconsistent with justice and the rule of law, which hinges on the impartial application of statutes as determined not by opinion or preference but by objective words and legislative history.

As Supreme Court Justice Antonin Scalia asserts, "I take the words as they were promulgated to the people of the United States, and what is the fairly understood meaning of those words."[14] Such an originalist view of the Constitution is buttressed, even made possible, by the conviction that

---

[12] Plato, *Laws,* translated by Benjamin Jowett, public domain Kindle book, location 5165.
[13] Aristotle, *Politics* 3.16. See http://en.wikipedia.org/wiki/Rule_of_law#cite_note-ari-3, accessed Feb. 15, 2014.
[14] A. Scalia, "A Theory of Constitutional Interpretation," speech at Catholic University of America, October 18, 1996.

absolute, objective truth exists, and that accordingly we must be governed by the rule of law.

The alternative is to either dominate others or be dominated by others' relative, subjective, ever-shifting opinions. Once a person rejects the existence of absolute truth, of objective standards, the only question that remains is, "Whose opinion, whose values will prevail?"

Personal preference and power replace the rule of law.

If God has not handed down to us His moral standards, His truth, as the basis for law and social order, then it is left to us to make our own "truth" and our own moral standards on which to base law. (Logically, of course, if "truth" is seen as subjective, then it cannot fairly be called truth but rather merely a perception, impression or opinion.) Unavoidably, human nature dictates that we will design and bend the rules we make up to fit our own views and desires.

Beginning with a denial of divine revelation, the worldview that denies objective truth is left with only autonomy, which inevitably devolves to dominance. We make up our own rules. When individuals' rules conflict, the stronger wins and the weaker loses. This is social Darwinism.

A worldview based on subjectivity ultimately serves to imperil every person who does not hold political power.

Apart from an outside, objective source for truth and law, what lawmaker will make laws and what judge will interpret laws in a way that does not align with his or her own personal preferences and benefit?

Let's say that a particular judge happens to disdain guns and those who use them. How likely is it that he or she will read the Second Amendment of the Constitution ("the right of the people to keep and bear Arms") as protecting gun ownership by citizens? If another judge who views the Constitution as malleable sees abortion as a key to women's career progress, what will prevent him or her from inventing a constitutional right to "privacy" to open the door to abortion on demand?

By contrast, those who hold a worldview that includes objective truth that transcends time and individual preference are much more likely to treat the U.S. Constitution as an objective contract that transcends time and individual preference. They will seek to interpret the Constitution not as a matter of what they wish it said but rather what its original framers actually said, based on the text and the historical record.

If one's view of the world allows for absolute, objective truth apart from our own perception or bias, one can also read laws as objective, seeking to determine their original meaning apart from one's own perception or bias.

A worldview based on objective truth ultimately serves to protect the weak, the vulnerable and all who do not hold a position of political power.

Autonomy is a wholly unsuitable ethic to guide a society. Yet many Americans have been sucked into the superficial attraction of autonomy, unaware of the tyranny and oppression lurking in its shadows.

Worldviews, whether faith-based or agnostic or atheistic, lead to significant consequences. Which worldview gets applied to human trafficking, as we have seen, can mean the difference between the rescue and life, or enslavement and death, of countless victims.

To choose life for ourselves and our nation, we need to know how to move toward God's worldview.

# Chapter 3:
# *Faith steps – Moving toward God*

*"...that which is known about God is evident within them..."*
–Romans 1:19

Often the words of Scripture plainly and clearly spell out key spiritual truths.

Romans 3:23, for example–"for all have sinned and fall short of the glory of God"–teaches plainly that our sin creates a chasm between us and our Creator. Romans 6:23 in similar fashion spells out the consequence and solution of this separation–"the wages of sin is death, but the free gift of God is eternal life in Christ Jesus our Lord." Romans 10:9 shows us in concrete terms how to take hold of this gift: "... if you confess with your mouth Jesus as Lord, and believe in your heart that God raised Him from the dead, you will be saved."

Occasionally, however, we have to dig beyond the actual words of the Scriptures to *deduce* spiritual principles.

For example, while the Scripture clearly commands us to pray, it does not explicitly direct us to pray three times daily, as Daniel did during his captivity in Babylon.[1] Yet as we examine the remarkable life and miracles that Daniel experienced, we can *deduce* that diligently maintaining regular prayer times is a profitable spiritual discipline.

Similarly, we can observe the pattern that Jesus often withdrew to a secluded place to pray and regain spiritual strength after times of concentrated ministry and interactions with crowds. We can *deduce* from His example that retreating in solitude for prayer is a vital spiritual practice, especially for those engaged in potentially exhausting ministry.

---

[1] "Now when Daniel knew that the document was signed, he entered his house (now in his roof chamber he had windows open toward Jerusalem); and he continued kneeling on his knees three times a day, praying and giving thanks before his God, as he had been doing previously."–Daniel 6:10.

Or we may come to understand that a certain moral action recounted in a biblical story results in a certain consequence. We can also learn by deducing the likely consequence of the *opposite* moral action.

For example, David had his general Uriah killed in order to take for himself Uriah's beautiful wife, Bathsheba. David's treachery severely undermined his credibility and moral authority in the kingdom. David's son Absalom imitated his father in willfulness and sexual sin, rebelled against David's throne and ultimately, died a violent death.

While the tragic story provides an obvious lesson about infidelity and loss of self-control, at the same time it teaches, by deduction, the protective merits of fidelity and self-control. If David had applied fidelity and self-control, we might deduce that his kingdom would have enjoyed unity and peace and that with a strong fatherly example, his son Absalom might have exercised the discipline and submission that could have prevented his moral offenses and saved his life. The book of Proverbs encourages such side-by-side comparisons of good and evil, often contrasting the consequences of wicked actions with the blessings of righteous actions.

The concept of *faith steps* is just such an example of a *deduced* spiritual principle. Once understood, however, this principle can be seen clearly and consistently throughout Scripture.

### Scriptural basis for faith steps

The book of Romans opens by explaining how God has revealed Himself to every human being, in a general sense, through nature and the human conscience:

> ...that which is known about God is evident within them; for God made it evident to them. For since the creation of the world His invisible attributes, His eternal power and divine nature, have been clearly seen, being understood through what has been made, so that they are without excuse.[2]

God provides in His creation a profound witness to His character and principles. We can observe the unmistakably intelligent design of the universe, from the systematic cycles of the winds, tides and seasons to our DNA code. We can witness the transformation of a caterpillar into a butterfly or the fearful and wonderful development of a tiny human embryo into a baby.

As the psalmist testifies, "The heavens declare His righteousness, and all the peoples have seen His glory."[3] God's natural world creation reveals His

---

[2] Romans 1:19-21.

greatness, His power and His invisible attributes. His creation invites us to respond to Him in worship.

Besides revealing Himself in nature, God also creates within us a *conscience* to guide our moral choices.

The Apostle Paul explains how, even absent the clear written revelation of Scripture, conscience serves as a moral guide:

> For when Gentiles who do not have the Law do instinctively the things of the Law, these, not having the Law, are a law to themselves, in that they show the work of the Law written in their hearts, their conscience bearing witness and their thoughts alternately accusing or else defending them....[4]

God graciously reveals Himself to everyone through nature and conscience. Yet many tragically respond to such revelation by refusing God's implicit entreaties. They choose instead to plow through life doing their own thing, as if gods in their own universe.

> For even though they knew God, they did not honor Him as God or give thanks, but they became futile in their speculations, and their foolish heart was darkened. Professing to be wise, they became fools.... And just as they did not see fit to acknowledge God any longer, God gave them over to a depraved mind....[5]

The result of rejecting God's revelation through nature and conscience is a darkened, hardened heart and a twisted, futile way of thinking.

God's principles reflect love, justice, mercy and peace. But a person or a culture that has rejected God often devolves to a life of loneliness, despair, self-indulgence, conflict and ruthlessness. Absent the providence and purpose of a Creator, man-made worldviews descend into narcissism, nihilism, hedonism, or social Darwinism.

That's the bad news. Daily we can see the evidence of these tragic choices, in people we know and on the nightly news.

### Defiance leads to alienation but compliance leads to relationship

The good news is found in a silver lining in the cloud of rejected revelation. Consider carefully this unspoken *corollary* of the process of revelation and response outlined in Romans:

---

[3] Psalm 97:6.
[4] Romans 2:14-15.
[5] Romans 1:22, 28.

**If we respond to God's revelation through nature and conscience
by making moral choices aligned with His creation and His law,
our thinking begins to align with God's principles and our hearts soften
toward Him.**

Perhaps a husband resists an adulterous temptation and devotes himself to loving his wife. A woman sacrificially cares for her elderly mother who suffers from Alzheimer's. A teenager makes a culture-challenging personal decision to save sex for marriage.

As individuals make choices aligned with God's principles, they step closer toward divine relationship and their providential purpose. Our gears mesh when aligned with our Maker's blueprint, yielding peace, satisfaction and fulfillment.

Conversely, when we make choices opposed to our Maker's principles, we experience negative results such as failure, loneliness and conflict. We cannot find peace, satisfaction and fulfillment. Adultery shatters marriages and families. Enmity with parents removes the crucial emotional support children need. Teenage sex results in emotional scars, disease and crisis pregnancies.

Each moral decision we make and action we take–to acknowledge God or not, to choose good or evil–either draws us closer to God or drives us farther from Him.

**Faith steps are the moral choices we make
and actions we take toward God,
as we respond to His revelation and invitation.**

A discerning and open individual will perceive readily the difference that moral choices make and the fruit they produce in his or her life. Such experience can begin to train the mind and conscience in the direction of God and His principles, as we learn through experience to choose the path that yields the best result.

Moses counseled Israel to review their experience and consider the practical results of following or rejecting God and His principles:

You have seen all that the Lord did before your eyes in the land of Egypt to Pharaoh and all his servants and all his land; the great trials which your eyes have seen, those great signs and wonders.
I have set before you life and death, the blessing and the curse. So choose life in order that you may live, you and your descendants, by loving the LORD

your God, by obeying His voice, and by holding fast
to Him....[6]

### *Good works can put us on the tracks that lead to the station*

Scripture makes clear that none of us by good works alone can bridge the chasm between a sinful individual and a holy God. At the same time, making moral choices consistent with His kingdom can serve to keep us moving down the tracks toward a personal relationship with God.

Reaching the station–a relationship with God–ultimately depends upon our responding to God's more specific revelation in Scripture and placing our faith and trust in His Son, Jesus Christ. But the first step in that journey for many begins with responding to God through the personal experience of His creation and to the conscience that guides us toward Him.

Philosopher and theologian Francis Schaeffer explains this principle in his classic, *The God Who is There:*

The truth that we let in first is not a dogmatic
statement of the truth of the Scriptures but the
truth of the external world and the truth of what man
himself is. This is what shows him his need. The
Scriptures then show him the nature of his lostness
and the answer to it. This, I am convinced, is the
true order for our apologetics....[7]

When Jesus came to earth, God appointed John the Baptist to "prepare the way" in the hearts of the people for Jesus' ministry. John laid the tracks to Jesus, "preaching a baptism of repentance for the forgiveness of sins." John fulfilled the Old Testament prophecy:

Behold, I send My messenger ahead of You, Who will
prepare Your way; The voice of one crying in the
wilderness, 'Make ready the way of the Lord, make His
paths straight.'[8]

Many who heard John's preaching began to realign their crooked and broken lives with God's principles. The people's response to John's message prepared the soil of their hearts for Christ.

**As individuals take faith steps
in response to God's natural revelation
and begin to align their lives with His principles,
this prepares the soil of their hearts to receive Christ.**

---

[6] Deuteronomy 29:2-3; 30:19-20.
[7] *The God Who is There*, Downers Grove: Intervarsity Press 30th edition, 1982, p.128
[8] Mark 1:2-3.

To review the principle of faith steps:

1. God reveals His character and His principles in nature and in our conscience.
2. We respond to this natural revelation either by aligning ourselves with His principles or by defying His principles.
3. These choices have consequences. Taking faith steps by choosing the good aligns us with God and His principles, yielding a sense of peace, satisfaction and fulfillment and keeping us on track toward a relationship with Him. Choosing the bad and going our own way results in a hardened heart and degraded thinking, yielding failure, loneliness and conflict.
4. The person who remains open to God will begin to recognize the link between good choices and good consequences and between bad choices and bad consequences. This realization marks the first step in recognizing that God exists and in inclining our hearts and minds toward Him.
5. Responding to God's general, natural revelation with faith steps can prepare the way to receiving His specific revelation in Scripture, which makes clear the path to a personal relationship with God by putting our faith and trust in Jesus Christ.

As we shall see, the principle of faith steps applies both to individuals and to nations. For this reason, the principle will help us assess the question of Christian involvement in culture and public policy.

First, we need to understand more concretely how faith steps work.

# PART TWO:
# How Faith Steps work

# Chapter 4:
# A personal journey

*"'Behold, I send My messenger ahead of You,*
*Who will prepare Your way before You.'"*
–Luke 7:27

As a teenager in tumultuous 1970's America, I harbored no intention of devoting my life to God.

In junior high, I had quit praying after God had failed to deliver on my earnest request for a girlfriend. By high school, I rebelled so vehemently at attending our mainline Presbyterian church, where neo-orthodox ministers treated the Bible as a fallible "faith story," that my parents eventually gave up and left me at home on Sundays.

I entertained few serious ambitions, other than to play sports, carouse with buddies and find the elusive girl of my dreams (a failure I could no longer pin on God after I stopped praying). The friends I caroused with drank Schlitz beer and Boone's Farm apple wine, smoked dope, dropped acid and stole cars.

I felt conservative by comparison to my gangsta pals, but I was hardly a saint, and my lifestyle yielded little satisfaction and no peace.

Then some tough experiences sent me into an introspective spiral–a sobering, literal existential angst. I looked around for some consolation of meaningful answers about life and purpose but found absolutely nothing.

I found myself living in the apparently meaningless, painful world described in the biblical book of Ecclesiastes:

```
"Vanity of vanities," says the Preacher,
"Vanity of vanities! All is vanity."
And I set my mind to know wisdom and to know madness
and folly; I realized that this also is striving
after wind. Because in much wisdom there is much
grief, and increasing knowledge results in increasing
pain.¹
```

---

[1] Ecclesiastes 1:2, 18-18.

### Revolution

The cultural revolution of the 1960's, launched during the tumult of the Vietnam War and fed by radical ideology and drugs, had shaken the traditional American foundations of faith, morality and even reality itself. It hadn't taken much, it seemed, to strip the nation of its religious facade, revealing superficial beliefs ungrounded in Scripture and a cultural religion that had drifted far away from the living God.

No one, as far as I could discern, seemed to come even close to offering any real answers to the meaning of life, the nature of man or the existence of a Creator.

Haight Ashbury hippies turned out to be better at turning on to drugs than offering any substantive alternatives to the American capitalism they simultaneously despised and depended upon. My parents' generation had won World War II and provided wonderfully for their families, but many couldn't muster much meaning in life beyond financial security. So their children, wise to their parents' emptiness and hypocrisy but not to their own, traipsed off into Zen, LSD and Woodstock.

American political leaders had launched a successful race to the moon and built an unrivaled economy but then violated the public trust with moral lapses and bungled burglaries. Mainline religious leaders had long since lost the biblical moorings for faith and taken to mumbling a social gospel that eschewed spiritual life for the latest hip political ideology. Educators were trading traditional scholastic disciplines for subjective, "relevant" explorations–like the high school course I took on Rock and Roll.

I found the silence of meaning terrifying.

### Good News / Strange News

In desperation, I took up reading a paperback copy of Good News for Modern Man–a loose, modern translation of the New Testament. I would read passages for a while but could only take so much of what struck me as bewildering, even bizarre.

I was looking to plant my feet on firm ground, not float off into spooky spiritualism. Angels and demons, prophecies and parables. That stuff practically made me shiver.

Yet after a time, for some reason, I would once again delve into the pages of the Strange Book.

Meanwhile, I had begun to figure out that the exciting friends in the "cool crowd" at high school that I had been hanging around with were not even remotely loyal or dependable friends. One incident that clued me in to this fact involved a street fight with a football player. I had rashly stood up to him at a party in a bold but ill-considered attempt to prevent him from attacking my best friend.

The football player later sucker- punched me in a parking lot and continued to pummel me while I managed just a few jabs, unable to unbutton my heavy overcoat that unfortunately functioned as a straitjacket. My "best friend" simply stood by and watched, as if some unwritten gentlemanly rule of street fighting precluded his intervention, while I took a pounding on his behalf.

The tumult without and within caused me to begin to shift values. I sought the company of the "forgotten crowd" instead of the cool crowd. The lifestyles of these friends were perhaps not as exciting, but they were far less likely to land in jail and much more likely to provide genuine friendship.

## Changing direction

I also began to significantly change my taste in music. I sensed in much of the music that I had been listening to with my friends the same darkness and terrifying absence of meaning that I was desperately trying to flee. Groups like Black Sabbath, Alice Cooper and other heavy metal icons that had once fueled late-night parties with friends now seemed shadowy, frightening, evil.

I had no idea at the time of such groups' association with the occult, but I was developing a spiritual sensitivity as I began to change the direction of my life. God was using my crisis of existential angst to rip away any vestiges of false security and to sensitize me to the spiritual realities around me.

He was essentially teaching me to recognize good and evil.

And I was responding by taking small but important faith steps in His direction.

Somehow I stumbled through the rest of my high school senior year without the mental breakdown I feared was imminent, and I headed for Penn State University. Hardly a bastion of evangelical fervor, the university at Happy Valley was known for frat parties, football and the freedom to do whatever your parents hadn't let you do at home.

I packed up my Good News for Modern Man, along with a tobacco pipe and a trash can painted to look like a beer can, and took up life as a young Nittany Lion. I straddled two worlds. My Mom would visit me occasionally, and to the utter astonishment of my dorm buddy from a teetotaling Mennonite background, drop off a case of beer. I think Mom's theory was that alcohol was a tried and true traditional alternative to hard drugs, or at least that it somehow complemented college studies.

College offered the chance to start a whole new life, to explore new interests and choose new friends. I trotted off to the music store and returned with a mild and melodic John Denver album.

The times, they were a'changin'.

## Drawn to the difference

During an evening in orientation week, I walked past a coed on the corner holding a lunch box and made a lame crack about her waiting for the bus to go to work. For some reason she responded to me, saying that she was looking for a certain building on campus, and did I know where it was? I assured her that I did (I had no clue), and we struck up a conversation as we walked together to who-knew-where.

Her name was Sarah Rush, and besides her good looks, there was something about this unique young woman that I felt attracted to. She exuded joy and wholesomeness. As I learned over the ensuing weeks, Sarah was a Christian.

During that first freshman semester, Sarah patiently talked to me about how faith in Jesus Christ could transform my life. I rudely retorted that Christianity was a crutch and a lot of, well, the phrase I chose wasn't polite.

If I had thought about it honestly, I would have admitted that I actually needed much more than a crutch; I needed a stretcher.

Another young woman I met on campus, Jeannine Forgette, possessed the same winsome essence that had drawn me to Sarah. Like Sarah, Jeannine gently and patiently encouraged me to consider Christ. And I in turn, like a jerk, rejected her kind entreaties as so much bunk.

I later learned that Jeannine told a friend in frustration that if anyone had had a chance to become a Christian and never would, it was Jonathan Imbody.

While Sarah and Jeannine both eventually seemed to despair of leading me into the Kingdom of God—who could blame them—thankfully, God did not. He continued to gradually and gently shape my desires, thinking and lifestyle.

God was encouraging me to take *faith steps* toward Him and His principles.

## Hallelujah linebackers

Our Hamilton Hall dormitory, located across from the old gymnasium (in which I unquestionably spent more time than in the library), served as living quarters for many Penn State football players. They were hard to miss: large, loud and occasionally obnoxious. Like the All-American linebacker down the hall whose room reeked of dope morning, noon and night and who reportedly pulled a gun during a fight one night in the dorm.

One freshman player a couple doors down from my room, however, seemed remarkably different from the jock stereotype. Ron Hostetler, nicknamed "Hoss," hailed from the tiny Pennsylvania hamlet of Holsopple, where his conservative and deeply religious Mennonite family raised seven children and hundreds of cows and chickens. Ron was without doubt one of the few linebackers to hail from the staunchly pacifistic sect.

Like Sarah, Ron also exuded joy. His laugh resounded a mile away. Unlike Sarah and Jeannine, Ron didn't talk much about Christ. He disappeared every Wednesday night and then returned fired up and friendly, rousing my roommate and me from our studies, in search of our large jar of pickles. (He would actually chug the brine. After later watching his brother pour a mountain of salt onto his dinner, I began to wonder if maybe Mennonites had some strange inherited salt deficiency.)

Hoss eventually told me that he went to a Wednesday night Bible study for football players and their friends. David Martin, the associate pastor of the State College Christian & Missionary Alliance Church, led the Bible study in an apartment affectionately known as "Saved Headquarters." Hoss invited me to attend, and I tagged along, not knowing what to expect but for some reason willing to take a chance.

I soon wished I had stayed safely back in the dorm.

About 15 of us, including a few gorilla-sized offensive linemen, sank down into old sofas, facing each other. Lots of smiling faces.

Why?

Suddenly to my dismay, someone started playing a guitar and the group, excepting me, joined in a rousing rendition of some religious song they all knew. After the chorus, I realized with acute panic that they were going around the room, taking turns individually and singing the words, "Oh yes, I love Jesus" in response to the song's question, "Oh, so-and-so, do you love Jesus?"

Arrgh! I didn't know if I loved Jesus, and I certainly didn't love singing in front of people I hardly knew. I desperately wanted to escape before my turn came. But I had sat near several very large offensive linemen who, by nature of their football training, had developed a singular talent for keeping people in place.

Finally my dreaded turn came and I meekly spurted out the words, "Oh, yes, I love Jesus."

A statement coerced by fear hardly qualifies as a true conversion experience, but I suppose it was oddly enough a start in the right direction.

## New life, new mission

After several visits to the athletes' fellowship at Saved Headquarters, I worried less about the awkward songs and thought more about a personal faith commitment. One night one of the players gave a devotional message on II Corinthians 5:20:

> Therefore, we are ambassadors for Christ, as though God were making an appeal through us; we beg you on behalf of Christ, be reconciled to God.

That night, I returned to my dorm room, knelt by my bed and prayed, "Lord, You know I am scared to do this, but I want You to make me a new person. I yield my life to you. I believe you are the Son of God and that you died for my sins. Please forgive my sins. Make me an ambassador for Christ."

When Hoss returned, I told him of my faith commitment.

"I knew something was different about you!" he exclaimed. "Wait till the guys hear about this."

Shortly after my commitment to Jesus Christ, the associate pastor who had organized the athletes' fellowship Bible studies, David Martin, knocked on our dorm door. He said the Lord had laid it on his heart to disciple us.

Heaven knows we needed it.

I had taken the faith steps of making that initial commitment, but now my whole world view needed reformation–a transformation by the renewing of my mind.

## Broken down for building up

I had moved from responding to God's general revelation to submitting to the authority of His specific revelation in His Word, the Bible.

In doing so, I would still be applying the principles of faith steps, but in a more specific and conscious way. God would still allow practical tests of character to lead me closer to Him–tests of the will, the body, the mind–but I would have solid, objective Scriptures to prepare me, equip me and deliver me safely from those tests.

So how had God used faith steps to lead me to Himself?

He took a haughty, self-centered teenager and gradually broke me down, first through challenging circumstances and then through the inner conviction of my conscience.

The high school football player who sucker-punched and pummeled me in a parking lot had disabused me of my illusions of invincible toughness. The faithless friends had revealed to me the inadequacy of human relationships for providing security. The tumult in American culture and existential crisis had knocked away the psychological props that blinded me to my true state of desperation and purposelessness apart from God.

As God ripped away my false supports and fallacies, He also sensitized my conscience. Our conscience functions to convict us of right and wrong and ultimately of our sin and our need for a righteous, loving God.

As God sensitized my conscience, I began to recognize evil in the raucous and rebellious music that had provided the backdrop for our parties. I began to turn away from that music and the values and the dark kingdom it preached.

I realized the folly of following the cool crowd and developed a bit more humility and grace in my choice of friends. As my goal morphed from rebellion to survival, I began to humbly reach out to consider God and His Word.

As we begin to see ourselves not in relation to our own measuring standards but in relation to a holy God, we begin to realize that we simply do not have the slightest ability to measure up. The conviction of our conscience heightens our awareness of the relational gap between us and God, and fuels the desire to have that gap bridged.

## Bridging the chasm

The Scriptures describe this growing realization that even our best efforts eventually fall prey to our miserable moral incompetence:

"For I joyfully concur with the law of God in the inner man, but I see a different law in the members of my body, waging war against the law of my mind….[2]

The result of this realization is that we recognize our own sin before God and the impossibility of obtaining salvation through moral perfection:

Now we know that whatever the Law says, it speaks to those who are under the Law, so that every mouth may be closed and all the world may become accountable to God; because by the works of the Law no flesh will be justified in His sight; for through the Law *comes* the knowledge of sin.

…for all have sinned and fall short of the glory of God….[3]

---

[2] Romans 7:22-23.

Conscience can lead us this far in our spiritual quest–to recognizing our deep, incurable dilemma and separation from our Creator. But the next step–actually healing our breach with God–requires the *direct revelation* of Jesus Christ and our faith step of receiving Him.

Three key passages in the book of Romans reveal the simple steps to a relationship with God through Jesus Christ:

- But God demonstrates His own love toward us, in that while we were yet sinners, Christ died for us.[4]
- For the wages of sin is death, but the free gift of God is eternal life in Christ Jesus our Lord.[5]
- ...if you confess with your mouth Jesus as Lord, and believe in your heart that God raised Him from the dead, you will be saved.[6]

Salvation by grace, through faith.

God restores our relationship with Him through faith and solely by His grace. No good works of our own could possibly bridge the gap. We come to God through the work of His Son, Jesus Christ, on the cross on our behalf. Taking the penalty Himself that we deserved for our sins, Jesus made a bridge to God for us.

We cross this bridge by putting our faith, our trust, in Christ.

### Faith in action

The Scriptures also make clear, from Abraham to Jesus, the Old Testament to the New, that true faith is demonstrated by deeds.

These deeds can be considered faith steps.

As an example, consider the story of Zaccheus, a tax-collecting cheat who climbed a tree to glimpse Jesus as He passed through town.

When Jesus came to the place, He looked up and said to him, "Zaccheus, hurry and come down, for today I must stay at your house." And he hurried and came down and received Him gladly.

When they saw it, they all began to grumble, saying, "He has gone to be the guest of a man who is a sinner."

Zaccheus stopped and said to the Lord, "Behold, Lord, half of my possessions I will give to the poor, and

---

[3] Romans 3:19-20, 23.
[4] Romans 5:8.
[5] Romans 6:23.
[6] Romans 10:9.

41

```
if I have defrauded anyone of anything, I will give
back four times as much."
And Jesus said to him, "Today salvation has come to
this house, because he, too, is a son of Abraham. For
the Son of Man has come to seek and to save that
which was lost."[7]
```
We can imagine the faith of Zaccheus–his desire for God–as he climbs
the tree to see the Lord. But we can *see* the sincere faith of Zaccheus as he
promises to pay back money to those he had defrauded. Zaccheus responded
to God's grace, manifested by Jesus coming to his home for a meal, with the
faith step of exchanging his dishonesty for honesty.

The biblical James explains this tandem of faith and works, illustrated in
the life of the patriarch Abraham, who believed God's promises to the point
of preparing to sacrifice the life of his own son, Isaac.

```
You see that faith was working with his works, and as
a result of the works, faith was perfected.[8]
```
The book of James makes clear that faith and works naturally go
together; they cannot be separated. Just as mere words cannot meet a
physical need, faith words severed from faith works do not comprise real
faith.

```
What use is it, my brethren, if someone says he has
faith but he has no works? Can that faith save him?
If a brother or sister is without clothing and in
need of daily food, and one of you says to them, 'Go
in peace, be warmed and be filled,' and yet you do
not give them what is necessary for their body, what
use is that? Even so faith, if it has no works, is
dead, being by itself.[9]
```
James emphasizes that faith is not ethereal but real. What we believe
manifests itself in what we do. Truly faithful priests don't leave beaten
victims lying in the ditch. The Good Samaritan manifests his faith and his
love for his neighbor by caring for the victim's physical needs.

The book of Romans clarifies that our works do not earn salvation,
which God offers us as a free gift, by His grace, through the death and
resurrection of His Son. Good works cannot regenerate our hopelessly sinful
nature; only God's Spirit can do that.

```
Therefore, having been justified by faith, we have
peace with God through our Lord Jesus Christ…. For
```

---

[7] Luke 19:5-10.
[8] James 2:22.
[9] James 2:14-17.

while we were still helpless, at the right time
Christ died for the ungodly. [10]

The principles of faith and works, expressed from different angles in the books of James and Romans, are not competing but complementary.

### Moving in God's direction

Jesus also explained that doing the works of God means putting our trust in Him.

Therefore they said to Him, "What shall we do, so
that we may work the works of God?" Jesus answered
and said to them, "This is the work of God, that you
believe in Him whom He has sent." [11]

So then, taking faith steps does not mean working our way to salvation, as if somehow we could do enough godly deeds to change our sinful nature and bridge the chasm between us and a holy God.

Taking faith steps simply means *making choices in God's direction.* Faith steps help prepare us for a relationship with God, as we begin to turn toward Him.

Putting our faith, our trust in the work of Jesus Christ–His life, death and resurrection–finally bridges the chasm and unites us in a new and living relationship with our loving heavenly Father.

Next, we examine more about how we as individuals practically take faith steps toward God.

---

[10] Romans 5:1, 6.
[11] John 6:28-29.

43

# Chapter 5:
# *How individuals take*
# *faith steps*

*"Peter said to Him, "Lord, if it is You,*
*command me to come to You on the water."*
–Matthew 14:28

In the city lived the shoemaker, Martuin Avdyeitch. …
Avdyeitch had always been a good man; but as he grew
old, he began to think more about his soul, and get
nearer to God.[1]

So Russian writer Leo Tolstoy begins his short story, "Where Love is,
God is." After Martuin Avdyeitch's son had died from an illness, he
had despaired of life and confided his sorrows in an old man from his village.
"But what shall one live for?" asked Martuin.
And the little old man said, "We must live for God,
Martuin. He gives you life, and for His sake you must
live. When you begin to live for Him, you will not
grieve over anything, and all will seem easy to you."
Martuin kept silent for a moment, and then said, "But
how can one live for God?
And the little old man said:– "Christ has taught us
how to live for God."[2]
Martuin begins to study the Scriptures and gradually changes his
perspective on life, himself and God.
As Tolstoy explains, "From that time Martuin's whole life was changed."[3]
One night Martuin reads about how the Pharisees showed disdain for
Jesus by neglecting to welcome Him into their homes with the customary

---

[1] Tolstoi, Lyof N. (Tolstoy, Leo), *"Where Love is There God is Also,"* translated from the
Russian by Nathan Haskell. New York: Thomas Crowell Company, 1887. Kindle edition,
locations 7, 13.
[2] Ibid, 26.
[3] Ibid, 36.

courtesies. Martuin recognizes himself in the Pharisees. Meditating on the lesson, he soon falls asleep.

"Martuin!" suddenly seemed to sound in his ears. Martuin started from his sleep. "Who is here?" He turned around, glanced toward the door-no one. Again he fell into a doze.
Suddenly, he plainly heard: "Martuin! Ah, Martuin! Look tomorrow on the street. I am coming."[4]

The next day, Martuin waits in eager anticipation of the Lord's appearance to him. But instead of seeing Jesus outside his shop, he sees an old man, weary and faint from shoveling snow.

"Pshaw! I must be getting crazy in my old age," said Avdyeitch, and laughed at himself. "Stepanuitch is clearing away the snow, and I imagine that Christ is coming to see me. I was entirely out of my mind, old dotard that I am!"[5]

Nevertheless, Martuin invites the old man to come in and share some tea. Martuin relates his vision and rehearses the kindnesses of Christ related in the Bible, moving the old visitor Stepanuitch to tears. Upon leaving, Stepanuitch exclaims,

"Thanks to you, Martuin Avdyeitch, for treating me kindly, and satisfying me, soul and body."[6]

A little while later a poor mother, shivering with a baby in her arms, happens by Martuin's shop and he invites her in. After receiving from Martuin hot food and warm clothing, the mother thanks him.

"May Christ bless you, little grandfather! He must have sent me to your window. My little baby would have frozen to death. When I started out it was warm, but now it has grown cold. And He, the Batyushka, led you to look through the window and take pity on me, an unfortunate!"[7]

In like fashion, Martuin helps to redeem a boy thief and encourages his captor to have mercy on the boy.

"God has commanded us to forgive," said Avdyeitch, "else we, too, may not be forgiven. All should be forgiven, and the thoughtless especially."[8]

---

[4] Ibid, 65.
[5] Ibid, 78.
[6] Ibid, 108.
[7] Ibid, 142.
[8] Ibid, 171.

Eventually nighttime arrives and, never having seen the One he expected, Martuin closes his cobbler shop and retreats inside.

```
Avdyeitch looked around, and saw-there, in the dark
corner, it seemed as if people were standing; he was
at a loss to know who they were.
And a voice whispered in his ear, "Martuin-ah,
Martuin! Did you not recognize me?"
"Who?" exclaimed Avdyeitch.
"Me," repeated the voice. "It was I."
Stepanuitch stepped forth from the dark corner; he
smiled, and like a little cloud faded away, and soon
vanished.
"And it was I," said the voice. From the dark corner
stepped forth the woman with her child; the woman
smiled, the child laughed, and they also vanished.
"And it was I," continued the voice; both the old
woman and the boy with the apple stepped forward;
both smiled and vanished.
Avdyeitch's soul rejoiced; he crossed himself, put on
his spectacles, and began to read the Evangelists
where it happened to open.
On the upper part of the page he read: "For I was an
hungered, and ye gave me meat; I was thirsty, and ye
gave me drink; I was a stranger, and ye took me in."[9]
```

Tolstoy offers us a wonderful literary gift of Scriptural insight into how we draw near to God.

Martuin Avdyeitch takes faith steps by responding to God's initiative toward him. God provided Martuin with an *opportunity*. Not a mandate, not a Hobson's choice, not even an irresistible predestination.

Needy friends and strangers pass by Martuin's shop. He easily could have ignored them. He could have busied himself otherwise so as to blot out their presence. But instead, he embraced the opportunities and welcomed each needy visitor into his shop.

### God in the "gentle blowing"

The unexpected, subtle manner in which God revealed Himself to the prophet Elijah offers another glimpse of how God reveals Himself to each one of us.

```
So He said, "Go forth and stand on the mountain
before the Lord." And behold, the Lord was passing
by!
```

---

[9] Ibid, 188.

> And a great and strong wind was rending the mountains
> and breaking in pieces the rocks before the Lord; but
> the Lord was not in the wind.
> And after the wind an earthquake, but the Lord was
> not in the earthquake.
> After the earthquake a fire, but the Lord was not in
> the fire; and after the fire a sound of a gentle
> blowing.
> When Elijah heard it, he wrapped his face in his
> mantle and went out and stood in the entrance of the
> cave.
> And behold, a voice came to him and said, "What are
> you doing here, Elijah?"[10]

When we respond to the "gentle blowing" of God as He introduces opportunities into our lives, we are taking faith steps.

### Responding to His invitations

Jesus presented just such subtle opportunities to His disciples. The sixth chapter of the biblical book of Mark relates that Jesus spent days teaching a large crowd in the wilderness. The disciples eventually began asking Jesus to send the crowd away.

At that time, Jesus had answered them, "You give them something to eat!"[11] They demurred and instead Jesus miraculously fed over five thousand men plus women and children by multiplying five loaves and two fishes.

Later Mark relates a similar teaching occasion:

> In those days, when there was again a large crowd and
> they had nothing to eat, Jesus called His disciples
> and said to them, "I feel compassion for the people
> because they have remained with Me now three days and
> have nothing to eat. If I send them away hungry to
> their homes, they will faint on the way; and some of
> them have come from a great distance."[12]

Jesus had subtly presented the disciples with another opportunity. Unfortunately, the disciples failed to respond to the opportunity God had provided—just as they often did and as we often do. If the disciples had responded to the opportunity, they would have taken a giant faith step toward the Lord. Instead they neglected the opportunity and demonstrated their dullness.

---

[10] 1 Kings 19:11-14.
[11] Mark 6:37.
[12] Mark 8:1-3.

48

At other times, Jesus proves far more direct and obvious in His invitations.

> As He passed by, He saw Levi the son of Alphaeus sitting in the tax booth, and He said to him, "Follow Me!" And he got up and followed Him.[13]

Couldn't ask for a clearer faith step opportunity and response.

## Persevering love

But what if we fail to respond to God's invitation to take faith steps toward Him?

Mark relates a remarkable account of Jesus' encounter with a Samaritan woman. While traveling in Samaria, the disciples head for town while Jesus remains behind at a local well.

> There came a woman of Samaria to draw water. Jesus said to her, "Give Me a drink."[14]

Rather than responding to the invitation, the woman sidesteps it. Instead, she raises raising an ethnic and religious issue related to Samaritans and Jews.

Jesus persists.

> "If you knew the gift of God, and who it is who says to you, 'Give Me a drink,' you would have asked Him, and He would have given you living water."[15]

The woman responds with what sounds like a sarcastic attempt to ground the spiritual talk.

> "Sir, give me this water, so I will not be thirsty nor come all the way here to draw."[16]

Jesus presses.

> "Go, call your husband and come here."[17]

Her face drops. The woman offers that she has no husband.

Jesus adjusts her response. He observes that she actually has had five husbands and is now living with a man to whom she is not married.

Her pretense uncovered, the woman finally turns in the direction of Jesus' invitation and stammers out a painfully obvious observation.

> "Sir, I perceive that You are a prophet."[18]

---

[13] Mark 2:14.
[14] John 4:7.
[15] John 4:10.
[16] John 4:15.
[17] John 4:16.
[18] John 4:19.

49

Scrambling to recover, the woman again diverts the conversation to ethnic and religious differences.

But Jesus continues to engage her with spiritual truth.

The woman turns yet a bit farther in the direction of Jesus' invitation. She allows that she knows that Messiah is coming.

`Jesus said to her, "I who speak to you am He."`[19]

What can we learn from this remarkable exchange?

God not only presents us with opportunities to take faith steps; He also *persists* so that we take them. In His love and grace He seek us out–and *keeps* seeking us out.

Jesus could have withdrawn the opportunity He was presenting the woman at the well at her very first resistance. He did not persist because she responded to Him; she avoided Him. Jesus persisted with the woman at the well because He *loved* her.

He loves us, too. He is not going to let our failure wreck His perfect plan for our lives. He keeps coming back, presenting more opportunities.

That is why a failure to take a faith step toward God does not doom us to a life apart from Him. We fail and we fail often, yet He remains *persistently merciful*.

`For He Himself knows our frame; He is mindful that we are but dust.`[20]
`The Lord's lovingkindnesses indeed never cease, for His compassions never fail. They are new every morning; great is Your faithfulness.`[21]

Undaunted by our failures, He continues to offer us opportunities to draw closer to Him. Opportunities to conform our daily decisions to His will. To practice practical kindnesses. To sacrifice self and serve others.

### We can take initiative

Besides responding to *God's* initiative and opportunities–as did Martuin Avdyeitch, Levi the disciple and the Samaritan woman at the well–faith steps can also involve *our* taking initiative toward God.

After feeding the five thousand, Jesus sends the crowds away and retreats to the mountain for prayer. The disciples take the boat out to sea, but it veers off course as winds buffet the craft.

`And in the fourth watch of the night He came to them, walking on the sea. When the disciples saw Him`

---

[19] John 4:26.
[20] Psalm 103:14.
[21] Lamentations 3:22-23.

walking on the sea, they were terrified, and said,
"It is a ghost!" And they cried out in fear.
But immediately Jesus spoke to them, saying, "Take
courage, it is I; do not be afraid."[22]

At this point, Peter takes an amazing initiative that would not have occurred to most of us:

Peter said to Him, "Lord, if it is You, command me to
come to You on the water."[23]

We can only guess Peter's motive; some might suspect the thrill of adventure. But a professional fisherman seems a highly unlikely candidate to choose the "thrill" of stepping out of a boat in the deep of a storm-tossed sea.

Peter was not a man of letters and contemplation but of zeal and action, as demonstrated just before Jesus' capture and crucifixion, in his proclamation of loyalty and readiness with the sword. He likely took the initiative on the storm-tossed sea as a zealous urge to prove his faith and fealty. He sought to show his love for the Lord by literally stepping out in faith.

Of course, Peter's zeal soon turned to fright in the face of the winds, and the Lord had to pluck His sinking disciple out of the drink. Jesus administered an admonition to believe and not doubt. It seems possible that Jesus also appreciated the fact that whereas the others remained in the boat, Peter had ventured out onto the water. This bold and brave, flailing and failing disciple demonstrated the spark of faith upon which Jesus said He would build His Church.

Peter's example reminds us that God honors even our imperfect faith steps as we take initiative toward Him. He enabled Peter to *walk on water*. It does not surprise Him that we often falter and fall. He picks us up and prepares us for the next opportunity.

### Trouble can prompt our initiative

God also casts a wide net, eager to seek and save the lost from even the most unlikely of quarters. Observe how Jesus responds to the faith steps of a Roman military officer:

And when Jesus entered Capernaum, a centurion came to
Him, imploring Him, and saying, "Lord, my servant is
lying paralyzed at home, fearfully tormented."
Jesus said to him, "I will come and heal him."

---

[22] Matthew 14:25-27.
[23] Matthew 14:28.

51

But the centurion said, "Lord, I am not worthy for
You to come under my roof, but just say the word, and
my servant will be healed. For I also am a man under
authority, with soldiers under me; and I say to this
one, 'Go!' and he goes, and to another, 'Come!' and
he comes, and to my slave, 'Do this!' and he does
it."
Now when Jesus heard this, He marveled and said to
those who were following, "Truly I say to you, I have
not found such great faith with anyone in Israel.[24]

God often uses illness, calamity and angst to prompt us to take initiative
to seek Him.

A woman with a hemorrhage comes up behind Jesus and touches His
cloak for healing. A synagogue official beseeches Jesus to heal his dying
daughter. A leper implores Him. Friends lower a paralyzed man down
through the roof to reach Jesus for healing.

## Step by step by step

Nicodemus, a Pharisee and ruler of the Jews, must have wrestled with
tremendous internal tension as he listened to the teachings of Jesus–teachings
that challenged the very core of his legalistic learning. Torn between
tradition and truth, Nicodemus comes to visit Jesus at night. His nascent faith
not yet bold enough to venture forth in the daylight of peer pressure,
Nicodemus takes a timid step of faith toward Jesus.

[T]his man came to Jesus by night and said to Him,
"Rabbi, we know that You have come from God as a
teacher; for no one can do these signs that You do
unless God is with him."
Jesus answered and said to him, "Truly, truly, I say
to you, unless one is born again he cannot see the
kingdom of God."[25]

Like the Samaritan woman at the well, Nicodemus first tries to blunt the
spiritual challenge by focusing on the physical, perhaps with a hint of
sarcasm.

Nicodemus said to Him, "How can a man be born when he
is old? He cannot enter a second time into his
mother's womb and be born, can he?"[26]

Jesus, as always, fixes the focus on the spiritual.

---

[24] Matthew 8:5-10.
[25] John 3:2-3.
[26] John 3:4.

Jesus answered, "Truly, truly, I say to you, unless one is born of water and the Spirit he cannot enter into the kingdom of God. That which is born of the flesh is flesh, and that which is born of the Spirit is spirit.

"Do not be amazed that I said to you, 'You must be born again.' The wind blows where it wishes and you hear the sound of it, but do not know where it comes from and where it is going; so is everyone who is born of the Spirit."

Nicodemus said to Him, "How can these things be?"[27]

As his religious presuppositions melt in the heat of Jesus' truth, Nicodemus has been moved from curiosity to conviction, yet still short of conversion. His faith steps continue over time, and we next hear of Nicodemus defending Jesus before a hostile gathering of Jewish officials.

This time Nicodemus faces in the daylight the peer pressure he had avoided in his previous night visit.

Nicodemus (he who came to Him before, being one of them) said to them, "Our Law does not judge a man unless it first hears from him and knows what he is doing, does it?"

They answered him, "You are not also from Galilee, are you? Search, and see that no prophet arises out of Galilee."[28]

We see the further progression of Nicodemus' faith steps immediately after the crucifixion.

After these things Joseph of Arimathea, being a disciple of Jesus, but a secret one for fear of the Jews, asked Pilate that he might take away the body of Jesus; and Pilate granted permission. So he came and took away His body.

Nicodemus, who had first come to Him by night, also came, bringing a mixture of myrrh and aloes, about a hundred pounds weight. So they took the body of Jesus and bound it in linen wrappings with the spices, as is the burial custom of the Jews.[29]

Gradually progressing from skeptic to defender to follower, Nicodemus keeps responding to God by taking initiative. He affirms his allegiance to the Messiah who had died for him, by burying His body.

---

[27] John 3:5-9.
[28] John 7:50-52.
[29] John 19:38-40.

53

## Concrete faith steps

Just as Nicodemus' third act of faith took the form of a practical ministry—anointing the crucified body of Jesus with myrrh and aloes—faith steps often involve practical, concrete actions. Observe how Jesus invites the rich young ruler to carry out a faith commitment:

As He was setting out on a journey, a man ran up to Him and knelt before Him, and asked Him, "Good Teacher, what shall I do to inherit eternal life?" And Jesus said to him, "Why do you call Me good? No one is good except God alone. You know the commandments, 'Do not murder, do not commit adultery, do not steal, do not bear false witness, do not defraud, honor your father and mother." And he said to Him, "Teacher, I have kept all these things from my youth up." Looking at him, Jesus felt a love for him and said to him, "One thing you lack: go and sell all you possess and give to the poor, and you will have treasure in heaven; and come, follow Me." But at these words he was saddened, and he went away grieving, for he was one who owned much property. And Jesus, looking around, said to His disciples, "How hard it will be for those who are wealthy to enter the kingdom of God!"[30]

Doubtless the rich young ruler would have preferred perhaps a simple salvation prayer or maybe merely raising his hand to confirm his faith. Yet Jesus went straight to the heart of the man's real obstacle to faith—his idolatrous worship of wealth—and called for a faith step. The rich young ruler's response sadly illustrates the truth of the book of James: faith without works is dead.

In another Gospel occurrence, Jesus pairs faith with giving:

And He sat down opposite the treasury, and began observing how the people were putting money into the treasury; and many rich people were putting in large sums. A poor widow came and put in two small copper coins, which amount to a cent. Calling His disciples to Him, He said to them, "Truly I say to you, this poor widow put in more than all the contributors to the treasury; for they all put in out of their surplus, but she, out of her poverty, put in all she owned, all she had to live on."[31]

---

[30] Mark 10:17-23.

Jesus also defends and commends a penitent prostitute whose financial sacrifice demonstrated her love and faith:

```
While He was in Bethany at the home of Simon the
leper, and reclining at the table, there came a woman
with an alabaster vial of very costly perfume of pure
nard; and she broke the vial and poured it over His
head.
But some were indignantly remarking to one another,
"Why has this perfume been wasted? For this perfume
might have been sold for over three hundred denarii,
and the money given to the poor." And they were
scolding her.
But Jesus said, "Let her alone; why do you bother
her? She has done a good deed to Me. For you always
have the poor with you, and whenever you wish you can
do good to them; but you do not always have Me. She
has done what she could; she has anointed My body
beforehand for the burial. Truly I say to you,
wherever the gospel is preached in the whole world,
what this woman has done will also be spoken of in
memory of her."[32]
```

## Consequential faith steps

Faith steps demonstrate our deepest desires. They reveal Whom or what we worship.

Faith steps carry eternal consequences. How we respond to God ultimately results in mercy or judgment.

When Zaccheus promised to repay those whom he had defrauded, Jesus exclaimed, "Today salvation has come to this house...."[33]

When the rich young ruler clung to his possessions, Jesus declared, "How hard it will be for those who are wealthy to enter the kingdom of God!"[34]

Christianity is not merely a belief system but an active relationship with the living God. Only faith saves us, yet true faith consummates belief with works.

As Jesus taught:

```
"So every good tree bears good fruit, but the bad
tree bears bad fruit. A good tree cannot produce bad
```

---

[31] Mark 12:41-44.
[32] Mark 14:3-9.
[33] Luke 19:9.
[34] Mark 10:23.

55

fruit, nor can a bad tree produce good fruit. Every
tree that does not bear good fruit is cut down and
thrown into the fire. So then, you will know them by
their fruits.
"Not everyone who says to Me, 'Lord, Lord,' will
enter the kingdom of heaven, but he who does the will
of My Father who is in heaven will enter."[35]

Faith steps hold consequences for individuals. As we shall see, faith steps
also hold consequences for nations.

---

[35] Matthew 7:17-21.

# Chapter 6:
# *How a nation takes faith steps*

*"See, I have taught you statutes and judgments just as the Lord my God commanded me, that you should do thus in the land where you are entering to possess it. So keep and do them, for that is your wisdom and your understanding in the sight of the peoples who will hear all these statutes and say, 'Surely this great nation is a wise and understanding people.'"*
–Deuteronomy 4:5-6

George Washington observed in his Farewell Address, "Can it be, that Providence has not connected the permanent felicity of a nation with its virtue?"

In his Second Inaugural Address, Abraham Lincoln demonstrated the deep and mature faith he had come to realize while grieving over his beloved son Willie, watching the dark emotional demise of his once-vibrant wife, and witnessing the casualties of a bloody civil war. Lincoln acknowledged God not as a divine favor-grantor but as the unsearchable, righteous Judge of men and nations.

> Yet, if God wills that [this war] continue until all the wealth piled by the bondman's two hundred and fifty years of unrequited toil shall be sunk, and until every drop of blood drawn with the lash shall be paid by another drawn with the sword, as was said three thousand years ago, so still it must be said, "The judgments of the Lord are true and righteous altogether."

Washington and Lincoln accepted what most Americans and many presidents have understood–that nations, like individuals, choose right or wrong and bear the consequences of good or ill. Whether one views these consequences as natural–the logical and necessary result of choices–or as supernatural, resulting from active blessings or punishments administered by God, does not affect the outcome. The result is the same.

Christians realize that the ultimate source of the consequences of choices also is the same. God created the natural laws that govern our lives and mete out natural consequences for our choices. We eat right and exercise and we lose weight. We overeat and park on the couch and we gain weight. We forgive and we gain peace; we bear a grudge and we suffer the effects of tension.

Students of the Bible know that God also brings to bear personal consequences, both in this life and the next, for our moral choices and deeds.

```
When I kept silent about my sin, my body wasted away
Through my groaning all day long.
For day and night Your hand was heavy upon me;
My vitality was drained away as with the fever heat
of summer.¹
But because of your stubbornness and unrepentant
heart you are storing up wrath for yourself in the
day of wrath and revelation of the righteous judgment
of God, who will render to each person according to
his deeds: to those who by perseverance in doing good
seek for glory and honor and immortality, eternal
life; but to those who are selfishly ambitious and do
not obey the truth, but obey unrighteousness, wrath
and indignation.²
```

## *Scriptural examples of nations' faith steps*

Scripture makes clear the importance of faith steps not only for individuals, but also for nations and cultures. Consider the following biblical examples of how God executes judgment or demonstrates mercy to nations and city-states as a result of the moral choices of their citizens and leaders:

- Egypt

```
God said to Abram, "Know for certain that your
descendants will be strangers in a land that is not
theirs, where they will be enslaved and oppressed
four hundred years. But I will also judge the nation
whom they will serve, and afterward they will come
out with many possessions."³
"When Pharaoh does not listen to you, then I will lay
My hand on Egypt and bring out My hosts, My people
```

---

¹ Psalm 32:3-4.
² Romans 2:5-8.
³ Genesis 15:13-14.

the sons of Israel, from the land of Egypt by great judgments."[4]

## • Israel

So the anger of the Lord burned against Israel, and He said, "Because this nation has transgressed My covenant which I commanded their fathers and has not listened to My voice, I also will no longer drive out before them any of the nations which Joshua left when he died, in order to test Israel by them, whether they will keep the way of the Lord to walk in it as their fathers did, or not."[5]

Moreover, the word of the Lord came to me saying, "And you, son of man, thus says the Lord God to the land of Israel, 'An end! The end is coming on the four corners of the land. 'Now the end is upon you, and I will send My anger against you; I will judge you according to your ways and bring all your abominations upon you.'"[6]

## • Judah

"So now let Me tell you what I am going to do to My vineyard: I will remove its hedge and it will be consumed; I will break down its wall and it will become trampled ground. I will lay it waste; it will not be pruned or hoed, but briars and thorns will come up. I will also charge the clouds to rain no rain on it. For the vineyard of the Lord of hosts is the house of Israel and the men of Judah His delightful plant. Thus He looked for justice, but behold, bloodshed; for righteousness, but behold, a cry of distress."[7]

Blessed is the nation whose God is the Lord, The people whom He has chosen for His own inheritance. Behold, the eye of the Lord is on those who fear Him, on those who hope for His lovingkindness, to deliver their soul from death and to keep them alive in famine.

Our soul waits for the Lord; He is our help and our shield. For our heart rejoices in Him, because we trust in His holy name. Let Your lovingkindness, O Lord, be upon us, according as we have hoped in You.[8]

---

[4] Exodus 7:4.
[5] Judges 2:20-22.
[6] Ezekiel 7:1-4.
[7] Isaiah 5:5-7.

- Sodom and Gomorrah

Now the men of Sodom were wicked exceedingly and sinners against the Lord.[9]

And the Lord said, "The outcry of Sodom and Gomorrah is indeed great, and their sin is exceedingly grave."[10]

Then [Abraham] said, "Oh may the Lord not be angry, and I shall speak only this once; suppose ten [righteous] are found there?"

And He said, "I will not destroy it on account of the ten."[11]

Then the Lord rained on Sodom and Gomorrah brimstone and fire from the Lord out of heaven, and He overthrew those cities, and all the valley, and all the inhabitants of the cities, and what grew on the ground.[12]

- Nineveh

Now the word of the Lord came to Jonah the second time, saying, "Arise, go to Nineveh the great city and proclaim to it the proclamation which I am going to tell you." So Jonah arose and went to Nineveh according to the word of the Lord. Now Nineveh was an exceedingly great city, a three days' walk.

Then Jonah began to go through the city one day's walk; and he cried out and said, "Yet forty days and Nineveh will be overthrown."

Then the people of Nineveh believed in God; and they called a fast and put on sackcloth from the greatest to the least of them.

When God saw their deeds, that they turned from their wicked way, then God relented concerning the calamity which He had declared He would bring upon them.[13]

## Principles that guide nations

In his inaugural address, Jimmy Carter said, "I have just taken the oath of office on the Bible my mother gave me a few years ago, opened to a timeless admonition from the ancient prophet Micah: 'He hath showed thee, O man,

---

[8] Psalm 33:12, 18-22.
[9] Genesis 13:13.
[10] Genesis 18:20.
[11] Genesis 18:32.
[12] Genesis 19:24-25.
[13] Jonah 3:1-5, 10.

61

what is good; and what doth the Lord require of thee, but to do justly, and to love mercy, and to walk humbly with thy God.'"[14]

The verse quoted from Micah lays out a simple moral foundation not only for individuals but also for a national government:

- *Do justice.* Apply the rule of law without favoritism or discrimination, for all persons are equal in God's sight.
- *Love mercy.* Marshall the resources of the community to help those who can't help themselves; show mercy to others in need, as God has shown mercy to us in our need.
- *Walk humbly with God.* Incorporate and submit to God's principles in law.

The American legal system, as in most of western civilization, draws heavily upon such biblical principles. Even though Ten Commandments plaques have disappeared from many court houses in recent years, America's historical documents and speeches leave little doubt about the foundation of core American principles.

The Declaration of Independence, for example, recognizes "the Laws of Nature and of Nature's God." The Declaration lays the foundation for community by promoting respect for individual human rights and dignity:

"We hold these truths to be self-evident, that all men are created equal, that they are endowed by their Creator with certain unalienable Rights, that among these are Life, Liberty and the pursuit of Happiness."

The United States Constitution lays out a system of checks and balances of power, expressed in a framework of three branches of government, pointedly designed to check the sinful nature of man and to help protect the citizenry against oppression and exploitation. In contrast to governments that joined powers of church and state, mandated religious payments, or proscribed the exercise of any faith or certain faiths, the establishment clause of the U.S. Constitution protected the God-given free will of every person from state coercion:

Congress shall make no law respecting an establishment of religion, or prohibiting the free exercise thereof....

Religious freedom is by design the very first amendment to the Constitution, the first of ten principles of human rights considered important enough to isolate for emphasis and highlight in the Bill of Rights.

---

[14] Micah 6:8.

## *Paper versus practice*

Articulating principles, of course, is one thing and following them is another. The former Soviet Union and communist China also formally espoused freedom of religion. Anyone who has lived in those countries, however, knows that words on paper do not automatically translate into actual practice.

Unfortunately, American leaders and we the people at times have proven hypocritical on principle as well. A determined minority of the 55 delegates to the Constitutional Convention, for example, lobbied relentlessly to ensure that slaves slipped through the Constitution's human rights safety net.

Thomas Jefferson owned hundreds of slaves and yet penned the glorious, revolutionary words of the Declaration of Independence, "We hold these Truths to be self-evident, that all Men are created equal, that they are endowed by their Creator with certain unalienable Rights, that among these are Life, Liberty and the Pursuit of Happiness...."

The Supreme Court likewise failed to cut the terminal cancer of slavery from the country, ruling in the infamous 1857 *Dred Scott* case that no black person, slave or free, could ever become a citizen. For political purposes, slaves counted only as three-fifths of a person. Such repeated moral failures set the stage for a bloody civil war.

Abraham Lincoln used his war powers in 1863 to issue the Emancipation Proclamation and begin to construct the road toward biblical human rights principles:

```
... all persons held as slaves within any State or
designated part of a State, the people whereof shall
then be in rebellion against the United States, shall
be then, thenceforward, and forever free....
And upon this act, sincerely believed to be an act of
justice, warranted by the Constitution, upon military
necessity, I invoke the considerate judgment of
mankind, and the gracious favor of Almighty God.
```

Two years later, the Thirteenth Amendment to the Constitution declared that "Neither slavery nor involuntary servitude, except as a punishment for crime whereof the party shall have been duly convicted, shall exist within the United States... ." The amendment set the stage for the legal integration of blacks as American citizens, provided for in the Fourteenth Amendment of 1868, which also remedied the *Dred Scott* decision.

Actual integration of blacks into society and culture, of course, would prove far more challenging than amending the Constitution. Still, vital social and moral movements often begin with documents that lay a legal framework that serves as a tool of cultural education. Consider the impact on the millions of school children who grew up daily reciting the Pledge of Allegiance, finalized in 1954, which promotes "liberty and justice for all" and declares that we are "one nation under God."

## Political principles

Political party platforms also say a lot about the values of party leaders and the citizens who align themselves with parties. While party platforms are not legal or even binding documents, they do serve to sketch the worldview of party leaders and members and to provide a general map of how party candidates will govern given the opportunity.

Consider the gulf of difference between the Democrat and Republican 2012 party platforms[15] on key social issues:

## Human life issues:

**Republican Party** - "…we assert the sanctity of human life and affirm that the unborn child has a fundamental individual right to life which cannot be infringed. We support a human life amendment to the Constitution and endorse legislation to make clear that the Fourteenth Amendment's protections apply to unborn children."

"We oppose using public revenues to promote or perform abortion or fund organizations which perform or advocate it and will not fund or subsidize health care which includes abortion coverage."

**Democratic Party** - "The Democratic Party strongly and unequivocally supports *Roe v. Wade* and a woman's right to make decisions regarding her pregnancy, including a safe and legal abortion, regardless of ability to pay."

"President Obama and the Democratic Party are committed to supporting family planning around the globe to help women care for their families, support their communities, and lead their countries to be healthier and more productive. That's why, in his first month in office, President Obama overturned the 'global gag rule,' a ban on federal funds to foreign family planning organizations that provided information about, counseling on, or offered abortions."

## Health care:

**Republican Party** - "We believe that taking care of one's health is an individual responsibility. To reduce demand, and thereby lower costs, we

---

[15] Party platforms are available online at ivotevalues.com/partyplatforms or democrats.org/democratic-national-platform and gop.com/2012-republican-platform_home

must foster personal responsibility while increasing preventive services to promote healthy lifestyles."

**Democratic Party** - "We believe accessible, affordable, high quality health care is part of the American promise, that Americans should have the security that comes with good health care, and that no one should go broke because they get sick...."

## Marriage:

**Republican Party** - "We reaffirm our support for a Constitutional amendment defining marriage as the union of one man and one woman."

**Democratic Party** - "We support marriage equality and support the movement to secure equal treatment under law for same-sex couples."

## Laws reflect values

Laws in a democratic republic like the United States, in which the people indirectly govern themselves through elected leaders who are bound to a constitution that enumerates inalienable rights, provide a measure of the *values* of the nation and its people. Of course, sometimes laws passed by elected leaders prove widely unpopular, such as the Alien and Sedition Act of 1798 or Prohibition or the more recent Affordable Care Act (Obamacare). Generally, however, the prospect of rewards or reprisals through elections means that politicians in the U.S. will most likely pass laws that reasonably reflect the values of many American people.

Evaluating contemporary American society under this assumption–that laws in a democratic republic generally reflect cultural values–one can conclude that Americans generally approve of the following, for example:

- strong punishment for violent crime;
- government aid for the poor at home and overseas;
- equal opportunity;
- individual freedom and free enterprise; and
- substantial investment in education.

Sectors of American society obviously debate the degree or method of implementing these values. Great internal debates rage over legalizing prostitution or pornography, workfare versus welfare, life imprisonment versus the death penalty, public versus private education and the amount of government taxes, regulation and power.

But Americans still possess a worldview and overarching values that the rest of the world recognizes as distinctly *American*.

National cultures are built on shared mores, on commonly held world views, on a dominant consensus of how people should live. Individuals may differ significantly from their country's culture, and rigid stereotypes are not helpful, but the fact remains that clear popular values emerge.

Nations are, after all, essentially groupings of people who not only share governments and geographical boundaries but also common values and cultural practices. The same pattern of sharp cultural contrasts depicted among the biblical-era nations still persists among modern nations. Who does not recognize that centuries of choices have made the United States culturally and religiously distinct from China, Iran or Vietnam?

Many of a nation's values arise from the faith commitments of its citizenry. Since the United States enjoys a heritage of Christian leaders and people, Americans historically have tended to take faith steps toward God when laying down our Constitution and laws. When we have failed to do so—such as in the case of slavery, racial discrimination and abortion—we have paid a heavy price for those moral failures.

## Consequences of faith steps

Americans as a nation over the centuries have taken faith steps toward God as well as steps away from God. These steps have borne consequences accordingly:

- In choosing to elevate the **rule of law** over the law of the ruler, America has enjoyed political and societal stability.
- By denying **equal rights** to blacks through slavery, an entire race suffered great harm and a bloody civil war cost countless lives.
- In choosing to protect **religious freedom**, America secured a rich and vibrant community of faith and moral strength.
- By denying the **right to life** to millions of unborn babies, our nation now faces a foreboding population and labor demographic that pits the young against the elderly.
- In choosing to **share wealth** with the poor at home and overseas, America has helped save millions of lives and lifted many out of poverty.

America's successes and failures have well borne out George Washington's admonition that "Providence has connected the permanent felicity of a nation with its virtue." Our future depends on whether we as a people will take steps toward God or, forsaking His principles for radical secularism and nihilism, away from Him.

So how can we encourage our nation and our friends to take faith steps toward God?

# Chapter 7:
# *How to encourage faith steps toward God*

*"I call heaven and earth to witness against you today, that I have set before you life and death, the blessing and the curse. So choose life in order that you may live...."*
–Deuteronomy 30:19

How can we encourage individuals and a nation to take faith steps toward God?

The function of the Old Testament Law–God's moral principles taught in the first five books of the Bible and summarized in the Ten Commandments–provides a model of how to encourage faith steps.

The Law functioned to *direct people toward God and prepare them for fellowship with Him.*

Through the Law, God taught people how to live as He had designed them to live. As people learned how to live according to God's Law, they learned about God's character, values and will.

The Law taught people right and wrong. Consequences–*harms and benefits*–reinforced the Law.

Following the Law yielded benefit. Transgressing the Law resulted in harm. By learning from these consequences and following the Law, people moved toward God.

The Law was limited, of course, in that it could only prescribe godly behavior; it could not empower a sinful people to live godly lives. The Law served to *prepare the way* for the time when God would write His laws on our hearts and put His Spirit within us, so that we could enjoy abundant life in fellowship with Him.

Christians today likewise can follow this very same principle in encouraging individuals and nations to take faith steps toward God. As we encourage our friends and government leaders to choose godly paths–honoring the sanctity of life, upholding equal justice for all, enforcing the rule of law–we are helping them to take steps toward God. Responding to God's principles keeps their hearts and minds open to Him.

## *Appealing to self-interest: blessing v. curse*

But how do we *communicate* these things to people who may not share our commitment to biblical principles?

We can learn from how Moses exhorted the nation of Israel shortly before he died. The nation Israel had been founded upon biblical principles, but the people had strayed far from those principles. The lessons of 40 years in the wilderness had taught them the consequences of turning toward or away from God. So as Moses neared the end of his earthly days, he delivered one last message to drive home those lessons and prepare the people to cross into the Promised Land.

First, Moses pointed to the path of living according to God's design:

"Now it shall be, if you diligently obey the LORD your God, being careful to do all His commandments which I command you today, the LORD your God will set you high above all the nations of the earth. All these blessings will come upon you and overtake you if you obey the LORD your God..."[1]

Then Moses presented a simple, pragmatic calculus of *self-interest*:

"See, I have set before you today life and prosperity, and death and adversity; in that I command you today to love the LORD your God, to walk in His ways and to keep His commandments and His statutes and His judgments, that you may live and multiply, and that the LORD your God may bless you in the land where you are entering to possess it.
"But if your heart turns away and you will not obey, but are drawn away and worship other gods and serve them, I declare to you today that you shall surely perish. You will not prolong *your* days in the land where you are crossing the Jordan to enter and possess it.
"I call heaven and earth to witness against you today, that I have set before you life and death, the blessing and the curse. So choose life in order that you may live, you and your descendants, by loving the LORD your God, by obeying His voice, and by holding fast to Him; for this is your life and the length of your days, that you may live in the land which the LORD swore to your fathers, to Abraham, Isaac, and Jacob, to give them."[2]

---

[1] Deuteronomy 28:1-2.
[2] Deuteronomy 30:15-20.

Life and prosperity. Death and adversity. The blessing and the curse.

A simple calculus of self-interest: Obey God and His principles and receive blessing and life; disobey and receive curses and death.

Moses' final exhortation demonstrates a simple formula for encouraging people to take faith steps:

1.  Point to the path for life.
2.  Outline the *benefit* of choosing and the *harm* of rejecting that path.

The pattern is quite simple. Choose the way of life and enjoy prosperity. Choose the way of death and experience adversity. The blessing or the curse hinge on your choice. The particulars of choices, harms and benefits will of course vary by issue, but the simple pattern remains the same.

### Observing evidence and learning from consequences

Around 1589, Galileo Galilei ascended the Leaning Tower of Pisa and dropped two balls of similar shape but differing weights (mass) to the ground. The two balls hit the ground at the same time, disproving the long-held Aristotelian theory of gravity–that objects fall at speed relative to their mass. Today anyone can replicate Galileo's classic experiment and observe the identical result.

A scientist makes a hypothesis (a choice), performs an action and observes the result. Consistently replicating this result time and again reveals a scientific fact. If the scientist learns and accepts this fact, he or she will begin to base future decisions on this discovered truth.

Similarly, an individual makes a moral choice, performs a behavior and observes the result. Over time, the results reveal a pattern, a moral principle. If the individual learns and accepts this moral principle, he or she will begin to base future choices on this discovered truth.

Even though this process in our everyday personal experience is not as systematic or tidy as in scientific experiments, the principle of learning by observing choices and consequences remains the same.

This learning pattern is especially true in the area of relationships.

A toddler disobeys his mother's warning to stay away from the stove and gets burned. A college student yields herself sexually to an insistent boyfriend, who causes her heartbreak and regret when he moves on to his next conquest. A husband mistreats his wife, creates a schism in their relationship and experiences the loneliness of alienation.

These lessons of life and relationships offer us an opportunity to observe which principles work and which principles fail.

69

## Choices and consequences

When the results of consequences prove consistent–when we see that our choices consistently yield a good or bad result–a moral principle emerges. We gain an opportunity to receive or reject that moral principle, to move toward Truth or away from Truth.

The result of our moral choices is, as Moses made clear, either blessing or curse.

Of course, people can choose whether or not to learn life lessons in this way. Some people stubbornly reject learning opportunities and become experts at suppressing or denying the consequences of their moral and relational behavior.

They are like the patient in a psychiatric ward who had convinced himself he was dead An intern at a hospital walks into the ward, determined to reason with the self-deluded patient. The intern had developed a strategy he was sure would outsmart the patient.

So the intern posed this clever challenge to the patient:

"Dead people don't bleed, right?"

The patient thought for a while. Finally, he nodded his head in agreement.

The intern produced a pin and pricked the patient's finger. A drop of blood formed on the patient's finger.

The patient looked at the blood and his eyes grew wide with astonishment.

The patient considered this unexpected result for quite some time. Suddenly, his puzzled brow arched upward and his eyes lit up.

"Why, that's incredible," he exclaimed. "Dead people *really do* bleed!"

## Learning or suppressing life lessons

Like the stubbornly self-deceived patient, we can persist in perverting the obvious lessons that our choices and consequences offer us. But the truth is that deep down, each of us actually apprehends the consequences of our choices.

We can kick against the goads, refuse to learn from the results of our choices and experience all kinds of pain. Prisons, divorce courts, debt collection agencies and rehab centers overflow with individuals who stubbornly fail to heed the consequences of bad choices. We may try to deny the lesson of touching the flame, but our scars daily remind us.

We can also learn from the consequences of our choices, submit to the lessons and adjust our behavior accordingly. An ex-con lands a job and launches a new life. An insensitive spouse learns to listen and love more selflessly. An undisciplined consumer develops self-control and saving. An addicted person seeks counseling and tackles the core issues contributing to addictive behavior.

Some individuals from a young age fairly consistently make good choices. They follow their parents' leadership, choose friends who stay out of trouble and avoid the temptation of negative cultural influences. Such choices naturally reward them with the approval of parents, protection from harms experienced by their risk-taking peers, and eventually success in adult and family relationships and career endeavors.

How about you?

Rewind the tape of your own life and review some of the key moral *choices* you have faced over the years. Think of the *consequences* you experienced as a result. Recall the responses you made to the *lesson*.

Those choices mapped out on a line would look like this:

Choice → Consequence → Lesson.

That's a picture of how *faith steps* have worked in your life.

You made choices, observed the consequences and learned principles. You deduced from the consequences you experienced which choices work and which don't. As you accommodated the lessons, you took faith steps toward God and His principles.

### *Outlining harms and benefits*

That's exactly how we can encourage faith steps by others and by our nation–in practical terms of which choices work and which don't. Outline the harms and benefits, or as Moses would say, the curses and the blessings. Appeal to self-interest.

Ensuing chapters illustrate what encouraging faith steps sounds like in a variety of public policy issues. For example:

- Engaging in sex before marriage risks sexually transmitted diseases and low self-esteem (*harm*). But saving sex for marriage can preserve your goals and self-esteem and protect you from physical disease and emotional trauma (*benefit*).

- Polling shows that eliminating conscience protections for physicians will cause many to drop out of medicine, thus decreasing patient access to physicians (*harm*). But preserving conscience protections allows patients to choose physicians who share their values–which

```
polling shows fulfills a high priority of most
Americans (benefit).
```

People make their own choices; we are simply informing their *self-interest*.

In encouraging individuals and a nation to take faith steps, we do not assume a position of moral superiority or judgment. We do not plead, cajole or threaten.

In love and compassion, offering evidence and reason, we simply present the clear choices and draw a line to the benefits or harms likely to result from those choices. Choosing this course of action will benefit you in this way, and choosing this course of action will harm you in this way.

This approach of allowing people to observe and consider the evidence mirrors the design of God's creation and how He communicates His principles to us. God does not force our choices. He lays out the evidence for us to observe. He shows us the harms and benefits to help us learn to make the right choices.

## Words and works

Jesus not only preached; He also performed miraculous works. He encouraged people to observe the works and draw conclusions.

```
"If I do not do the works of My Father, do not
believe Me; but if I do them, though you do not
believe Me, believe the works, so that you may know
and understand that the Father is in Me, and I in the
Father."3
```

Sometimes those of us who value so dearly the words of Scripture can neglect this principle. Knowing the power of God's Word, we tend to expect that words alone will win over others. Yet in fact, we face the same skeptical audience that Jesus faced. We can imitate His approach by educating not only with words, but also with works—in the sense of showing concrete consequences of choices.

People who do not yet know how to look toward heaven focus on their daily experience here on the earth. That's where we must begin—in the pragmatic, experiential sphere in which people live. Sometimes before people can experience spiritual principles through the eyes of faith, they need to see those principles demonstrated in the concrete reality they can see every day.

---

3 John 10:37-38.

So now we turn to applying the principles of faith steps to current public policy issues, with the goal of learning how to encourage our friends and our countrymen to make good choices and thus take faith steps toward God.

# PART THREE:
# Faith Steps in vital issues

# Chapter 8:
# *Euthanasia and assisted suicide*

*"Thou shalt not kill."*
– Exodus 20:13 (KJV)

Public policy offers Christians an opportunity to demonstrate biblical truth through practical principles. As an example of what encouraging faith steps looks like in the public square, consider the issue of medical killing–assisted suicide and euthanasia.

Christians know well the clear biblical commandment, "Thou shalt not kill" and the core biblical theme of God's sovereignty over life and death. But what about those who do not view the Bible as their moral authority?

For communicating with those individuals, we remember the pattern set by Moses. We want to show how choices result in curses or blessings, or in contemporary terms, *harms* or *benefits*.

## The power of stories

Explaining harms and benefits need not be relegated only to dry presentations of statistics, polling and other evidence. It can also involve the telling of *stories*.

Some years ago, I tired of watching on television the propagandist portrayals of euthanasia in the Netherlands. The story always went something like this: A "compassionate" family doctor complies with the repeated request of patient to end his suffering while family members look on with gratitude.

So I spent several months in the Netherlands, conducting interviews with real people about their experiences with the heralded Dutch euthanasia. I uncovered completely different stories than the media and Dutch authorities had been propagating.

When I returned to the United States, I shared those untold stories with then-Senator Sam Brownback. Moved by the tragic stories, Senator Brownback asked me to testify before the U.S. Senate Committee on the

Judiciary, Subcommittee on the Constitution, Civil Rights and Property Rights.

## My Senate testimony:[1]

Senators, thank you for the privilege of testifying today.

I spent several months in the Netherlands a few years ago researching personal accounts of euthanasia.

I knew from published medical studies that Dutch doctors admitted, on condition of anonymity, to putting approximately 1,000 patients to death a year *without* the patients' request.[2]

I interviewed Dr. Zbigniew Zylicz, a Polish-born internal medicine and oncology specialist who has practiced in the Netherlands since 1979.

Dr. Zylicz told me about his experience with an elderly patient in an academic hospital:

> "[My patient] was afraid to go to the hospital because she was afraid of euthanasia. She was not asking for this; she did not even want this. And they promised her that nothing would happen to her.
>
> "I admitted her on the weekend to a bed of another patient who would be coming back Monday morning. I had no other facility for her. She was very ill, and I expected she would die on the weekend.
>
> "But she improved. With good treatment and pain control, she started to talk and she was not dead.
>
> "On Monday morning when I went off from my shift and went home, my colleague came and did something. I don't know exactly what he did, but she died within ten minutes.
>
> "And the nurses called me at home. They were very upset about this. And I was very upset about this, too.

---

[1] Testimony of Jonathan Imbody, U.S. Senate Committee on the Judiciary, Subcommittee on the Constitution, Civil Rights and Property Rights, May 25, 2006. http://www.judiciary.senate.gov/hearings/testimony.cfm?id=e655f9e2809e5476862f735da115 4c57&wit_id=e655f9e2809e5476862f735da1154c57-2-3 Web accessed Sep. 3, 2012.

[2] Paul J. van der Maas, et. al., "Euthanasia, Physician-Assisted Suicide, and Other Medical Practices Involving the End of Life in the Netherlands, 1990–1995," *New England Journal of Medicine*, Volume 335:1699-1705 November 28, 1996 Number 22; Table 1. Basing calculations on data from surveys of physicians under promise of anonymity, authors account for between .5% and .8% of 135,546 (thus totaling between 678 and 1,084) deaths in the Netherlands were attributable to "Ending of life without patient's explicit request."

"And this was not the only single case. This was
the *whole system* working like this."

The Dutch have a lot of faith in their dikes and in their regulations. But euthanasia introduces dangerous gray areas of decision-making by doctors and by vulnerable patients who feel pressured to die.

These gray areas defy regulation.

I interviewed a Dutch couple, Ed and Xandra, who told me about Ed's father, Franz.

Franz was a Dutch sailor who had reluctantly entered the hospital for pain relief. Doctors discovered that Franz had a terminal illness. Franz's son Ed recalls,

"We were all invited to the hospital when [the
doctors] said the diagnosis. The doctors told my
Dad, 'Well, you don't have too long to live. We
can't guarantee anything, but if we operate, you
could live longer and have more time to be with
your kids.'"
"When the doctors left, my sister said it very
bluntly, just putting it on the table: 'What about
euthanasia?' she said."

Franz's wife did not protest. Xandra suggests that's because Franz's wife was angry with him and thought Franz had been unfaithful in their marriage.

So Franz agreed to euthanasia.

Xandra remembers the day the doctor came to put her father-in-law to death.

"[The doctor] had all those little vials, and she
had two injections—one to put him to sleep, and
one for the killing part.
"She was very, 'OK, I need to do this *now*.'
Probably she had another appointment after that.
"Then she started injecting him.
"While she was giving the injection, I was
standing at [my father-in-law's] feet. He was
really looking at me and at our baby—I was holding
the baby at the time."

Then, Xandra says, her father-in-law suddenly cried out.

He said, "I don't want to die!"

Xandra frantically looked to the doctor and at the others in the room.

"But no one was reacting."

She didn't know what to do.

"And then he was like he was in a deep sleep. So then
the doctor started getting the other injection. Then
I left the room."

Franz died from that second injection, whether he really wanted to or not.

Once a country casts off millennia of Hippocratic and Judeo-Christian prohibitions against suicide and euthanasia, the ship drifts farther and farther out to sea with no anchor.

If we assume the power to kill patients who ask for it, why not kill disabled patients who cannot ask for it? If we assume the power to kill patients with physical illnesses, why not kill patients with emotional illnesses? If we assume the power to kill the elderly who have medical problems, why not kill infants and children who have medical problems?

This slippery slope is not theoretical; this is exactly what has happened in the Netherlands and nearby Belgium, which now euthanizes children.[3,4,5,6]

And it can happen anywhere, unless we provide truly compassionate alternatives to state-sponsored suicide:

1. More doctors need advanced training in palliative care.
2. In certain cases, more aggressive pain-relief prescribing regulations will help doctors provide more effective relief for patients.

---

[3] The article, "Dutch take courage in debate on euthanasia," published in *The Times of London*, 2/26/00, notes:

- "Controversial cases have tested the boundaries of euthanasia's application, none more so than that of a 25-year-old woman who had suffered anorexia for 15 years and who had been in hospital and through therapy without success. She repeatedly begged her doctor to help her die and threatened violent suicide if he would not. She went so far as to videotape her plea for euthanasia and the doctor agreed."
- Euthanasia is also administered apart from consideration of whether or not the recipient is experiencing pain.
  "Professor Paul van der Maas, who led the first study into his country's euthanasia policy, said... 'Euthanasia is not given to spare pain; it is to preserve a patient's dignity.'"
- Critics believe that "many doctors still lie about the true number of euthanasia cases they perform and falsify statistics of the handicapped infants killed each year. Officially it is ten, but Professor [Roel] Kuiper said, 'So many statistics and studies on euthanasia are manufactured to promote it is as a sound idea.'"

[4] The article, "Hospital performs euthanasia on infants," Associated Press, 11/30/2004, reveals, "A hospital in the Netherlands — the first nation to permit euthanasia—has proposed guidelines for mercy killings of terminally ill newborns and then made a startling revelation: It already has begun carrying out such procedures, which include administering a lethal dose of sedatives."

[5] Eduard Verhagen, M.D., J.D., and Pieter J.J. Sauer, M.D., Ph.D., "The Groningen Protocol — Euthanasia in Severely Ill Newborns," *The New England Journal of Medicine*, Volume 352:959-962 March 10, 2005 Number 10.

[6] "Belgium extends euthanasia law to children," EuroNews, Feb. 13, 2014. http://www.euronews.com/2014/02/13/belgium-extends-euthanasia-law-to-children/, web accessed March 15, 2014.

3.  Hospice care can provide tremendous benefits for patients and families.

Perhaps the most important help for terminally ill patients transcends medicine. The unconditional, persevering love of family, friends and God can provide us with incomparable strength, courage and hope beyond our physical condition.

### *Dutch grandfather killed before family could stop the doctor*

Accompanying me to the Senate hearing was Henk Reitsema, a Dutch intellectual I had interviewed in the Netherlands. Henk's grandfather tragically had succumbed to a medical system too eager to hasten death.

Henk Reitsema's grandfather had received a diagnosis of non-Hodgkin's lymphoma, a disease that naturally would have taken his life within a few years. He had moved into a nursing home in Blauwborgje, in the northern province of Groningen. When he developed a painful thrombosis in his leg, he asked the attending physician at the nursing home for help with the pain.

The nursing home physician, however, responded to the request for help by quietly instructing nurses to administer overdoses of morphine while withholding food and water. Rather than providing healing or comfort, and without consulting Grandfather Reitsema or his loved ones, this doctor aimed to kill.

Henk's soft-spoken wife, Riana, had been regularly visiting Grandfather Reitsema at the time. She relates that one of Henk's aunts who was also visiting suddenly stumbled upon the plan—but too late.

```
The day before he died, she tried to give him water,
and the nurse came in. And the nurse said, "Don't
give him water."
They asked her, "Why not give him water? That's one
thing that he can drink if he doesn't want to have
food, out of his own choice."
But the nurse said, "No, you're not allowed to give
anything to drink."
```

Looking back on the event, the family now realizes why the nurse intervened to stop the aunt's simple act of compassion.

Riana notes,
```
They were in that stage of the euthanasia already,
when they don't give him anything to eat or drink.
They had stopped giving food, and then that day they
had stopped giving drink.
```

The aunt asked why and then the whole thing came out.
That's when they discovered the whole thing. But that
was too late. They couldn't reverse it at that time.

Henk interjects, "They tried, but he died from pneumonia." Pneumonia
can follow heavy morphine dosing, as the lungs fill with fluid because the
drug suppresses the muscular action needed to cough up phlegm.

The Reitsema family reeled from the revelation. Henk's father, a
missionary living overseas, had scheduled a plane trip several months later to
visit his ailing father. The doctor's deadly intervention meant he would not
see his father one last time before he died.

### Concrete evidence of harm and benefit

None of this testimony presented to the Senate included Bible verses or
theological themes. The testimony simply presented concrete evidence, in
both stories and statistics, against the choice of euthanasia and in favor of the
choice of compassionate care. Harms and benefits.

*Harms* of choosing assisted suicide and euthanasia include:

- patients lose personal autonomy while doctors gain a dangerous
  power to kill;
- patients lose the ethical protections provided for by millennia of
  Hippocratic medicine;
- unscrupulous heirs, profit-focused insurers and even cold-hearted
  medical personnel can pressure terminally ill patients or handicapped
  persons to "choose" a premature death.

The reality of assisted suicide and euthanasia is the exact *opposite* of
"death with dignity" and "compassionate choices" propaganda, which paints
the picture of autonomous patients triumphantly exercising their free will
while caring and compliant doctors carry out their wishes.

*Benefits* of choosing the alternative of palliative care (focused on making
a patient nearing the end of life comfortable) instead of euthanasia or assisted
suicide include:

- experiencing the unconditional love of family members;
- receiving comforting pain control from ethically guided physicians;
- living one's last days with true dignity, thereby providing a heritage
  of courage for the family.

Lobbying against medical killing with pragmatic arguments works. For
example, when liberal Massachusetts voters in 2012 considered Proposition
Two, which would have legalized assisted suicide, faith-based groups kept a
low profile while a public relations campaign stressed practical concerns.

As *The Washington Times* reported,

> The No on 2 camp argued that the [assisted suicide]
> initiative had too many flaws. No psychiatrist was
> required to screen patients for depression. There was
> no family-notification provision, and patients would
> fill their prescriptions at local pharmacies, leading
> to worries about unused pills falling into the wrong
> hands.

Once the public understands the harsh reality of medical killing, and the positive alternative of palliative care, through a rational explanation of such harms and benefits, support drops significantly and lifesaving patient protections remain in place.

Advocates of assisted suicide and euthanasia often gain an early advantage in assisted suicide drives by presenting carefully crafted, emotional stories that make it seem like medical killing is actually a compassionate act rather than an act of abandonment. In our desire to dispassionately and accurately present facts and evidence to appeal to the rational citizen, we cannot afford to cede to our opponents the ground of emotional appeal through stories.

Because human beings are both rational and emotive, effectively communicating harms and benefits requires both *statistics and stories*. Convincing our fellow citizens means driving home the rational message of medical evidence and statistics with accurate and compelling, emotional personal stories.

This public policy battle is not simply a matter of theory. We are not merely fighting for a principle on paper. The cold reality is that you or a loved one may someday land in a vulnerable health situation where an early demise poses a financial temptation to people who do not have your or your loved one's best interest at heart. Real people in such cases need the protection of life-honoring laws and of a society that elevates the value of life over cost and convenience.

While fighting to halt the relentless drive toward assisted suicide and euthanasia, Christians also have an opportunity to encourage our culture to value human life unconditionally, regardless of physical ailment or disability. If we can help our nation to step away from the temptation to approve medical killing and embrace instead a culture of life, we will be helping our countrymen take faith steps toward God.

# Chapter 9:
# *Sexual risk avoidance*

*Therefore do not let sin reign in your mortal body so that you obey its lusts,
and do not go on presenting the members of your body to sin as instruments
of unrighteousness; but present yourselves to God as those alive from the
dead, and your members as instruments of righteousness to God.*
–Romans 6:12-13

S arah, a 17-year-old student from Tennessee, offers a personal
testimony of the consequences of sexual choices:
When my mom and my step-dad got a divorce toward the
middle of the year, it turned my world upside down.
It had been my biggest fear for a long time, and I
just knew that I couldn't go through divorce myself.
In the same month, I received a phone call from
Alicia [a friend in college]. She was pregnant. She
was getting married. And she didn't think that she
could finish college.
I'll always remember her telling me, "You're lying to
yourself if you think that you can have sex with
someone without giving a part of your heart away,
too."
I believe in second chances, but I know that Alicia
probably won't get one.
Personally, Alicia's story scared me to death. I
didn't want to have to look my mother in the eye to
tell her that I was pregnant. I can't put my dreams
on hold because of one bad decision.
In the future, I want to marry the guy that I can
connect with on spiritual, emotional, intellectual,
and physical levels. And I'm not satisfied with just
one level. I'm doing all that I can now to make sure
that I start my future relationships on a basis of
trust.
I will be able to tell my husband-to-be that I was
faithful to him, even before I met him. And I will
not become a part of the 43% of children of divorced
parents whose marriages end in divorce as well.

I set my physical and emotional boundaries for myself
in ninth grade so that I was proactive in my decision
making. I choose where my life goes, and that means
not just letting "whatever happens happen." Setting
and knowing my own boundaries has made dating
relationships stronger and healthier in my life.
My boyfriend of six months knows exactly how far I'll
go, and that physical part of our relationship has
never been pressured. It really frees us up to get to
know each other on deeper levels and to be supportive
of each other's futures.[7]

## *Giving up about giving in*

For years, left-leaning sex education activists and many in academia
have considered teens like Sarah almost abnormal, adopting a view that boils
down to this: "Teens are going to have sex no matter what, so the best we can
do is teach them how to have sex safely." Besides giving up without reason,
this view also assumes that teens are good candidates to "have sex safely."

Never mind that no sane person would apply such an approach to other
risky teen behaviors, such as smoking, drinking or drug abuse. Imagine what
such a curriculum would sound like:

"Smoking is a natural part of growing up, so just
make sure to use a filter every time you light up."
"Drinking is part of expressing who you are, so just
be sure to only get drunk with a partner who
practices safe driving."
"Heroin is irresistibly pleasurable, so just be sure
to use clean needles."

Imagine also teaching teens that smoking a pipe isn't really smoking
because you don't inhale, that friends can have fun playing drinking games
without really getting drunk, and it's fun to experiment with different kinds
of drugs.

The prevailing "comprehensive sex education" model, however, takes
exactly this approach to child and teen sex.

"Comprehensive sex education" essentially surrenders to pop culture's
message that virtually every normal person has sex outside marriage, that sex
need not involve a committed relationship and that there is no reason to resist
sexual impulses. Starting with this faulty premise, "comprehensive sex ed"

---

[7] mychoice2wait.org website, http://mychoice2wait.org/testimonials.html accessed November
22, 2014.

emphasizes the *wrong aspects* of sex and sends the *wrong messages* about sex.

Rather than learning about building self-respect and self-control to protect themselves and to save sex for their marriage partners, students of "comprehensive sex ed" programs instead focus on the technical aspects of sex and mechanical strategies to reduce rather than avoid harm. Students learn to see bananas and cucumbers in new ways, as condom rehearsals reinforce the mistaken mantra of "safe sex."

A U.S. Department of Health and Human Services (HHS) study[8] of nine "comprehensive sex education" curricula found that two-thirds of the "comprehensive sex ed" curricula reviewed contained medically inaccurate information and that curricula often downplayed the risks and failures of condoms. The HHS review concluded that most of the programs demonstrated virtually no impact on teen sexual activity, and examples cited helped reveal why.

The "comprehensive sex ed" curricula, for example, encouraged teens to shower together, promoted methods for sexual stimulation of partners, encouraged sexual role-play on how to help a partner maintain an erection, and described how to eroticize condom use with a partner.

In one curriculum, the teacher was instructed to say to the student, "Pretend I am your sexual partner … and I want you to convince me to use a condom."[9]

One curriculum actually advised teens to "hide [condoms] on your body and ask your partner to find it …wrap them as a present and give them to your partner before a romantic dinner … tease each other manually while putting on the condom."

### FDA: Sex with condoms isn't "safe sex"

The Food and Drug Administration (FDA), while highlighting the potential risk reduction of consistent condom use, hardly recommends risking one's life on condoms:

> Will a condom guarantee I won't get a sexually transmitted disease? No. There's no absolute guarantee even when you use a condom. But most experts believe that the risk of getting HIV/AIDS and other sexually transmitted diseases can be greatly

---

Review of Comprehensive Sex Education Curricula, The Administration for Children and Families, HHS, May 2007.[8]
http://www.abstinenceworks.org/images/stories/pdfs/hhs_review_of_cse.pdf
[9] Ibid, citing "Making Proud Choices" curriculum, p. 157.

reduced if a condom is used properly. Condoms are not 100% safe, but if used properly, will reduce the risk of sexually transmitted diseases, including AIDS. Protecting yourself against the AIDS virus is of special concern because this disease is fatal and has no cure.

If you know your partner is infected, the best rule is to avoid intercourse (including oral sex). If you do decide to have sex with an infected partner, you should always be sure a condom is used from start to finish, every time.

Government testing cannot guarantee that condoms will always prevent the spread of sexually transmitted diseases. How well you are protected will also depend a great deal on which condoms you choose and how you store, handle and use them.

Condoms may be more likely to break during anal intercourse than during other types of sex because of the greater amount of friction and other stresses involved.

[B]eware of drugs and alcohol! They can affect your judgment, so you may forget to use a condom. They may even affect your ability to use a condom properly.

In other words, sex with condoms isn't totally "safe sex," but it is "less risky" sex.

The surest way to avoid these diseases is to not have sex altogether (abstinence).[10]

Nor does the FDA recommend relying on condoms to prevent sexually transmitted diseases such as the human papillomavirus (HPV):

HPV (human papillomavirus) is a sexually transmitted virus. It is passed on through genital contact (such as vaginal and anal sex). It is also passed on by skin-to-skin contact. At least 50% of people who have had sex will have HPV at some time in their lives. It is not known how much condoms protect against HPV. Areas not covered by a condom can be exposed to the virus.[11]

---

[10] "Condoms and Sexually Transmitted Diseases, Brochure," U.S. Food and Drug Administration.
http://www.fda.gov/ForConsumers/byAudience/ForPatientAdvocates/HIVandAIDSActivities/ucm126372.htm Web accessed Mar. 2, 2013.
[11] FDA web site http://www.fda.gov/forconsumers/byaudience/forwomen/ucm118530.htm accessed Feb, 10, 2013.

Likewise, the Centers for Disease Control and Prevention (CDC) acknowledges that the only surefire way to prevent HPV is to abstain from sexual activity:

> HPV can infect areas that are not covered by a condom-so condoms may not fully protect against HPV. HPV is passed on through genital contact, most often during vaginal and anal sex. HPV may also be passed on during oral sex and genital-to-genital contact. Most infected persons do not realize they are infected, or that they are passing HPV on to a sex partner.[12]

Finally, the FDA stresses no less than 20 critical safety factors the violation of which can nullify or significantly diminish the effectiveness of condoms. The factors include proper condom sources, labeling, storage, handling and inspection; special procedures related to non-circumcised males; timing of application; ensuring a reservoir tip; proper use of spermicides and lubricants; breakage; timing and method of withdrawal; disposal; contraindicated lubricants; temperature considerations; contraindicated types of intercourse; and finally and especially relevant to teens, the effect of drugs and alcohol on condom use.

How many teens do you think will meticulously follow these 20 crucial guidelines (and others omitted for the sake of brevity)? Most parents can't get their teens to clean their rooms or take out the trash on a consistent basis. Yet their very lives may be at stake if they miss any one of these condom cautions.

That's the rub with depending on "safe sex." Teens are hardly known for consistently following procedures, emotional control, sound risk assessment and careful decision making. Teen sex often occurs under rushed, drunken, drugged or emotionally charged conditions.

Expecting condoms to reliably protect this highly unreliable population and under these circumstances is like expecting a safety belt to protect a five-year-old driving a car full-speed the wrong way down the highway at rush hour. Yet many sex education advocates seemingly have plugged their ears to parents' clear preference for sexual risk avoidance education[13], labeling it "unrealistic."

---

[12] Centers for Disease Control and Prevention web site, http://www.cdc.gov/std/HPV/STDFact-HPV.htm. accessed Mar. 2, 2013.

[13] "Abstinence Education Supported By 76% of Democratic Parents and 87% of Republican Parents," NAEA, October 13, 2012 http://www.abstinenceassociation.org/newsroom/both_parties_agree_on_sra_ed.html Web

87

## The shocking revelation: Abstinence does it better

Imagine the shock and dismay of "comprehensive sex ed" advocates when researchers at the University of Pennsylvania–hardly a bastion of abstinence advocacy–suddenly trumpeted this news flash:

A new study weighs in on the controversy over sex education, finding that an abstinence-only intervention for pre-teens was more successful in delaying the onset of sexual activity than a health-promotion control intervention. After two years, one-third of the abstinence-only group reported having sex, compared to one-half of the control group. The study by researchers at the University of Pennsylvania appears in the February 1 edition of the *Archives of Pediatrics & Adolescent Medicine*.[14]

Not only did sexual risk avoidance (abstinence) education achieve impressive results; it also outperformed the competing approaches favored in federal funding—condom training and "comprehensive sex ed."

Ideologically and financially motivated groups had attempted to blame sexual risk avoidance programs for teen pregnancies without any evidence whatsoever of a causal link. By contrast, scientists with no ideological axe to grind and no profit to make reported the objective results of a randomized controlled trial.

Thomas, a teen from Arkansas, relates how sexual risk avoidance education turned his life around through its emphasis not just on sex but on character and skills for life. Thomas had been involved in gangs, violence, drinking and other high-risk behaviors when abstinence educators took a personal interest in him.

I had gotten involved with gangs and violence and drugs. I was not making the right choices that I needed to make in my life. We were making all the bad decisions you could possibly make.
Once I got into the eighth grade, an abstinence education program came into my classroom and did a workshop. And they brought in this group of kids that were 15, 16, 17 years old, and they did all of these cool skits that had a message behind them. That told me that I could make good choices and have fun, but I didn't have to keep doing what I was doing.

---

accessed Mar. 2, 2013.
[14] University of Pennsylvania Perelman School of Medicine news release, http://www.uphs.upenn.edu/news/news_releases/2010/02/theory-based-abstinence-education/, accessed November 22, 2014.

It seems like they just saw something in me, and they just started trying to mentor me and to show me the right way.
So I grabbed onto that. I started to participate in various programs they had going on in the community-summer camp and conferences and things like that.
I grabbed onto that because they were nurturing to me. It wasn't all about abstinence. They were trying to change my *life*. Yeah, they talked to me about premarital sex, but they also talked to me about staying away from drugs and alcohol and showed me negative things that could happen to me if I continued doing what I was doing. They showed me if I kept on doing the things I was doing, I could end up in jail.
But now, I'm happy to say, I'm a freshman in college. Recently there was a campus shooting. It just so happened that the four guys that committed the campus shooting were the four guys that I had started to hang out with. So all of my former friends, at the ages of 19 and 20, are facing life in the penitentiary for killing two people that night.
So who's to say that if this program did not come into my eighth-grade classroom that I would not be facing life in jail right now?
So abstinence education isn't just all about sex-it's about changing lives, and helping people around you, and nurturing and mentoring. [15]

Small wonder that parents want sexual risk avoidance (abstinence) education for their children. As Zogby polling revealed, when parents learn what abstinence education vs. comprehensive sex education actually teaches, their support for sexual risk avoidance programs reaches 60%, while support for "comprehensive sex" programs drops to 30%."[16]

Politicians should take note: When it comes to sex education, Mom and Dad really do know best.

Unfortunately, Congress and the Obama administration have bought into the propaganda about abstinence programs. Lobbyists for "comprehensive sex education" convinced President Obama in his first term and many Members of Congress to completely eliminate federal funds for abstinence education, instead devoting funding exclusively to condoms-and-

---

[15] Video testimony at Abstinence Works. http://abstinenceworks.org/teen-quotes-interviews-aamp-videos-mainmenu-53 Web accessed Feb. 16, 2013.
[16] http://www.abstinenceassociation.org/newsroom/pr_050307_parents_prefer_2to1.html

contraceptives programs. Politicians claimed to be following science in doing so, since a number of limited studies up to that point had purported to dismiss the value of sexual risk avoidance education.

## Science versus scientists

What can we learn from the misplaced animus toward effective sexual risk avoidance education?

While science itself remains objective, individual scientists can be as biased as politicians. The eagerness of researchers to prove their own ideologically driven assumptions or to secure grant funding too often seeps into study designs and results reporting. Biased journal editors can effectively shut out studies countering their biases. When the subject of research challenges the status quo consensus of researchers and policy advocates, as has been the case with abstinence programs, objective analysis is especially hard to come by.

When President Obama promised in his first Inaugural address to "restore science to its rightful place,"[17] he would have done better to acknowledge the limitations as well as the promise of science. If anti-abstinence partisans in Congress and the President can muster the humility to admit their mistake and restore funding for effective abstinence education, our nation's teens can gain a rock-solid wall of defense not only against HPV but also other potentially deadly sexually transmitted diseases.

Our teens can also learn how to set and reach higher goals and live more fulfilling lives. Teens need a counterculture message—not only to thrive but also to stay alive.

They can experience the transformation of perspective that Karla did, who tells how sexual risk avoidance education provided a platform from which to pursue much more in life than she had been settling for:

At the age of 15, I was making really poor choices and I was involved with risky behaviors. The fact that I was doing that led me to drop out of high school at the age of 15.
At the age of 17, I returned; I was 17 years old in the ninth grade. I started all over.
It was that day when the abstinence program came to my classroom. And they spoke to me about abstinence. The first thing that comes to your head when you say "abstinence" is obviously sex. But it wasn't just about not having sex. It was about making healthy

---

[17] Transcript, President Barack Obama's Inaugural Address, January 20, 2009.

choices, having a positive attitude. Staying away not just from drugs, not just from sex, but from negativity in your life.
And that's when they set my expectations and my standards higher.
I graduated from high school in three years, with scholarships. Who would have ever known I would have achieved all these things? I was the first female to graduate [from college] in my family, and I have opened the door for many others behind me in my family that are now going to be graduating and also have scholarships and have done well for themselves. So this abstinence education changed my life. [18]

Thankfully, more and more students like Thomas and Carla are seeing the value of saving sex for marriage and have grown tired of "safe sex" strategies that just don't work.

I met 2011 Miss America Teresa Scanlan at a lunch briefing at the U.S. Capitol, on sexual risk avoidance. (It's probably the only imaginable instance in which a wife would allow her husband to have lunch with a Miss America.) We had all gotten soaked in a driving rain while heading into the Capitol, and I joked with Teresa that she should use her Miss America status to launch a retro fashion explosion: galoshes.

That day Teresa, unfazed by the typically skeptical legislative staffer wonks in attendance, instead used her Miss America status to deliver a message about the tried and true method of saving sex:

I remember doing a radio interview with Sirius XM and the deejay was sarcastically asking me, "So, you're Miss America, so you're a virgin, right?" And I said, "Yes, actually, I am," and he didn't know what to say.
It's one of those things that people are surprised at because they think it's not possible. But then you see the numbers—that almost 75 percent of 15-to-17-year-olds are wanting to wait. That's pretty incredible.
This attitude that people have that "everybody is doing it" is not necessarily the case. It takes some people to stand up and say the truth—that you can 'survive' until you're 20 years old [as I am] and that you can wait until you're married. And yes, it's difficult, but having not only parents but school as

---

[18] Video testimony at Abstinence Works. http://abstinenceworks.org/teen-quotes-interviews-aamp-videos-mainmenu-53 Web accessed Feb. 16, 2013.

91

well communicating that message makes a huge difference.

We're now seeing the results and consequences of [sexual activity]. Our parents grew up in an environment of 'free sex for everyone.' Well, guess what—we've had enough of that; we don't want to try that anymore. We want [sex] to be something special; we want it to be something more. Young people are searching for relationships that mean more. Young girls are searching for men who are going to value them more.

This is about the health issues and should be taught the same way that drug and alcohol prevention are taught. It's not just 'okay' to do—the health risks are too high. There is nothing that will protect against pregnancy or an STD 100 percent except abstinence.

Now for me it's mostly for moral and theological reasons, but you don't have to agree with me theologically to believe that this is the best route to take. There is no reason we should not be presenting this side of the story. Young people are wanting it; they are needing it. I have seen the ramifications firsthand, with so many friends and family members. I've had many teenage friends get pregnant just in the past six months.

It is possible to make smart decisions and to be responsible, and young people need to be encouraged in that.

They will rise to the challenge when we say, "Your future and your health are in your hands."

# Chapter 10:
# *Abortion*

*For You formed my inward parts;*
*You wove me in my mother's womb.*
–Psalm 139:13

E very year in the United States alone, over a million women
experience the life-changing trauma of abortion. The issue is a
lodestone for public policy battles, but it carries a deep and tragic private and
personal impact. Women like Pamela relate a painful story that reflects the
personal tragedy experienced by millions of women and men:

When I was 17, I thought I was pregnant and finally
told my mom.
She called my dad who said, "Get rid of it or I'm
leaving."
She called a friend of hers, a nurse. Next thing I
know, I'm at the doctor's office thinking I'm getting
a checkup to see if I am pregnant. And he gives me a
shot and tells my mom to bring me back in tomorrow to
finish the procedure.
There was no chance to talk, to run away... it was
done.
I guess I was just numb. Because I can't remember
anything but lying on a table, staring at the ceiling
with tears coming out of my eyes, and the nurse
saying over and over, "Are you okay?" And me not
saying anything.
She told the doctor "Oh, she's fine-she just won't
talk."
I remember my dad driving us there. His name was
well-known around the community because of being
involved in youth sports. He didn't want to ruin "his
name" with a pregnant daughter.
I ended up drinking, doing drugs, sex-I just didn't
care.
Later I was married to an abuser and divorced two
years later. Found out during that time that the
boyfriend who got me pregnant was trying to hire

someone to push me down the stairs at school for $500 so I would miscarry.

I later remarried and got pregnant. They thought I miscarried and put me in for a D&C [dilation and curettage, a surgical procedure often performed after a first trimester miscarriage] with a bunch of other girls getting abortions, laughing and joking about it. Well I ended up in an emergency room and it was a tubal pregnancy which they removed.

Felt this was my punishment.

Got divorced and later remarried. Had another emergency surgery on my other tube that was twisted and full of cysts. So I no longer could have children.

I'm 52 and have never had a day where I haven't felt guilt.

I was raised in a very Catholic environment, so as I got older it was hard to understand how my parents could make this choice. Granted, my mother still to this day apologizes and says it is the biggest regret. And I end up trying to make her feel better. I guess I have forgiven them and myself.

But it's just a pain that never goes away.

My heart breaks for those getting abortions because they don't realize the effect it will have, if not now, then later. The one thing that keeps me going (though I did try suicide and by the grace of God the doctors brought me back after my heart stopped twice) is knowing I will see Anthony and Joseph someday.

I had I guess what you could call "The Light" moment when I was lying on the table when they were pumping my stomach. Jesus was standing there next to me with a white robe, and the hood was over his face.

He said, "This is who you need to love." I expected to see His face. When I looked over, it was my face.

I'm still in a marriage that is...well, we're married. He could care less about kids, so it's not an issue. I would have liked to adopt but never felt worthy. Now it's not even an option in my situation. So I'm just patiently waiting with my 'pet' kids to see my children someday.

I am now 52 and still cry about it.

I could go on and on about the messed up life I've had, but that just is expected with such guilt-ridden feelings.

I'm still healing and will be till the day I die.[1]

### Abortion as empowerment?

The reality experienced by Pamela and many others who account for the over 55 million abortions since the legalization of abortion in the United States[2] hardly matches the picture portrayed by the abortion industry. That savvy and well-financed industry has peddled abortion as a sterile medical procedure that simply excises a "blob of tissue."

Abortion ideologues also hail abortion as a socioeconomic tool, a cornerstone of women's rights and progress. The early women's rights movement advanced the notion that preventing babies through contraceptives and abortion holds the key to women's independence, economic advancement and empowerment.

Kate Michelman, president emerita of the abortion group, NARAL Pro-Choice America, explained in a 2013 *USA Today* column marking *Roe's* 40th anniversary,

> The goal of *Roe v. Wade* was to ensure a woman's right to control the most intimate aspect of her life. Without this right, women are unable to participate equally with men in the nation's social, political and economic life.[3]

That would be news, of course, to the millions of women who have had children while also making meaningful contributions to society, politics and professional enterprises.

Yet the Supreme Court in its 1973 *Roe v. Wade* decision accommodated the view of empowering women through the death of their babies, inventing a "constitutional right to privacy" where none had previously existed. The Court's unilateral and legally inventive decision abridged the right to life, expressed in the Declaration of Independence ("...endowed by their Creator with certain unalienable Rights, that among these are Life...") and the US Constitution ("nor shall any State deprive any person of life..."). It also tore

---

[1] Pamela X, testimony on Silent No More website, http://www.silentnomoreawareness.org/testimonies/testimony.aspx?ID=2615, accessed November 22, 2014.

[2] "Roe foes add up 55 million legalized abortions," Washington Times, Jan. 23, 2013. Figures based on Guttmacher Institute reports. http://www.washingtontimes.com/news/2013/jan/23/roe-foes-add-up-55-million-legalized-abortions/ Web accessed Jan. 27, 2013.

[3] "'Roe v. Wade' about much more than abortion," Kate Michelman and Carol Tracy, *USA Today*, Jan. 22, 2013. http://www.usatoday.com/story/opinion/2013/01/21/roe-v-wade-about-much-more-than-abortion-column/1852701/ Accessed Jan. 23, 2013.

decision-making power away from the citizens of individual states and opened the door to nationwide abortion on demand.

The decades-long fight to overturn that unjust decision has included not only public advocacy, but also personal outreach. Thanks to the compassionate work of thousands of pregnancy centers around the country, women who face financial and personal challenges during pregnancy and after giving birth are receiving financial, medical and practical help plus emotional and spiritual support. Young fathers are learning, through pregnancy centers' education, counseling and mentoring, to share in the responsibility and fulfillment of bringing a new life into the world.

### Ending or enabling "back-alley" abortions?

Abortion advocates assert that the *Roe* ruling ended dangerous "back-alley" abortions. In fact, however, *Roe* simply spread unregulated abortion clinics nationwide, as politicians exempted them from reasonable government health oversight as a way to curry favor with deep-pocketed political supporters like Planned Parenthood.

To Planned Parenthood and other abortion outlets, ending the lives of developing babies is not only a matter of ideology; it's also big business. As a "nonprofit" enterprise, Planned Parenthood in one year alone raked in well over a *billion* dollars, including over a third of a billion dollars in taxpayer funding.[4] In just three years, Planned Parenthood performed roughly a million abortions.[5]

My pro-life colleague Carol Everett, a former co-owner of a franchise abortion clinic in Dallas, Texas, explains the business strategy:

> Abortion is a skillfully marketed product sold to women at a crisis time in their life. If the product is defective, she can't return it for a refund.[6]

Norma McCorvey, whose false allegations as plaintiff "Jane Roe" in the Supreme Court's *Roe v Wade* decision provided pro-abortion attorneys with a perfect pretext for their case, testified at a U.S. Senate hearing in 1998 about her subsequent experience working in abortion clinics:

> I saw procedure rooms where sanitation and hygiene were after-thoughts. I worked with a doctor who

---

[4] "Planned Parenthood Federation of America Annual report 2008-2009." http://www.plannedparenthood.org/about-us/annual-report-4661.htm
[5] Planned Parenthood Services fact sheet, current as of Feb. 2011. http://www.plannedparenthood.org/files/PPFA/PP_Services.pdf
[6] See also Carol Everett's interview and others in "To Save a Life," a pro-life video exposing the inside operations of the abortion industry. http://www.youtube.com/watch?v=MNJmpQSbFeE Web accessed Jan. 28, 2013.

```
operated on women while he was barefoot. I've worked
in the clinics where drug use was rampant among
clinic workers.[7]
```

Statistical and videotaped evidence by innovative organizations such as
Live Action[8] have documented the apparently endemic corruption in abortion
outlets like Planned Parenthood. Investigations and undercover exposés of
the behemoth abortion business reveal a conglomerate more fit for a federal
investigation than a federal subsidy.

As Ohio Republican Rep. Jean Schmidt has noted,

```
For the sake of abortion, Planned Parenthood holds
itself above the law, ignoring mandatory reporting
requirements, skirting parental consent, and aiding
and abetting child sex trafficking.[9]
```

Partly as a reaction to scandalous abortion operations, in 2011, the U.S.
House of Representatives voted 240-185[10] to cut off federal subsidies to
Planned Parenthood. The Democrat-controlled Senate refused to follow suit,
however, and President Obama would have vetoed the bill.

Meanwhile, several states have enacted women's health regulations that
impact abortion clinics, thanks to the work of cutting-edge groups like
Americans United for Life and their stalwart attorneys Dan McConchie,
Denise Burke, Mailee Smith, Anna Paprocki, Bill Saunders and others. Such
state laws protect women's health by addressing dismal conditions in
previously unregulated clinics. Apart from proper state regulation and
oversight, abortion clinics can hide grossly unsanitary conditions, hire
unqualified practitioners and foist predatory practices on vulnerable women.

### Abortion clinic horrors

Philadelphia abortion doctor Kermit Gosnell, for example, operated a
squalid abortion clinic where he killed live babies with concentration camp
inhumanity. Women suffered and died in a filthy facility described as "a bad
gas station restroom." The abuses continued for years under the noses of pro-
abortion state officials who had curtailed state health and safety inspections.

---

[7] McCorvey, Norma. Testimony to the Senate Subcommittee on the Constitution, Federalism
and Property Rights (January 21, 1998), quoted by Muriel Patterson in a May 20, 1998
parliament of Western Australia session, transcript, p. 2826,
http://www.parliament.wa.gov.au/hansard/hans35.nsf/(ATT)/A4C48AF367A417A84825661A
007776E1/$file/C0520006.PDF accessed November 22, 2014.
[8] See http://www.liveaction.org.
[9] Speech by Rep. Jean Schmidt on House floor Feb. 17, 2011. http://www.c-
spanvideo.org/videoLibrary/clip.php?appid=599570975
[10] Feb. 18, 2011 House vote on the Pence Amendment.

Eventually, the law caught up with Gosnell, as *ABC World News* reported in 2011,

> Gosnell, 69, and nine employees from his West Philadelphia Women's Medical Society were arrested Jan. 19 and charged with several offenses. Gosnell was charged with eight counts of murder for allegedly killing babies born alive and giving a lethal dose of Demerol to a woman. [11]

According to Philadelphia District Attorney Seth Williams, Gosnell:

> "induced labor, forced the live birth of viable babies in the sixth, seventh, eighth month of pregnancy and then killed those babies by cutting into the back of the neck with scissors and severing their spinal cord."[12]

Shockingly, the Grand Jury report from the Gosnell case cites testimony revealing that when Pennsylvania pro-abortion Republican governor Tom Ridge took office, "high-level government officials" decided to discontinue abortion clinic inspections because "there was a concern that if they did routine inspections, that they may find a lot of these facilities didn't meet [health and safety standards] and then there would be less abortion facilities, less access to women to have an abortion."[13]

Abortion advocates commonly contend that health and safety regulations, such as regulations required of other surgical facilities, would shut down their clinics. What does that tell you about the level of safety women encounter in abortion clinics? Such tacit admissions should spur legislators to action to protect women by enacting clinic regulations. Otherwise any abortion clinic, shrouded in secrecy and protected by special interest lobbies, remains a "back alley clinic."

---

[11] "Alleged Victim Calls Philadelphia Abortion Doc Kermit Gosnell a 'Monster'," ABC World News, Jan. 25, 2011. Accessed 1/1/2013 at http://abcnews.go.com/US/alleged-victim-calls-philadelphia-abortion-doctor-kermit-gosnell/story?id=12731387#.UOMPpiqF9gw

[12] "'House of horrors' alleged at abortion clinic," NBC News, Jan. 19, 2011, http://www.nbcnews.com/id/41154527/ns/us_news-crime_and_courts/t/house-horrors-alleged-abortion-clinic/ accessed Apr. 18, 2014.

[13] "Report of the Grand Jury," R. Seth Williams, District Attorney, in the Court of Common Pleas, First Judicial District of Pennsylvania, Criminal Trial Division, in re : misc. no. 0009901-2008, County investigating: Grand Jury xxiii: c-17, p. 147, http://www.phila.gov/districtattorney/pdfs/grandjurywomensmedical.pdf accessed Apr. 18, 2014.

### What motivates abortionists?

Relatively few physicians in the United States blatantly transgress the Hippocratic oath and kill their unborn patients. What motivates those who do?

Former abortionist Dr. Anthony Levatino, now an outspoken pro-life physician, offers insights from personal experience:

> In my practice, we were averaging between $250 and $500 for an abortion, and it was cash. That's the one time as a doctor you can say, either pay me up front or I'm not going to take care of you. When somebody's going to have an abortion, it's an elective procedure. Either you have the money or you don't, and they get it.
>
> The resident on call got the job of doing the saline [abortions] and there would usually be two or three of those. They were horrible because you saw one intact, whole baby being born, and sometimes they were alive.
>
> That was very, very frightening. It was a very stomach-turning kind of existence.
>
> Yet, I was doing that at the same time that my wife and I were trying to have a child, and we were having difficulty with that. So we started desperately looking for a baby to adopt, and I was throwing them in the garbage at the rate of nine and ten a week.[14]

Dr. Levatino and his wife eventually had a daughter but lost her in an automobile accident.

> Let me tell you something. When you lose a child, your child, life is very different. Everything changes. All of a sudden, the idea of a person's life becomes very real. It is not an embryology course anymore. It's not just a couple of hundred dollars. It's the real thing.
>
> It's your child you buried.
>
> The old discomforts came back in spades. I couldn't even think about a D&E abortion [dilation and evacuation, a procedure done in the second trimester of pregnancy] anymore.
>
> [Y]ou start to realize this is somebody's child. I lost my child, someone who was very precious to us.

---

[14] Testimony given at "Meet the Abortion Providers" workshop sponsored by the Pro-life Action League of Chicago (see http://pro-lifeaction.org/providers). Accessed online Oct. 18, 2012 at http://www.silentnomoreawareness.org/testimonies/testimony.aspx?ID=1127

And now I am taking somebody's child and I am tearing
him right out of their womb.
I am killing somebody's child.
That is what it took to get me to change. My own
sense of self-esteem went down the tubes. I began to
feel like a paid assassin. That's exactly what I was.[15]

## Biblical basis for protecting life

While the Bible may contain some mysteries and passages hard to
comprehend, the sanctity of human life is not among them.

In the beginning, the book of Genesis reveals, God created us as a
reflection of Himself:
God created man in His own image, in the image of God
He created him; male and female He created them.[16]

Later in Genesis, God explains to Noah the implications of this divine
creation and imputation:
Whoever sheds man's blood, by man his blood shall be
shed, for in the image of God He made man.[17]

In Exodus, God lays down a simple, bedrock command:
"You shall not murder."[18]

Apart from cases of self-defense and war, the Bible is clear that a willful
attack on another human being is the equivalent of an attack on God, in
whose image man is made. Murder attacks God's own creation.

Scripture reveals God's sacred hand on early human life, in passages such
as Psalm 139, in which David reflects on the wonder of God's creation and
His plan for David's life before the beginning of time:
For You formed my inward parts; you wove me in my
mother's womb. I will give thanks to You, for I am
fearfully and wonderfully made; wonderful are Your
works, and my soul knows it very well.
My frame was not hidden from You, when I was made in
secret, and skillfully wrought in the depths of the
earth; Your eyes have seen my unformed substance; and
in Your book were all written the days that were
ordained for me, when as yet there was not one of
them.[19]

---

[15] Ibid.
[16] Genesis 1:27.
[17] Genesis 9:6.
[18] Exodus 20:13.
[19] Psalms 139:13-16.

The New Testament prophecy concerning John the Baptist makes clear that a developing baby is no mere "blob of tissue" but a person, a human vessel whom God will fill with His divine life:

...he will be filled with the Holy Spirit while yet in his mother's womb.[20]

The Gospel of Luke reveals how John the Baptist responded from within the womb when Mary greeted John's expectant mother, Elizabeth:

When Elizabeth heard Mary's greeting, the baby leaped in her womb; and Elizabeth was filled with the Holy Spirit.[21]

The apostle Paul explains that God had established a plan for his life even before his birth:

... God, who had set me apart even from my mother's womb and called me through His grace....[22]

Nor is the sanctity of life reserved only for developing babies without defect. When Moses complains to God that he lacks speaking ability, God's response reveals that He is the One who oversees human capabilities:

"Who has made man's mouth? Or who makes him mute or deaf, or seeing or blind? Is it not I, the Lord?[23]

The book of Isaiah highlights the danger of interfering with God's design:

Woe to the one who quarrels with his Maker — an earthenware vessel among the vessels of earth! Will the clay say to the potter, "What are you doing?"
Or the thing you are making say, "He has no hands"?
Woe to him who says to a father, "What are you begetting?"
Or to a woman, "To what are you giving birth?"[24]

### Science also provides a basis for protecting life

Politicians and activists may dispute whether an unborn baby is a human being, but the verdict of science is unequivocal.

Even the tiniest human embryo is a human being. As one embryology textbook explains, a zygote is the cell that "results from the union of an

---

[20] Luke 1:15.
[21] Luke 1:41.
[22] Galatians 1:15.
[23] Exodus 4:11.
[24] Isaiah 45:9-10.

oocyte and a sperm during fertilization. A zygote is the beginning of a new human being."[25]

Another leading embryology textbook teaches,

"Although life is a continuous process, fertilization (which, incidentally, is not a moment) is a critical landmark because, under ordinary circumstances, a new, genetically distinct human organism is formed when the chromosomes of the male and female pronuclei blend in the oocyte."[26]

To help a skeptical person reason through the humanity of the unborn baby, ask that person to consider the baby at birth. Is that baby human? Of course. What about a few days before birth? A few months before birth? At the beginning of embryonic development?

A reasonable person will quickly recognize that there is no scientific or logical point in human development before which the organism was not human and after which "it" suddenly became a human being. Human development from an observable, scientific perspective is a *seamless* process from fertilization to birth.

The "blob of tissue" deception proffered by some abortion apologists hardly comports with embryology or genetics. The tiniest human embryo already has a complete genetic makeup. The amazing journey of human biological development remains, but the map of that journey is complete at fertilization.

As my friend and colleague Dr. Bill Cheshire, a neurologist with Mayo Clinic, has written,

The Human Genome Project has not demystified human nature. Rather, the astonishing detail it has revealed about the human organism gives us new reasons to respect human life at all stages of development.

No longer can an observer familiar with the science of the human genome reasonably hold to the belief that a biologic discontinuity separates the embryo from the human adult, for development occurs along a continuum of at least genetic identity.[27]

---

[25]Keith L. Moore and TVN Persaud, *The Developing Human: Clinically Oriented Embryology*, 7e , Philadelphia: Saunders / Elsevier, p. 2.

[26] Ronan O'Rahilly & Fabiola Muller, *Human Embryology & Teratology*, 3rd Ed., New York: Wiley-Liss, p. 10, copyright Elsevier, 2001.

[27] William P. Cheshire, Jr., MD, MA, FAAN, "Human Embryo Research after the Genome," Center for Bioethics and Human Dignity website, posted 11/14/2002.
http://cbhd.org/content/human-embryo-research-after-genome accessed 12/17/12.

### See for yourself

Science, prominently aided in recent years by enhanced ultrasound technology, has been providing increasingly clear evidence of the developing baby's obvious humanity. As I wrote for *Today's Christian Doctor* magazine, this incredible glimpse into the womb leaves no doubt about the baby inside. A General Electric commercial[28] for its 4D ultrasound imaging device beautifully illustrates this miracle, beginning with these soft lyrics:

```
"The first time ever I saw your face, I thought
the sun rose in your eyes."
As Roberta Flack softly coos her 1973 Grammy-winning
song in the background, the 2011 TV commercial slowly
unveils a stunning, color image of a developing,
gently moving baby in utero. The baby's tiny arm
curls upward, framing her glorious face.
The video shifts to the faces of a beaming young
woman and a wide-eyed young man. A wider shot pans to
reveal a physician applying a corded ultrasound
device to the woman's pregnant belly. The parents
watch with wonder as the monitor shows their newest
family member opening and closing her mouth.
"When you see your baby for the first time on the new
GE 4D ultrasound system, it really is…a miracle."
The final shot shows mother cradling her newborn baby
as father looks on with wonder.
Fade with music: "The first time ever I saw your
face."
Such eye-opening medical technology really is
awakening our culture to the reality of early life.[29]
```

### Law limits humanity–again

But while science is clear–a developing baby clearly is a human being–the law remains specious. Abortion in America hinges on the flawed legal rationale developed by non-scientist justices on the Supreme Court, explained in the landmark 1973 *Roe v. Wade* decision.

Again, from my *Today's Christian Doctor* article:

```
In 1973–the same year that "The First Time Ever I Saw
Your Face" won a Grammy–the Supreme Court handed down
```

---

[28] GE 4D Ultrasound TV Commercial - YouTube available on YouTube at http://www.youtube.com/watch?v=a7B6C_0_rBs.

[29] Jonathan Imbody, "Post-Roe v Wade: Overt war on conscience rages," *Today's Christian Doctor*, Winter 2012.

a landmark decision that deemed an early developing baby a virtually faceless non-person. In *Roe v. Wade*, the Court revisited its egregious error in the Court's infamous 1857 *Dred Scott v. Sandford* decision. The Scott ruling, which essentially valued a slave as just three-fifths of a person, divided the nation over the issue of federalism (the division of powers between the states and the national government) and spawned a bloody fratricide.

After the war in 1868, Americans attempted to reconstruct the constitutional protection of persons by enacting the Fourteenth Amendment:

> "…nor shall any State deprive any person of life, liberty, or property, without due process of law…"

Yet just over a century later, the Supreme Court once again divided the Republic and reignited the fight over federalism, by creating a whole new class of non-persons deemed ineligible for constitutional protection. The Court unilaterally declared that an unborn human being is not a person.

Writing for the majority, Justice Harry Blackmun asserted,

> "The appellee and certain amici argue that the fetus is a 'person' within the language and meaning of the Fourteenth Amendment. In support of this, they outline at length and in detail the well-known facts of fetal development. If this suggestion of personhood is established, the appellant's case, of course, collapses, for the fetus' right to life would then be guaranteed specifically by the Amendment… [But we are persuaded that] the word 'person,' as used in the Fourteenth Amendment, does not include the unborn.

In *Roe*, the Court cast aside not only federalism but also more than two millennia of medical ethics, under which physicians who followed the Hippocratic oath had determined to adhere to this ethical commitment:

> "I will use treatment to help the sick, according to my ability and judgment, but I will never use it to injure or wrong them. I will not help a patient commit suicide, even though asked to do so, nor will I suggest such a plan. Similarly, I will not perform abortions."

In *Roe*, the Court asserted the indifference-perhaps
even the animus-of the modern secular state to both
secular and biblical foundations of medical ethics
and personal conscience.
In analyzing medical ethics, Justice Blackmun
acknowledged the later confluence of the Hippocratic
oath with Christian biblical principles, but he chose
to cast his lot with ancient Greeks who rationalized
killing.
Blackmun observed,

> "Most Greek thinkers ... commended abortion, at
> least prior to viability." He agreed with an
> analysis that characterized the Hippocratic oath
> as merely "a Pythagorean manifesto and not the
> expression of an absolute standard of medical
> conduct."

By returning to the ancient Greek's rationalization
of killing, the Court undermined more than 2,000
years of medical ethics and the objective bases for
training physicians' consciences.
The Court also taught a whole generation that killing
one's developing baby is not only legally
permissible; it is a Constitutional right.[30]

Like the Court's flawed decision in *Dred Scott* dehumanizing African-
Americans, its flawed decision in *Roe* dehumanizing the unborn may
eventually fall, potentially returning the battle for life to each of the 50 states.

The good news of that eventuality is that we the people rather than a few
elite justices would decide the matter. The bad news is that because the pro-
abortion forces have considerably more money and manpower than the pro-
life forces, a state-by-state battle over abortion could stretch pro-life
organizations very thin. While a number of the larger pro-life organizations
can afford to base a policy advocate in Washington, DC to cover federal
issues, few if any pro-life organizations can afford 50 times that number to
cover all the states.

That's why it's vital that state-based pro-life organizations continue to
develop and expand, preparing for a post-*Roe* battle and meanwhile
advancing pro-life measures in their states.

---

[30] Imbody, "Post-Roe v. Wade."

## What about cases of rape?

We need not shrink from the difficult questions raised by abortion, such as cases of rape–provided we articulate our position reasonably and compassionately. In the 2012 elections, a couple well-meaning pro-life politicians with an undisciplined message lost voters and caused angst and division in the pro-life community.

Republican Rep. Todd Akin, the frontrunner candidate for a Missouri Senate seat, said during an interview,

> First of all, from what I understand from doctors [pregnancy from rape] is really rare. If it's a legitimate rape, the female body has ways to try to shut that whole thing down.
> But let's assume that maybe that didn't work, or something. I think there should be some punishment, but the punishment ought to be on the rapist and not attacking the child.[31]

In a statement following the explosive "legitimate rape" interview, Mr. Akin said,

> In reviewing my off-the-cuff remarks, it's clear that I misspoke in this interview and it does not reflect the deep empathy I hold for the thousands of women who are raped and abused every year.[32]

Then in a general election debate, Indiana Republican candidate Richard Mourdock responded to a question about banning abortion:

> The only exception I have to have an abortion is in that case of the life of the mother. I just struggled with it myself for a long time but I came to realize: Life is that gift from God that I think even if life begins in that horrible situation of rape, that it is something that God intended to happen.[33]

*USA Today* reported on Mr. Mourdock's news conference, during which he attempted to deflect criticism for his remarks:

---

[31] "Todd Akin, GOP Senate candidate: 'Legitimate rape' rarely causes pregnancy," *Washington Post*, April 10, 2012, http://www.washingtonpost.com/blogs/the-fix/wp/2012/08/19/todd-akin-gop-senate-candidate-legitimate-rape-rarely-causes-pregnancy/, accessed Apr. 18, 2014.
[32] Ibid.
[33] "Richard Mourdock under fire for rape remarks," *Politico*, Oct. 23, 2012. http://www.politico.com/blogs/on-congress/2012/10/richard-mourdock-under-fire-for-rape-remarks-139411.html accessed Jan. 19, 2013.

Mourdock, who at times appeared teary during his news
conference, said he regrets that his comments have
been "twisted."

"I said life is precious. I believe life is precious.
I believe rape is a brutal act. It is something that
I abhor. That anyone could come away with any meaning
other than what I just said is regrettable, and for
that I apologize," Mourdock said.[34]

Delete keys don't work on oral statements, however, and voters deserted both candidates in enough numbers to hand the elections to their opponents.

It's easy to play the armchair quarterback and critique candidates' gaffes, but the truth is that most of us stumble and make misstatements we regret; they're just not usually captured on videotape and replayed for the nation.

A pro-life colleague, Ryan Bomberger,[35] an Emmy Award-winning movie maker who was conceived through rape and adopted into a multi-racial Christian family of 15, offers this perspective for a rape victim:

Although you may be in this immediate moment of pain
and chaos, there is another side of the story.
There's something beautiful that can rise from the
ashes of such a violent act.[36]

To Ryan's biological mother and to his adoptive family, he was the something beautiful that rose from the ashes of rape.

Another pro-life colleague, Dr. Alveda King, a niece of the Rev. Martin Luther King, Jr. who herself has experienced abortion, notes that "rape and abortion are both violent acts"[37] and that answering one act of violence with another act of violence does not bring healing—only more heartache.

When we speak about abortion and cases of rape, we empathize with the woman victimized by the horrific crime. We speak out against the rapist and the subculture that condones and encourages sexual aggression and acts of violence against women. We also plead for the violence to stop there.

---

[34] "GOP's Mourdock says rape, abortion comments 'twisted,'" *USA Today*, Oct. 24, 2012. http://www.usatoday.com/story/news/politics/2012/10/24/mourdock-rape-god-intended-indiana-senate/1653745/ Web accessed Jan. 19, 2012.

[35] For Ryan's story, see http://www.theradiancefoundation.org/our-story/our-bios/ryan-scott-bomberger/.

[36] "Rape Victim's Child Speaks Up for Right to Life," *LifeNews*, Nov. 9, 2011, news report of video of a talk given by Ryan Bomberger, Nov. 9, 2011 at the Family Research Council in Washington, D.C. http://cnsnews.com/news/article/rape-victims-child-speaks-right-life Web accessed Jan. 19, 2013.

[37] Alveda King, "Let Truth Clear the Air around Todd Akin," Newsmax.com commentary Aug, 23, 2012. http://www.newsmax.com/DrAlvedaCKing/Todd-Akin-rape-pro-life/2012/08/23/id/449564 accessed Jan. 19, 2013.

We encourage empathy for the innocent baby. We compassionately point to safety net ministries like pregnancy centers and to thousands of loving couples seeking to adopt. Highlighting individuals like Ryan Bomberger and others conceived in rape yet raised in love keeps our focus on life-honoring alternatives to abortion.

## *Join the new generation of "Esthers"*

Winning pro-life victories, especially at the state level, may well hinge on individual citizens not previously engaged in public policy taking a stand in their communities and state legislatures to advance the cause of life. Physicians, mothers, attorneys, media and marketing experts, pastors, educators, writers, students and many others will need to band together to supplement existing and create new state pro-life organizations.

While combatting abortion as an evil, we must also treat pregnant women with loving compassion and respect while offering life-honoring alternatives. The expansive network of pregnancy centers offers a practical and visible alternative. Organizations such as Care Net,[38] Heartbeat International[39] and the National Institute of Family & Life Advocates[40] help shepherd thousands of community-based pregnancy centers that offer counseling, testing, education and provisions to pregnant women.

For example, an organization I've appreciated and supported for years, the Capitol Hill Pregnancy Center,[41] provides at no charge:

---

[38] https://www.care-net.org/ "Care Net is a Christ-centered ministry whose mission is to promote a culture of life within our society in order to serve people facing unplanned pregnancies and related sexual issues. Our vision is a culture where lives are transformed by the Gospel of Jesus Christ and every woman chooses life for herself and her unborn child."

[39] http://www.heartbeatinternational.org/ "Heartbeat International works to inspire and equip Christian communities worldwide to rescue women and couples from abortion through the development of neighborhood pregnancy help centers, maternity homes, and adoption services. These ministries provide life-saving help in a truly life-changing way by assisting women who are at risk for abortion with the life-affirming, practical support they need to choose life, then prepare them to parent or to place for adoption. Heartbeat serves as the leadership supply line for the Pregnancy HELP Movement worldwide."

[40] www.nifla.org/ "Founded in 1993, the National Institute of Family and Life Advocates (NIFLA) provides life-affirming PRCs with legal counsel, education, and training. NIFLA has dramatically grown and now represents approximately 1,200 member PRC's across the country. NIFLA provides critical legal counsel to PRCs to enable them to avoid legal pitfalls in their operations. NIFLA is the national leader in the development of legal guidelines to help PRCs convert to licensed medical clinics."

[41] http://www.capitolhillpregnancycenter.org "Capitol Hill Pregnancy Center is a Faith based 501(c)3 non-profit organization offering help and support to women, men and their families who are in a crisis pregnancy. Our goal is to provide compassionate care as well as complete, accurate information pertaining to pregnancy and pregnancy options. We provide counseling,

- Childbirth classes
- Maternity and baby clothing and supplies
- Parenting classes
- Ongoing pregnancy support (counseling and mentoring)
- Post abortion peer support
- Bible studies
- Medical, legal, adoption, and housing referrals

Since Americans place so much trust in science, those who can present compelling scientific evidence hold an advantage. The American College of Obstetrics and Gynecologists (ACOG) unfortunately aggressively promotes abortion rights, and other leading medical specialty organizations cannot be counted on to provide objective scientific evidence supporting a pro-life position. That means that courageous pro-life individuals with scientific and medical backgrounds will play a vital role in advancing the culture of life in the individual states.

Not everyone will receive our apologetic for life. Many have hardened their minds and hearts seemingly beyond reason or repair.

But we can reach some.

We can build a culture of life, brick by brick. We can stand firmly in the truth, reach out in love and pray for God to work in hearts. The more winsomely and wisely we do this, the more likely truth, love and life will prevail.

This is a time for a new generation of "Esthers"–women and men called by God to influence public policy in order to protect and preserve life.

If God is calling you to help establish or participate in such a movement in your state, be strong and courageous. Do not hide but stand up, depending on God and His power to accomplish through you above and beyond your own imagination or capabilities.

> Then Mordecai told them to reply to Esther, "Do not imagine that you in the king's palace can escape any more than all the Jews. For if you remain silent at this time, relief and deliverance will arise for the Jews from another place and you and your father's house will perish. And who knows whether you have not attained royalty for such a time as this?"[42]

---

mentoring, childbirth classes and parenting classes (which includes a fatherhood initiative program). We also support families and their babies by offering free material resources."
[42] Esther 4:13-14.

# Chapter 11:
# *Stem cells and human cloning*

*"[King Solomon] said, 'Divide the living child in two,*
*and give half to the one and half to the other.'*
*"Then the woman whose child was the living one spoke to the king,*
*for she was deeply stirred over her son and said,*
*'Oh, my lord, give her the living child, and by no means kill him.'"*
−1 Kings 3:25-26

S tem cell research involves harvesting special human cells for
potential purposes of patient therapies and research. For example,
*adult* stem cell research, which uses cells from various parts of our bodies
without harming the donors, has been proven effective in treating over 70
diseases.[1]

Highly controversial *embryonic* stem cell research, by contrast, harvests
stem cells from living human embryos, destroying a genetically complete
human being in the process. Some theorize that such cells could be used
some day to replace body parts or cure disease. So far they have not.
Embryonic stem cells by their nature have a stubborn tendency to form
tumors, casting serious doubts on their applications in humans. Yet many
researchers persist, because they want to experiment on embryonic stem cells
to see what secrets the cells might hold about early life and to test how
diseases progress in the human organism.

Some ethically concerned scientists contend that alternative cells very
similar to embryonic stem cells offer great potential while avoiding the
unethical destruction of human embryos. Scientific breakthroughs over the
past few years have buttressed these claims. New research avenues include,
for example, induced pluripotent stem (iPS) cells and also an acid bath
procedure called stimulus-triggered acquisition of pluripotency (STAP).[2]

---

[1] For a complete listing, see http://www.stemcellresearch.org/stem-cell-research-treatments/
accessed Apr. 19, 2014.
[2] See "Acid bath offers easy path to stem cells: Just squeezing or bathing cells in acidic

Yet many scientists doggedly cling to the branch they climbed out on over a decade ago, insisting on aggressively pursuing embryonic stem cell research despite ethical and proven alternatives. After decades of research and billions of dollars, embryonic stem cell research has yet to fulfill the sky-high speculations of politicians and scientists who promised "biblical" cures, paralyzed patients leaping out of wheelchairs and the end of AIDS.

A video produced by the Alliance for Medical Research, for example, illustrates how researchers attempt to gain grants and public approval by constantly linking embryo-destructive research, including human cloning, with cures for disease:

Now with this revolutionary breakthrough of regenerative medicine doctors will actually be able to cure diseases, not just treat them with pills and shots.

Insulin-producing cells will be injected into the diabetic child to cure diabetes. Retinal cells will be injected to make the blind see. Nerve cells will be used to make the quadriplegic walk again.

Stem cell research has the potential to cure over 130 million Americans plagued by chronic degenerative diseases and conditions. This is the potential that [embryonic] stem cell research holds for us.[3]

In reality, embryonic stem cell boondoggles instead have diverted precious research dollars away from ethical and proven effective alternative stem cell research that likely would have helped millions of real patients with *real* therapies and cures.

### Dearth of critical thinking

The fact that so many leaders and much of the public bought into what has turned out to be a marketing ploy for a highly speculative and seriously flawed product suggests a dangerous dearth of critical judgment in our nation. Trained by television, we seem ready to buy just about anything on the basis of a one-minute commercial with a moving celebrity testimonial.

A history of incredible scientific accomplishments doubtless contributes to the pass we give scientists. Americans don't say no—we say "Why not?"

---

conditions can readily reprogram them into an embryonic state," *Nature*, January 29, 2014, http://www.nature.com/news/acid-bath-offers-easy-path-to-stem-cells-1.14600 accessed Apr. 19, 2014.

[3] Transcript included in "Science and Spin," by Wesley J. Smith, *The Weekly Standard*, Nov. 23, 2006. Accessed Apr. 30, 2013 at http://www.weeklystandard.com/Content/Public/Articles/000/000/012/990cuqpf.asp.

Don't handcuff scientists–they may be on the verge of the next amazing breakthrough.

But in our justifiable admiration of scientists' accomplishments, we forget that scientists are subject to the same human frailties and temptations we all face. Scientists also want to get rich, to gain the acclaim of their peers and to crown their reputations with notable accomplishments.

Most scientists and researchers do not simply wake up one morning and consciously determine to deceive the public in order to secure their ambitions. Nor do they all eschew ethical concerns. Many doubtless convince themselves that killing human embryos will be justified by some day curing diseases. Others try to skirt ethical concerns by defying embryological science and logic, contending that the human embryo is something less than human–something perhaps worthy of "respect" but not protection.[4]

### *Cloning human beings*

Discussions of human cloning typically focus on the technical process of somatic cell nuclear transfer (SCNT), which basically involves taking genetic information (DNA) from a donor and inserting that donor's DNA into an egg that has been emptied of its own DNA.

In reporting on human cloning, the media tend to depend on researchers themselves for descriptions and analysis of cloning research.

An April 17, 2014 Reuters news story lead made for a fitting editorial straight out of the talking points of researchers who treat embryonic human beings as mini laboratories:

```
Scientists have moved a step closer to the goal of
creating stem cells perfectly matched to a patient's
DNA in order to treat diseases, they announced on
Thursday, creating patient-specific cell lines out of
the skin cells of two adult men.
The advance, described online in the journal Cell
Stem Cell, is the first time researchers have
achieved "therapeutic cloning" of adults. Technically
```

---

[4] A minority of President Bush's Council on Bioethics took this position with regard to killing embryos in the process of human cloning for the purpose of biomedical research. They noted, "We believe the embryo has a developing and intermediate moral worth that commands our special respect, but that it is morally permissible to use early-stage cloned human embryos in important research under strict regulation. These embryos would not be 'created for destruction,' but for use in the service of life and medicine. They would be destroyed in the service of a great good...." Comments published in "Human cloning and human dignity," President's Council on Bioethics, July 2002 position paper, pre-publication version, p. 85.

called somatic-cell nuclear transfer, therapeutic
cloning means producing embryonic cells genetically
identical to a donor, usually for the purpose of
using those cells to treat disease.[5]

The news is framed primarily as a wonderful advance toward "the goal of
creating stem cells perfectly matched to a patient's DNA in order to treat
diseases." Only later does the reader discover that the "advance" actually is
an ethical regression involving the deliberate cloning of human embryos for
purely utilitarian purposes:

"But nuclear transfer is also the first step in
reproductive cloning, or producing a genetic
duplicate of someone—a technique that has sparked
controversy…."

Controversy. You think?

Rather than quoting the dissenting views of an expert who actually views
what these researchers are doing as unethical, the article instead only quotes
one of the researchers, who feigns moral caution:

"Without regulations in place, such embryos could
also be used for human reproductive cloning, although
this would be unsafe and grossly unethical," said Dr.
Robert Lanza, chief scientist of Massachusetts-based
biotech Advanced Cell Technology and a co-author of
the new study.[6]

No, what Dr. Lanza himself is doing is "unsafe and grossly unethical."
He is creating living human beings as experiments and then destroying them
as if they were lab rats. The fact that he doesn't take the even more
horrifically unethical next step of implanting the embryos with the goal of
birthing a clone hardly exonerates him from his utilitarian and lethal
treatment of living human beings.

At no point does the story even mention that to use stem cells from
cloned human embryos, the researchers destroy the embryos. Instead, the
story focuses merely on the technical success achieved through the
experimentation on human beings:

It worked: They generated two healthy embryos, one
from each adult donor, aged 35 and 75.[7]

And, as usual, the "news" story ends with a researcher's marketing
pronouncement:

---

[5] "In a cloning first, scientists create stem cells from adults," Reuters, April 17, 2014
http://news.yahoo.com/cloning-first-scientists-create-stem-cells-adults-160302258—
finance.html accessed Apr. 19, 2014.
[6] Ibid.
[7] Ibid.

"100 human embryonic stem cell lines would generate a complete match for over half the (U.S.) population," said Lanza.[8]

No mention is made of the fact that because the cloning technique requires human eggs, it accelerates the exploitation of women who, lured by compensation, will endure dangerous and potentially life-threatening procedures to supply their eggs. My colleague Jennifer Lahl of the Center for Bioethics and Culture has produced a revealing documentary, "Eggsploitation,"[9] that chronicles the harms to women involved in harvesting their eggs.

Growing awareness of these harms and the exploitation of women, many of them students and poor, has generated liberal as well as conservative opposition to egg-harvesting procedures. Whether such opposition can triumph over the extremely well-financed marketing masked as scientific information, however, remains to be seen.

### More media obfuscation

In an oddly titled *Washington Post* editorial, "Stem cells: Good or evil?"[10] the usually clear and readable *Post* suddenly reverts to sterile, technical language ("something called somatic cell nuclear transfer") to describe a new human cloning process. The *Post* coyly notes that the new process involves "creating stem cells cloned from the normal skin cells of adults," when in fact researchers actually clone and kill living human embryos like utilitarian lab rats.

Gallup polling shows that 83 percent of Americans oppose human cloning;[11] hence the obfuscation.

Several decades of grant-seeking researchers' scandalous propaganda and hundreds of millions of research dollars thrown at embryo-destructive research have produced zero cures. Yet the *Post* persists in promoting the hype, asserting that human cloning will at long last produce "extraordinary new treatments."

Following this yellow brick road unfortunately diverts precious funds away from ethically non-controversial and proven effective non-destructive

---

[8] Ibid.

[9] See http://www.eggsploitation.com/. Accessed Apr. 19, 2014.

[10] *Washington Post* editorial, Apr. 20, 2014, http://www.washingtonpost.com/opinions/in-stem-cell-research-the-potential-health-benefits-outweigh-the-ethical-risks/2014/04/20/dabdc824-c73c-11e3-8b9a-8e0977a24aeb_story.html accessed May 1, 2014.

[11] "Cloning," Gallup poll conducted May 2013, http://www.gallup.com/poll/6028/cloning.aspx accessed May 1, 2014.

stem cell research. Moreover, if human cloning is technically perfected, no law will prevent rogue scientists from cloning a baby, along with potential horrific physical defects and unspeakable psychological trauma.

Science is a powerful tool that can serve us well within ethical boundaries and critical scrutiny. Without such boundaries and scrutiny, we will become its victims–and in the case of cloned human beings, its slaves.

### "Scientists behaving badly"

Financial allurements, a materialistic philosophy and personal ambition too often combine to rationalize just about any means to achieve a researcher's ends. While I've arrived at this conclusion through years of observing the stem cell wars from the front lines in Washington, I am not alone in viewing some scientists as startlingly prone to unethical behavior.

A jarring article in the highly regarded scientific journal *Nature*, entitled, "Scientists behaving badly," provided abundant evidence that human sin nature applies without partiality to scientists:

> We surveyed several thousand early- and mid-career scientists, who are based in the United States and funded by the National Institutes of Health (NIH), and asked them to report their own behaviors. Our findings reveal a range of questionable practices that are striking in their breadth and prevalence. Our findings suggest that US scientists engage in a range of behaviors extending far beyond falsification, fabrication and plagiarism.[12]

The researchers consulted with compliance officers at five major research universities to identify ten serious types of unethical professional behavior that would normally carry serious sanctions if discovered. When the researchers tabulated the anonymous responses of US scientists, the results proved astonishing. While noting that the disturbingly high numbers of admitted instances of unethical behaviors by scientists is likely even *lower* than actual (since many perpetrators would not likely respond to the survey), the authors concluded,

> With as many as 33% of our survey respondents admitting to one or more of the top-ten [unethical] behaviors, the scientific community can no longer remain complacent about such misbehavior.[13]

---

[12] Joseph Bottum and Ryan T. Anderson, "Stem Cells: A Political History," *First Things*, November 2008. http://www.firstthings.com/article/2008/10/001-stem-cells-a-political-history-27 accessed Apr. 3, 2013.
[13] Ibid.

If scientists fail to resist the temptation to unethical behavior for purposes of self-aggrandizement, how much easier to rationalize lying and deceiving when they see themselves as "saving civilization from diseases" through lethal stem cell research? As Joseph Bottum and Ryan T. Anderson explained in a retrospective of the stem cell wars during the Bush administration, no one needed to shove grant-hungry scientists into the political pot:

> They rushed to be used. Offered a public platform, they begged to be exploited, and the politicians, newspapers, and television talk shows merely obliged them. In the summer before the 2004 presidential election, Ron McKay, from the National Institutes of Health, admitted that he and his fellow scientists had generally failed to correct the media's false reports about the promise of stem cells—but that was all right, he told the *Washington Post*, since ordinary people "need a fairy tale." They require, he said, "a story line that's relatively simple to understand."[14]

Here's the real story line we need to understand: *Science is always objective, but all too often, scientists are not.*

So the next time you hear a scientist make a claim about embryonic stem cell research—or anything, for that matter—take a cue from Ronald Reagan's proverbial quip to the Soviets at the signing of the Intermediate-Range Nuclear Forces (INF) Treaty: "Trust, but verify."

### When scientists replace prophets

Scientists' unethical hype and the public's incredible gullibility in the stem cell debate suggest a deeper, theological problem.

When a person refuses to worship God, he needs to create an object to worship, since God has designed us to worship. When someone rejects God's revealed Word, the Scriptures that explain the world and our place in it, he needs to create a framework from which to view the world.

The ancients who rejected their Creator worshiped nature instead—the moon or the sun or animals—and crafted idols with their own hands. Modern, "enlightened" persons who reject their Creator and assert that material life here on earth is all there is may replace God by elevating science to a quasi-religious status.

---

[14] Joseph Bottum and Ryan T. Anderson, "Stem Cells: A Political History," *First Things*, November 2008. http://www.firstthings.com/article/2008/11/001-stem-cells-a-political-history accessed November 24, 2014.

In this idolatry of science, scientists replace prophets and research supplants revelation.

Scientists who embrace this materialistic philosophy, limiting the universe to matter and denying the Source of the wonders they discover, can become demigods–at least in their own eyes and the eyes of those who idolize them. Francis Crick, the British scientist who co-discovered DNA, seems to have succumbed to just such an illusion.

He once summed up the implications of his landmark work in human genetics by brazenly asserting, "The god hypothesis is rather discredited."[15]

Crick's American partner and fellow atheist James Watson ventured one step further, suggesting that scientists like himself were on the verge of filling functions traditionally attributed to God:

> Only with the discovery of the double helix and the ensuing genetic revolution have we had grounds for thinking that the powers held traditionally to be the exclusive property of the gods might one day be ours.[16]

I offered an analysis of the comments of these two scientists, in a commentary published by *The Washington Times*:

> How odd. One scientist discredits God while his partner claims to be God.
> Both scientists seem to have inherited a mutant gene for vanity. Having witnessed firsthand the divine mystery and majesty within our genes, they have missed altogether the Author of the evidence. They might as well maintain that reading the works of Shakespeare proves that Shakespeare never existed. How much wiser and more productive is the humble approach of Dr. Francis Collins, a Christian believer who replaced Mr. Watson to head the Human Genome Project. Dr. Collins describes the human genetic code as a "very large book written in a language that we don't yet understand very well. The interesting and challenging part is figuring out what it all means."[17] Understanding that fallible human beings are far from gods, Dr. Collins has emphasized protecting patients

---

[15] "DNA pioneers lash out at religion," *The Washington Times*, March 24, 2003. Accessed on the web April 2, 2013: http://www.washingtontimes.com/news/2003/mar/24/20030324-090202-5705r/

[16] Ibid.

[17] Francis S. Collins, M.D., Ph.D., "Reflections from the Director of the National Human Genome Research Institute," *Dignity* newsletter of the Center for Bioethics and Human Dignity, Summer 2001.

from potential abuses of genetic medicine while
advancing toward its disease-conquering potential.
At the ages of 74 and 86, scientists Watson and Crick
may soon have an opportunity to test their hypotheses
about who is God. Hopefully, each will exchange
arrogance for grace before his helix of hubris
unravels.[18]

## Communicating stem cell research harms and benefits

While we cannot control the machinations of unscrupulous researchers or lazy reporters who slavishly reproduce researchers' talking points, we can present evidence. We can highlight the wondrous nature of the human embryo, the genetic completeness of an embryo and the fact that every one of us began life as an embryo.

My friend Dr. Bill Hurlbut of Stanford University put it eloquently in his statement for the President's Council on Bioethics, in a committee paper on human cloning:

When looked at through the lens of science, it is
evident that human existence cannot be defined
atemporally, but must be recognized in the full
procession of continuity and change that is essential
for its development.
From conception, our unique genetic endowment
organizes and guides the expression of our particular
nature in its species and individual character.
Fertilization initiates the most complex chemical
reaction in the known universe: a self-directing,
purposeful integration of organismal development.
In both character and conduct the zygote and
subsequent embryonic stages differ from any other
cells or tissues of the body; they contain within
themselves the organizing principle of the full human
organism.[19]

Besides emphasizing this continuum of human development, we can also present the harms of embryo-destroying research and the benefits of ethical research, as we attempt to convince policy makers and our countrymen to choose the ethical path:

---

[18] Imbody, Jonathan, "DNA and God," commentary published in *The Washington Times*, March 27, 2003.
[19] Hurlbut, William, "Personal Statement," in the appendix of "Human cloning and human dignity," President's Council on Bioethics, July 2002 position paper, pre-publication version, p. 176.

**Harms** of *embryo-destroying* research, including human cloning:

- Treats human beings as mere <u>commodities</u> for experimentation, deliberately creating, exploiting and destroying one human being for the benefit of another.
- There is <u>no bright line</u> to stop lethal human research at the two-week human embryo stage. Sacrificing one human being for the sake of another can quickly expand beyond human embryos to already born human beings, including cloned babies and babies born naturally but considered by some as unfit for continued life.
- Human cloning requires the potentially harmful and deadly <u>exploitation of women</u> for their eggs.
- Once the human cloning technique is perfected, no one can stop a <u>rogue researcher</u> from implanting a cloned human embryo in a womb. The human being born as a result, if she lives, will likely experience horrific unanticipated physical consequences. She will also suffer emotionally as she learns that she was not born as a unique individual springing from the love of parents but rather as a copy of another human being, created in a laboratory by researchers.
- Once human clones can be born, the prospect of cloning human beings for the sole purpose of producing organs for harvesting becomes a potential reality.
- After decades of embryo-destructive research, researchers' wild promises of healing, deployed to overshadow ethical concerns, have never been realized. Yet such research meanwhile has been <u>siphoning off funds</u> better used for non-lethal stem cell research that has been proven effective and is providing real therapies for real patients.

**Benefits** of *non-lethal* stem cell research:

- <u>Proven effectiveness</u> in therapies and cures for patients. Adult stem cells, for example, have already provided over 70 research treatments for cancers, autoimmune diseases, heart damage, metabolic disorders, wounds and injuries, liver and bladder diseases, blood conditions, Parkinson's Disease, spinal cord injury, stroke damage and more.[20]
- Ethically <u>non-controversial</u>, so that all can unite behind the drive for cures.

---

[20] http://www.stemcellresearch.org/stem-cell-research-treatments/ accessed Apr. 19, 2014.

119

Besides communicating harms and benefits, we can also teach our children and encourage our peers not to blindly accept what researchers or the media feed us. We all need to do our own research and think critically– especially about what new technologies may *enable* us to do and what we ethically *should* do.

Scientific discoveries pursued ethically offer us tremendous potential benefits in line with God's design, but science unbridled by ethical constraints and unmindful of unintended consequences takes us down a dark and deadly path no one wants to discover.

# Chapter 12:
# *Human trafficking*

*He sits in the lurking places of the villages;*
*In the hiding places he kills the innocent;*
*His eyes stealthily watch for the unfortunate.*
*He lurks in a hiding place as a lion in his lair;*
*He lurks to catch the afflicted;*
*He catches the afflicted when he draws him into his net.*
*He crouches, he bows down,*
*And the unfortunate fall by his mighty ones.*
*He says to himself, "God has forgotten;*
*He has hidden His face; He will never see it."*
*You have seen it, for You have beheld mischief and vexation to take it*
*into Your hand.*
*The unfortunate commits himself to You;*
*You have been the helper of the orphan.*
*Break the arm of the wicked and the evildoer,*
*Seek out his wickedness until You find none.*
*–Psalm 10: 8-11, 14-15*

The following stories of Ashley, Camila and Raju are examples of
human trafficking, or modern-day slavery. The worldwide trade in
human beings fuels organized crime and terrorism, operates underground and
likely is happening right now in your own community.

Human trafficking may involve forced labor, sex trafficking, bonded
labor, debt bondage among migrant laborers, involuntary domestic servitude,
forced child labor, child soldiers and child sex trafficking.[1]

---

[1] To better understand this issue, consider the *what, how* and *why* of human trafficking:
1. *What*: The exploitation of someone involving force, fraud and/or coercion.
2. *How*: Recruiting, transporting, transferring, harboring, and/or receiving the person.
3. *Why*: The goal of human trafficking is prostitution, pornography, violence and/or sexual exploitation, forced labor, involuntary servitude, debt bondage or slavery.
Examples of What / How / Why:
    1.   A man kidnaps a child and takes her to another country, where someone forces her into prostitution (Force / Transporting / Prostitution).
    2.   A deceptive aunt convinces her own niece to go with men to another country, falsely

## Ashley

When Ashley was 12 years old, she got into a fight with her mother and ran away from home. She ended up staying with her friend's older brother at his house and intended to go home the next day, but when she tried to leave he told her that he was a pimp and that she was now his property.

He locked her in a room, beat her daily, and advertised her for sex on websites. Once she looked out a window and saw her mother on the street, crying and posting flyers with Ashley's photo.

When Ashley tried to shout her mother's name from the window, her pimp grabbed her by the hair and yanked her back, threatening "If you shout, I'll kill you." Ashley eventually escaped her confinement and is now at a treatment center for girls who have been sexually trafficked in New York.

## Camila

Camila was only 14 when she was persuaded to leave her job as a maid and forced into prostitution in a bar in the Amazon.

She was repeatedly restrained, raped and drugged. The traffickers coerced and bribed Camila with her freedom to get her to recruit her friend Sandra into sex trafficking as well.

Camila was given her freedom but Sandra was then sexually exploited and humiliated. One night, while out riding with a customer, Sandra made a break from the car and shouted for help from the police.

Instead of being rescued, they took her to a center for juvenile offenders, where she was detained for two years.

Camila was finally able to return home and filed a criminal complaint against her traffickers, but says she still feels trapped in her memories.

---

promising a good and decent job upon arrival—which turns out to be stripping (Fraud / Recruiting and also Receiving / Sexual exploitation).

3. A seven-year-old boy is forced to make bricks in the hot sun all day long because his father has been indentured with no realistic way to pay off the debt, resulting in subjecting his family to living in a laborers' camp and performing hard labor (Coercion / Harboring / Debt bondage).

### Raju

Raju, a migrant worker from Burma, traveled to Thailand after being falsely promised 6,000 baht per month as a restaurant or factory worker—if he could first pay a 12,000 baht brokerage fee. Out of options, he agreed to borrow money for the fee and use his future earnings to repay it.

Raju was instead forced and threatened at gun-point to board a fishing boat.

On board the Thai vessel, Raju and the other workers were forced to work day and night, lived in cramped quarters and were beaten if they took fish to cook and eat. Already saddled by debt, Raju never received his promised wages.

Each time the fishing boat docked, the workers were taken to a house and locked in a room so that they could not escape.

Raju recalled one worker who attempted to run away but was caught: "The man was tied to a post...the man was electrocuted and tortured with cigarette butts...later he was shot through the head."

Raju was finally able to escape the Thai fishing vessel by tying himself to a buoy, jumping overboard, and swimming six hours to shore.[2]

## "Hidden in plain sight"

After our West Wing meeting on human trafficking described in the first chapter, our group of four abolitionists left the White House and debriefed in a nearby coffee shop. We planned the crucial next practical steps that, we hoped, would turn our encouraging meeting into solid action. We knew we were sailing in unchartered waters, since to our knowledge, no government had ever significantly engaged the medical community in the fight against human trafficking.

We also knew that we would face opposition from many on the left and even in the medical community who categorized prostituted individuals as "sex workers." We would be challenging established researchers and entrenched activists who espoused a "harm reduction" strategy rather than rescue and abolition.

---

[2] U.S. Office to Monitor and Combat Trafficking in Persons, "Victims' Stories," *Trafficking in Persons Report 2012*. http://www.state.gov/j/tip/rls/tiprpt/2012/192360.htm accessed Mar. 5, 2013.

One of our group of four abolitionists, Dr. Laura Lederer, had come up against the harm reduction notion during her years as a pioneer in fighting commercial sexual exploitation. Having landed in the anti-trafficking office at the U.S. State Department, she began to focus on strategies to persuade the medical community to adopt a "rescue and restore" strategy rather than the harm reduction approach that left victims enslaved in brothels.

Laura had invited me to a private meeting at the State Department, early on during the Bush administration, to strategize about engaging the medical community. Laura knew then what studies would eventually document—that trafficking victims frequently end up in medical offices and hospitals because their traffickers hold a vested financial interest in keeping them healthy.[3] A sick prostituted victim doesn't bring in much cash.

The problem was that most medical professionals didn't even know what human trafficking was, much less how to report and treat victims. Golden opportunities to rescue victims were slipping away because of ignorance, allowing traffickers to keep their victims "hidden in plain sight."[4]

So over a series of meetings, we developed a multi-pronged plan to engage the medical community:

1. Conduct **medical studies** abroad to document the need for medical interventions with trafficking victims. Data speaks to doctors.
2. Invite leaders of key medical **specialty colleges** (professional associations such as the American Medical Association) to the White House for a high-level briefing and a challenge to develop awareness-building materials for their members. By engaging

---

[3] Years later, Dr. Lederer published the results of a study that found that nearly 88 percent of victims interviewed had seen a healthcare professional while in captivity (Lederer, L. and Wetzel, C.A. "The Health Consequences of Sex Trafficking and Their Implications for Identifying Victims in Healthcare Facilities," (2014) *The Annals of Health Law* 23:1. 61-91; p. 77.) An earlier study of fewer victims had noted, "In all, 28 percent of the trafficking victims that we interviewed came into contact with the health care system during their time in captivity—each one of those visits represents a missed opportunity for potential intervention or education about trafficking." *Turning Pain into Power: Trafficking Survivors' Perspectives on Early Intervention Strategies.* San Francisco, CA, 2005. Available at http://www.childhood-usa.org/upl/files/4109.pdf, accessed Aug. 1, 2011.

[4] A study examining the experience of emergency room personnel regarding trafficking victims found that although 29 percent thought it was a problem in their emergency department population, only 13 percent felt confident or very confident that they could identify a TIP victim, and less than 3 percent had ever had any training on recognizing TIP victims. Chisolm-Strike M, Richardson L. Assessment of emergency department provider knowledge about human trafficking victims in the ED. *Acad Emerg Med* 2007; 14(suppl1):134.

medical specialty groups, we could reach potentially hundreds of thousands of health professionals—and at no cost to taxpayers.

3. Establish a **national center** for victim treatment, research and development of a national education program. The center would provide a best practice example to be emulated in the U.S. and around the world.

4. Engage the Surgeon General to conduct a national **awareness campaign**—just as Dr. C. Everett Koop had done on the issue of smoking.

I worked closely with the Bush administration on this agenda, gaining high-level White House support for the goals. Administration officials who recognized the huge opportunity in engaging the medical community on human trafficking and proved particularly receptive to our plans included Claude Allen, President Bush's Domestic Policy Advisor; Dr. Mark Dybul, an ambassador who led the President's Emergency Plan for AIDS Relief; and former Congressman John Miller, the U.S. ambassador at large for human trafficking.

Despite the best intentions and enthusiasm of key administration officials, however, it seemed that we could never hit the target and fully engage medical professionals.

### White House meeting

Claude Allen arranged a White House meeting with top administration social services and health officials, including Centers for Disease Control and Prevention (CDC) Dr. Julie Gerberding and the president's chief speechwriter, Michael Gerson. Claude followed the outline I had provided, which sketched out the plans we had developed during the initial summer meeting in the West Wing.

The meeting, though filled with promise and potential, proved unproductive. Dr. Gerberding skeptically questioned the FBI's numbers of human trafficking victims, perhaps unconvinced that the problem warranted a significant public health intervention. We never heard from her again.

Then Claude abruptly resigned from his Domestic Policy Council post at the White House. Within weeks, a scandal emerged involving charges of theft. Thankfully, Claude worked through the crisis and with new humility seemed to emerge strengthened in his faith. Meanwhile, however, the loss of our friend and colleague as an advocate within the White House cost our anti-trafficking strategy precious momentum and influence.

As a State Department official, Ambassador Dybul's welcome enthusiasm for our idea of a White House summit could only go so far, since outreach to the US medical community is largely the domain of the US Department of Health and Human Services (HHS). Washington is infamous for turf battles.

The State Department eventually hosted a White House summit on human trafficking, but it lacked a medical focus. HHS held a medical conference, but it did not include the medical specialty college leaders crucial to reaching the medical community. Missed opportunities.

Another roadblock hindering government action on any long-term project is high turnover, notably among political appointees. Just when key personnel would finally catch the vision for our human trafficking plan, they would move on in the constant career moves that political appointees make in Washington. Each personnel change meant the education cycle would begin all over, meeting with their replacements to once again cast the vision.

Of course, the biggest shakeup comes every four years, when either a brand new administration takes over with all new people, or a continuing administration replaces worn-out appointees with fresh faces.

### *Courts thwart anti-prostitution requirement*

Our group of abolitionists realized early on that some also might oppose our efforts simply because we represented Christian organizations and a Christian president, George W. Bush. Many simply despised President Bush for his evangelical persuasions, which often resulted in policies counter to the worldview of academic elites, liberals and many health activists.

The conflict over what worldview would determine public policy on sex trafficking and other forms of prostitution came into sharp focus when Congress included a clear anti-prostitution pledge policy in the United States Leadership Against HIV/AIDS, Tuberculosis, and Malaria Act of 2003. President Bush had signed the bill into law. Under the new law, groups seeking US anti-trafficking grants had to demonstrate that they were not undermining the whole purpose of those grants by advocating for or condoning prostitution.

Consistent with that law, President Bush had issued a National Security Presidential Directive (NSPD-22) that asserted,

"Our Policy is based on an abolitionist approach to trafficking in persons…. The United States Government opposes prostitution and any related activities, including pimping, pandering, or maintaining brothels as contributing to the phenomenon of trafficking in persons."[5]

---

[5] George W. Bush, National Security and Homeland Security Presidential Directive 22,

Hardly a radical notion—or at least one would think.

The anti-prostitution requirement passed by Congress and the administration's formal position against prostitution touched off a firestorm of protest, led in part by those who would allow prostitution as a libertarian choice. A coalition of leftist organizations wrote a letter to President Bush to protest the anti-prostitution policy. The International Planned Parenthood Federation, International Gay and Lesbian Human Rights Commission, the Center for Reproductive Rights, the Episcopal Church USA, the Feminist Majority Foundation, Human Rights Watch, Sexuality Information and Education Council of the United States and others joined the protest, painting the policy as judgmental.

The protesting groups asserted that requiring groups seeking U.S. funding to fight human trafficking to agree not to promote prostitution somehow would "exacerbate stigma and discrimination against already marginalized groups. Any anti-prostitution declaration by organizations working in the sex sector has the potential to judge and alienate the very people these organizations seek to assist, making it difficult or impossible to provide services or assistance to those at risk."

The leftist groups concluded with quite a stretch of rationality, asserting that the "U.S. government policy compels speech, which is an unconstitutional condition on government funding in violation of the First Amendment." In other words, these groups held that the government had no right to stipulate how taxpayer funds could be used—including preventing the use of tax dollars from being used to promote prostitution.

## Affirming abolition

To highlight the policy, and also to encourage wobbly political operatives within the White House to stand firm on the President's anti-prostitution stand, I drafted a policy-affirming letter to the President. I organized a campaign inviting like-minded organizations to sign onto the letter to show widespread support for the policy.

Over 100 groups and individuals representing tens of millions of constituents worldwide joined the effort, including Focus on the Family, National Association of Evangelicals, Family Research Council, The Salvation Army, Concerned Women for America, Southern Baptist Ethics & Religious Liberty Commission, Sex Industry Survivors, The Medical Institute, World Hope International, World Relief, the Christian Medical Association and others. The letter also included the signatures of 50 physicians and prominent feminists such as Donna M. Hughes, Ph.D.; Diana E. H. Russell, Ph.D.; and Phyllis Chesler, Ph.D. I hand-delivered the letter to President Bush's Domestic Policy Advisor.

Meanwhile, the prostitution pledge protestors took their case to court and presented their spurious argument. Incredibly, a judge actually agreed and ruled that the law and administration policy–requiring grantees to certify that they would not undermine the grant by promoting prostitution–violated the First Amendment free speech rights of organizations seeking funding.

On appeal, however, U.S. Circuit Judge A. Raymond Randolph restored sanity. Judge Randolph recognized that Congress had authorized the funding "on such terms and conditions as the president may determine." He concluded that the law "does not compel [organizations seeking funding] to advocate the government's position on prostitution and sex trafficking; it requires only that if [they wish] to receive funds it must communicate the message the government chooses to fund. This does not violate the First Amendment."

The case wound its way to the US Supreme Court, which in a split decision ruled against the government and struck down the anti-prostitution requirement as wrongly compelling speech.[6] I summarized in a blog entry

---

[6] To my regret, a few of my esteemed colleagues, legal advocates who focus on religious liberty issues, had filed briefs opposing the "prostitution pledge" provision. They reasoned that its allowance would let the government unconstitutionally dictate the ideological views of any organization that receives government funding. These groups understandably feared strengthening the Obama administration's attacks on religious liberty, buttressing local governments' attacks on pregnancy centers through speech requirements, and squeezing out campus student groups that decline to conform to university dogma on social issues. The groups reasoned that even the tax exemption status of charitable groups, seen (oddly) as a form of government subsidy, could be jeopardized if groups opposed the social policies of the government.

Other religious liberty advocates, such as the American Center for Law and Justice, reasoned– rightly, in my view–that requiring grantees to supply proof of opposition to prostitution was an eminently reasonable requirement to further the goals of a government health program that hinges on stopping prostitution. The anti-prostitution requirement, in this view, does not restrict the free speech of anyone–it just keeps the government from paying for speech opposed to the goals of this particular program, which provides funding on a completely voluntary basis. Justices Scalia and Thomas agreed in their dissent: "But here a central part of the Government's HIV/AIDS strategy is the suppression of prostitution, by which HIV is transmitted. It is entirely reasonable to admit to participation in the program only those who believe in that goal."

In a comment relevant to the funneling of government funds to groups that support prostitution, abortion and other evils, the dissenting Justices noted, "Money is fungible. The economic reality is that when NGOs can conduct their AIDS work on the Government's dime, they can expend greater resources on policies that undercut the Leadership Act."

my deep disappointment with the logic and also with the practical effect of the ruling:

> What remains undeniable and real are the immediate harms, from a pro-life, anti-trafficking and anti-AIDS perspective, that result from this ruling:
> - more money to groups that see prostitution as legitimate "sex work" rather than as an evil to be eradicated-including pro-abortion and pornography groups;
> - a blow to efforts to eradicate prostitution, along with prostitution's threat to public health and its degradation of and violence against women and children;
> - the prospect of yet more forced and elective abortions, resulting from relying on condom distribution programs and unionization of prostituted women and children rather than rescuing them out of sex trafficking and other forms of prostitution.

### Homeland Security Secretary meeting

When the Obama administration came to power in 2009, we found ourselves back at square one for the human trafficking plan—and without many friends in high places.

The Department of Homeland Security (DHS) took up the cause of building awareness for human trafficking, since organized crime and terrorists reap huge profits from the sale of human beings. I again raised our medical community engagement strategy with DHS and other administration officials, who received it gladly.

In a subsequent meeting with DHS Secretary Janet Napolitano, I again explained the concept of engaging the medical community through medical specialty colleges. Alice Hill, Senior Counselor to Secretary Napolitano, noted that DHS had been working on the idea of outreach to the medical community since I had suggested the plan a year ago at the launch of the DHS Blue Campaign.

I outlined the plan during our meeting to Secretary Napolitano, who had just been summoned by President Obama to a cabinet meeting.

She responded positively to the plan and told me, "I'll be in a cabinet meeting with [U.S. Secretary of Health and Human Services (HHS), Kathleen] Sebelius in about 20 minutes and I'll ask her to be involved."

My hopes faded at that point, since as an ardent advocate for abortion and Obamacare, HHS Secretary Kathleen Sebelius would not likely heartily welcome a plan from any pro-life advocate. Besides, the top leadership at HHS seemed less enthusiastically engaged on the human trafficking issue than Homeland Security, where top officials had caught the vision and run with it.

Not surprisingly, a response from Secretary Sebelius never came. I have continued to promote the plan (see Appendix B) with human trafficking public officials and organizations any chance I get.

## *Injecting abortion into the fight against trafficking*

Meanwhile, Secretary Sebelius and the Obama administration inserted abortion ideology into the fight against human trafficking. The Obama Department of Health and Human Services began to alter federal grants policies in accordance with the administration's aggressive abortion agenda. One notable change involved an insidious new requirement tied to a federal grant intended to provide health and social services for victims of human trafficking, or modern-day slavery.

The administration's funding opportunity announcement for the competitive grant stipulated,

> [P]reference will be given to grantees under this [grant program] that will offer all victims referral to medical providers who can provide or refer for provision of treatment for sexually transmitted infections, family planning services and the full range of legally permissible gynecological and obstetric care.[7]

Offering the "full range of legally permissible gynecological and obstetric care" translates thus: "participate in abortion or lose the grant."

To enforce submission to the president's abortion ideology, HHS used the new language to refuse to renew a federal grant to the U.S. Conference of Catholic Bishops (USCCB), despite USCCB's unquestioned qualifications. In previous years, the USCCB had used the grant to provide excellent care, by all reports, for victims of human trafficking. The USCCB proposal for

---

[7] Dept. of Health and Human Services, Administration for Children and Families, Office of Refugee Resettlement, National Human Trafficking Victim Assistance Program 2011 funding opportunity announcement
HHS-2011-ACF-ORR-ZV-0148 http://www.acf.hhs.gov/grants/open/foa/files/HHS-2011-ACF-ORR-ZV-0148_0.htm web accessed March 29, 2014.

renewing that grant had declined to agree to the new Obama administration's explicit preference for participating in abortions.

An objective grant proposal review committee, which included experts outside the administration, had scored the USCCB proposal highest among all competitors for the human trafficking services grant. Top HHS officials, however, overrode the objective reviewers and refused to renew the grant for the USCCB. Instead, HHS officials awarded the grant to an abortion-compliant organization whose proposal the grant review panel had scored, on a 100-point scale, 20 points *lower* than USCCB.

Besides the injustice of the USCCB losing the opportunity to compete fairly for the grant, victims of human trafficking lost the proven effective care the organization had been providing.

In a Congressional hearing[8,9] examining the travesty, Pennsylvania Republican Rep. Mike Kelly declared, "This is so obviously to me a way of eliminating faith-based people from being able to participate by structuring language that would leave them out."

Michigan Republican Rep. Tim Walberg warned that through the biased HHS grant process, "we have broached something that we never countenanced here in the past in this great country, where on the basis of strongly held religious moral belief, you will be discriminated against."

### One person can make a difference

William Wilberforce and his companions in Britain had to fight for decades in myriad and unfair battles with a slavery-promoting Parliament before finally securing abolition. Cultures tend to change slowly and governments do not typically respond quickly to initiatives. Besides that, government bureaucracies often seem singularly ill-suited for doing anything creative.

Yet once a government as huge as ours finally takes up a cause, it brings to bear resources that can turn the tide of the battle. And that's worth working for years to attain, all the while educating the public and key leaders about the issue.

---

[8] Govt. Printing Office transcript, Committee on Oversight and Government Reform hearing, "HHS and the Catholic Church: Examining the Politicization of Grants," Dec. 1, 2011, http://www.gpo.gov/fdsys/pkg/CHRG-112hhrg73939/html/CHRG-112hhrg73939.htm accessed May 1, 2014.

[9] I detail highlights of this hearing in a Dec, 7, 2012 article for *National Right to Life News*, "Abortion Ideology Trumps Aid for Victims of Human Trafficking," http://www.nationalrighttolifenews.org/news/2011/12/abortion-ideology-trumps-aid-for-victims-of-human-trafficking/#.U2Kv9SqF_u4 accessed May 1, 2014,

Meanwhile, nongovernment groups and especially faith-based organizations can accomplish much with comparatively meager resources, through creativity and devotion. Several physicians within the Christian Medical Association volunteered and developed an 11-module online training program to educate health care professionals on human trafficking.[10]

One of those physicians, Dr. Jeffrey Barrows, had felt God's stirring to get involved in the issue in an unusual way. Jeff's unexpected journey into the fight against human trafficking began in 2004, when I sent him an email asking his perspective, as a physician and leader of overseas medical ministries, on the scourge of modern-day slavery.

Jeff wrote to me,

What is human trafficking? I honestly didn't know much about it prior to reading a few of your emails, but lately it's something I can't get out of my mind.

He later explained how a remarkable journey evolved:

Even though I had traveled all over the world, I had not yet heard about the issue of human trafficking. I began to research the issue and was horrified to learn just how prevalent it was and how little was being done to fight it. Initially, like most people, the human trafficking I learned about was the trafficking occurring overseas, not the trafficking that is happening right in our neighborhoods.

After several months of research, I began to develop an interest in helping young victims of child sex trafficking in other countries-perhaps helping to provide medical care for them. This led me to a pivotal phone conversation with an expert in the field of child sex trafficking.

I began the conversation thinking that I would be traveling to places like Cambodia and Thailand to render care to these young victims.

But as the conversation progressed, this expert asked, "Why are you going overseas to help the girls?"

I answered, "Because that's where the girls are-right?"

He then asked me what state I lived in. When I answered Ohio, he informed me that Ohio was one of the leading states in terms of victims of child sex trafficking within the U.S.

---

[10] The human trafficking modules for health care professionals is available at www.cmda.org/tip.

I was dumbfounded!

I then asked him what was being done to help these girls. When he answered "nothing," it was then that the Lord gave me the idea of the name "Gracehaven" and called me to start an organization that would bring the love of Christ to these lost and forgotten children.

Over the course of the next several years, Jeff's commitment to helping human trafficking victims intensified. I brought him to Washington to meet with officials at the White House and the State Department, and he continued to research victims' health and personal needs.

Within three years, Jeff had decided to trim back his medical practice in obstetrics and gynecology in order to found and lead Gracehaven, a shelter and rehabilitation center in Ohio for prostituted girls. As of this writing, he is helping to lead Abolition International,[11] an organization that among other ministries helps establish critically needed medical protocols to help health professionals recognize, report and treat victims of human trafficking.

### President raises awareness

President Bush and his administration ramped up public awareness of human trafficking while also making a concerted effort to educate those on the front lines most likely to encounter victims. As a guest of the US Department of Justice, I attended a conference in Miami on human trafficking where President Bush addressed us, saying:

Human life is the gift of our Creator – and it should never be for sale. It takes a special kind of depravity to exploit and hurt the most vulnerable members of society. Human traffickers rob children of their innocence, they expose them to the worst of life before they have seen much of life. Traffickers tear families apart. They treat their victims as nothing more than goods and commodities for sale to the highest bidder.

We've got a problem; we need to do something about it.

The American government has a particular duty, because human trafficking is an affront to the defining promise of our country. People come to America hoping for a better life. And it is a terrible tragedy when anyone comes here, only to be

---

[11] http://abolitioninternational.org/

133

forced into a sweatshop, domestic servitude,
pornography or prostitution.
We're working to make sure you have the support you
need in Washington, D.C. … because the struggle
against human trafficking is more than a fight
against crime. This is more than a criminal justice
matter. It's a struggle for the lives and dignity of
innocent women and children. And that's why all of us
must be dedicated to the strategies that will enable
us to prevail. [12]

## A family responds

As public awareness about human trafficking spread nationwide, and as
the Christian Medical Association (CMA) continued to educate health care
professionals, more physicians also caught the vision. CMA member Dr. Bill
Bolthouse and his family felt so moved by meeting human trafficking victims
overseas that they produced a Hollywood-quality movie focused on the topic.

The movie's lead actress, Academy Award winner Mira Sorvino, has
served as United Nations ambassador on human trafficking, using her
celebrity status to draw attention to the issue. Ms. Sorvino also serves as a
United Nations ambassador for the cause of raising awareness. She has
noted,

Trafficking is everywhere in the world, and the
United States is one of the worst offenders. It's
tied with the illegal arms trade as the second
largest criminal industry on the earth, just after
drugs. It makes $32 billion a year worldwide. There
are about 300,000 kids at risk in the US every year,
and only one in 100 victims are ever rescued.
Once you find out about it, you can't look away, and
once you've met someone who has been bought and sold
as an object, been beaten and denied their basic
human rights, you can't ever forget that. You meet
these survivors of human trafficking and they blow
you away with their courage and the misery that
they've lived through. [13]

---

[12] Bush, George, Remarks at the National Training Conference on Human Trafficking, Tampa,
FL, July 16, 2004, http://www.gpo.gov/fdsys/pkg/PPP-2004-book2/pdf/PPP-2004-book2-doc-pg1350.pdf accessed May 2, 2014.
[13] "Mira Sorvino Reflects on Roles as Actress, Activist, Mother," *Hamptons Magazine*,
undated, http://hamptons-magazine.com/personalities/articles/mira-sorvino-union-square
accessed May 2, 2014.

At the New York City premier for the movie, entitled "Trade of Innocents,"[14] I discussed with Ms. Sorvino the huge potential for more health care professionals to aid in identifying, reporting and treating victims. She immediately understood the opportunity.

I pray that many more in government and the health care community would likewise understand the opportunity–and act on it to save lives. Thankfully, the Christian community has helped lead the anti-trafficking movement from its early days. Faith-based organizations including the Salvation Army, World Relief, Abolition International Shelter Association, the U.S. Conference of Catholic Bishops, World Hope International, the Triple S Network, Transport for Christ, The Samaritan Women, International Justice Mission and many more are fully engaged in rescuing and rehabilitating victims.

These organizations bring to victims what government and secular groups cannot–spiritual healing and hope. Besides caring for their physical and sociological needs, Christian ministry workers can share God's love, His healing touch and His grace, forgiveness and new life in Jesus Christ.

Some local churches and entire denominations, like the Evangelical Lutheran Church in America (ELCA), have made concerted efforts to address problems such as sexual commercial exploitation (i.e., sex involving money). The ELCA statement notes,

Sexual exploitation in any situation, either personally or commercially, inside or outside legally contracted marriage, is sinful because it is destructive of God's good gift [of sexuality] and human integrity.

Commercial sexual exploitation is an organized form of this sinful behavior. It is especially demonic when it exploits children and youth. Commercial sexual exploitation is widespread throughout the United States and around the world, and it continues to grow. To a large extent, this exploitation remains hidden from public attention and ignored by Church and society. It includes what customers do by:

- viewing pornographic videos
- downloading pornography from the Internet
- visiting strip clubs
- engaging in simulated sex by phone or computer
- using escort services
- participating in sex tourism

---

[14] See http://tradeofinnocents.com.

> While customers may think they harm no one but themselves, the truth is that they are swept up in a system of sexual exploitation that degrades all participants, both providers and customers.[15]

Determine not to support human trafficking in any way. Learn the clues and signs that suggest someone may be a victim. Sexual exploitation of minors, forced labor and other forms of human trafficking may be occurring right now at your own doorstep. The following information will help you learn more about what *you* can do to recognize and report victims of human trafficking.

### *What you can do about human trafficking.*

*Guidelines provided by the U.S. Department of Homeland Security:*
Everyone has a role to play in combating human trafficking. The Blue Campaign created a variety of resources[16] for its partners and stakeholders across government, law enforcement, first responders, prosecutors, judges, non-governmental organizations and the private sector to inform people of potential "red flags" or indicators of human trafficking. We encourage you to get involved in combating human trafficking by taking a few simple steps:

1. **Learn the indicators of human trafficking.**[17] Recognizing these signs of human trafficking is the first step to identifying a victim.
2. **Take human trafficking awareness trainings**[18] to learn more about this crime and how to identify victims and report suspected cases of human trafficking.
3. **Educate others about the indicators of human trafficking.** Conduct your own five-minute general awareness Coffee Break Training[19] on human trafficking among coworkers, community members, or friends. Simply discuss the material on the one-page sheet to raise awareness of the issue, victim indicators and how to report the crime.

---

[15] "Commercial Sexual Exploitation," policy statement adopted by the Church Council of the Evangelical Lutheran Church in America on November 11, 2001. Complete statement available at http://www.elca.org/What-We-Believe/Social-Issues/Messages/Commercial-Sexual-Exploitation.aspx.

[16] http://www.dhs.gov/blue-campaign-materials-catalog, accessed May 2, 2014.

[17] http://www.dhs.gov/human-trafficking-indicators, accessed May 2, 2014.

[18] See www.cmda.org/TIP and also http://www.dhs.gov/human-trafficking-awareness-training accessed May 2, 2014.

[19] http://www.dhs.gov/xlibrary/assets/blue-campaign/ht-blue-campaign-coffee-break-training.pdf, accessed May 2, 2014.

4.  **Report suspected human trafficking.** To report suspected human trafficking activity or get help from federal law enforcement (available 24/7, in over 300 languages and dialects):

# Call 1-866-347-2423 (toll-free)

Call 1-802-872-6199 (non-toll free international)

## Report online at www.ice.gov/tips

*Anonymous tips may be reported on the online form and may also be reported to ICE via the toll-free HSI Tip Line.*

Call the National Human Trafficking Resource Center (NHTRC) at 1-888-3737-888 to get help or connect with a service provider in your area. The NHTRC is not a law enforcement or immigration authority and is operated by a nongovernmental organization. For more information, please contact the Blue Campaign at BlueCampaign@hq.dhs.gov. "Like" us on Facebook[20] to receive Blue Campaign updates and share updates with your friends.

### A proposal to engage the medical community

I developed the following proposal to increase the awareness and response by medical professionals:

A Proposal for Medical - Law Enforcement Partnerships to Enhance TIP Victim Rescues, Health and Cooperation

### Problems and opportunities

1.  Increasing victim recognition and reporting by educating medical professionals

A study published by Dr. Laura Lederer documented that 88 percent of victims actually visited a healthcare professional during their time of victimization.[21] Yet victims taken to medical professionals during their captivity often are not recognized and reported, because most medical professionals do not know the signs of trafficking victims or how and where to report suspected cases.

Healthcare professionals–especially those who work in emergency rooms, clinics in low-income areas and Obstetrics and Gynecology–need training to learn how to help recognize, report, rescue and restore victims of

---

[20] www.facebook.com/bluecampaign accessed May 2, 2014.

[21] Lederer, L. and Wetzel, C.A. "The Health Consequences of Sex Trafficking and Their Implications for Identifying Victims in Healthcare Facilities". (2014) *The Annals of Health Law* 23:1. 77.

trafficking in persons (TIP) brought to hospitals and clinics for health needs. Knowing how to identify and work with law enforcement officials plays a key role in this effort to increase the number of victims reported, rescued and rehabilitated. To conform to the continuing medical education (CME) requirements and expectations of medical professionals, the training should be developed and overseen by medical professionals.

2.   Gaining the trust and cooperation of victims by meeting their health needs

Because victims often evidence the Stockholm syndrome and have been conditioned to view law enforcement officials as enemies rather than allies, a lack of trust can impede initial interviews, cooperation in prosecutions and attempts to persuade victims not to return to traffickers. Law enforcement officials need to be able to enlist the help of healthcare professionals to initially interface with and medically examine victims immediately following raids and rescues, and also to provide ongoing medical care for victims.

By assisting in initial interviews of rescued victims, medical professionals can provide a readily trusted contact for victims who have been conditioned to mistrust law enforcement officials and even men in general. If one of the first persons a victim encounters is a caring medical professional who helps meet her health needs–for example, a female health professional caring for a female victim–that victim will much more likely cooperate with questioning and prosecution efforts.

3.   Diagnosing diseases to treat victims and protect agents and caregivers

Absent medical protocols for interfacing with trafficking victims during intake interviews, victims may not receive immediately needed medical help, and law enforcement officials and caregivers unknowingly risk exposure to infectious diseases such as tuberculosis and typhus.

Developing protocols to immediately identify and address health problems, including infectious diseases, will help victims receive potentially lifesaving help while also protecting law enforcement officials and caregivers from potentially life-threatening exposure.

### Solution

*Summit:* Medical and Law Enforcement Partnerships to Stop Human Trafficking

**Goal:**

Engage medical specialty group leaders and other healthcare leaders to educate and motivate healthcare professionals to partner with law enforcement officials in recognizing, reporting, treating and earning the cooperation of victims of human trafficking.

**Invite:**
1. Leaders of medical specialty organizations whose members are most likely to see victims of human trafficking (e.g., American College of Emergency Physicians, American Congress of Obstetricians and Gynecologists, American Association of Public Health Physicians, etc.). Medical specialty groups reach hundreds of thousands of professionals.
2. Leaders of community and faith-based organizations that work with victims and/or are likely to have contact with victims.
3. Leaders of influential medical educational institutions.
4. Top officials representing public health agencies.
5. Healthcare specialists serving in crisis relief agencies, community health and faith-based programs and others working with vulnerable populations.

**Speakers:**
- Secretary of the Department of Homeland Security
- U.S. Surgeon General
- Member of Congress who sponsored TVPRA

**Panels:**
1. Medical-law enforcement partnering to identify, report, treat and engage victims
    - Outline steps to recognizing victims in healthcare settings.
    - Explain methods and considerations for reporting victims to law enforcement authorities.
    - Discuss the process of rescuing, interviewing, treating and earning the cooperation of victims in prosecutions, and how medical professionals can participate.
2. Federal TIP resources and how to customize them for specific medical audiences
    - Overview medically related TIP education materials developed by federal agencies.
    - Encourage attendees to customize the agency materials and develop their own national awareness education resources, adapted for the various medical specialty groups (e.g., Ob-Gyn, emergency medicine, public health) and types of medical professionals (e.g., physicians, nurses and support staff).
3. TIP medical working groups
    - Solicit volunteers for two TIP medical working groups to develop:

139

o   a formal medical protocol for use nationwide with victims immediately following raids and rescues;[22] and,

o   a plan for a registry of medical professionals who will interface with victims immediately following raids and rescues.

---

[22] U.S. Department of Justice notes, "Another safety consideration is whether the victim has been exposed to infectious diseases such as tuberculosis, HIV, and typhus (Salvation Army, 2006) and the risk of exposure to others. This should be determined as part of an initial assessment or screening of the victim."

# Chapter 13:
# *Freedom of faith, conscience and speech*

*"...let it be known to you, O king,*
*that we are not going to serve your gods*
*or worship the golden image that you have set up."*
–Daniel 3:18

While governments throughout history have often viewed the Church as a competitor for power and have sought to restrict her freedom, religious freedom as public policy dates back to medieval times.

In the first clause of the groundbreaking Magna Carta of 1215, King John acknowledged that "the English church shall be free, and shall have its rights undiminished and its liberties unimpaired." (Notably, the King signed the document only under duress, as his barons threatened revolt against his reign.)

The First Amendment to the U.S. Constitution follows this freedom, providing that "Congress shall make no law respecting an establishment of religion, or prohibiting the free exercise thereof...." Accordingly, U.S. courts have consistently upheld the right of religious organizations to make internal employment decisions apart from government interference. The Supreme Court has issued stinging rebukes to administrations that succumb to the temptation to extend their power by tramping religious freedom.

This temptation to restrict religious freedom, however, seems to hold a particular allure for the Obama administration.

### Gutting conscience protections in healthcare

President Obama announced early in his first term that he intended to replace the "conscience regulation"–the only federal regulation protecting pro-life healthcare professionals from discrimination and firings for declining to participate in abortions on grounds of conscience.

To craft a strategic response to the President's assault on the conscience freedoms of healthcare professionals, I helped organize a meeting of pro-life and pro-family leaders and former Bush administration health officials. We gathered at the Family Research Council offices in Washington, DC to plan legal, political and public relations strategies to fight the discrimination.

Individuals with years of experience in Congress, the White House and federal agencies joined what are known as "outside groups"–nonprofit and charitable organizations dedicated to advancing values on specific topics such as pro-life and family issues. As a result of the plan that arose from that meeting, we formed a new coalition focused on conscience rights, Freedom2Care, which eventually grew into 50 organizations and 30,000 individuals. We developed a website, www.Freedom2Care.org, to serve as a one-stop shop of education, news and action opportunities for anyone interested in conscience rights.

We determined to educate the public about the religious freedom principles that had prompted three bipartisan federal laws over three decades and a federal regulation designed to prevent discrimination against life-affirming healthcare professionals and institutions.

### Personal testimonies illustrate discrimination

Realizing the power of personal stories, I began to collect testimonials from healthcare professionals who had experienced discrimination on the basis of conscience values. Here's a sampling from the dozens of personal stories that helped drive home the need for conscience protections:

Dr. James Joyce wrote of discrimination simply for being Catholic:

Many medical school students who trained with me avoided Ob/Gyn [Obstetrics and Gynecology] residency because their Catholic beliefs would not be respected. I carefully screened 11 Ob/Gyn programs by mail and personal visit at great expense.
After being selected for my top choice program, I was attacked by chief residents who were suspicious that Catholicism had something against women and targeted me for a four-month "probation" where all of my preceptors were "warned of my Catholic [views]."
In spite of all of this, I was successful in passing the in-training exam. But I was again attacked by the assistant director of the program, who indicated that he did not believe that it was possible to be an Ob/Gyn and be a practicing Catholic.
He refused to recommend me to any other program in Ob/Gyn. At this vulnerable point in residency training, I was unable to afford to move to a new

program and (although I was encouraged to do so) unable to afford a lawsuit for discrimination.[1]

An obstetrician who requested anonymity related his experience of discrimination for simply teaching about abortion complications:

I have been discriminated against during my Ob/Gyn residency. I gave a grand rounds [case presentation] on abortion complications and was fired for it. It was in San Diego, and I was a chief resident in Ob/Gyn at [a local] hospital.

I gave the talk at the Grand Rounds at [another] hospital. I was fired for "creating morale problems and insubordination." That was in 1980, but it is still happening.

I was suspended by [a large medical employer] in the 1980s twice for assisting teen clients who were being forced by their families to undergo abortions. I have been discriminated against in my career advancement. Being pro-life is not politically correct. Directorship of departments, fellowships, etc. are out of the question.[2]

The experience of a medical student, Trevor K. Kitchens, offers insight as to why the field of obstetrics is increasingly repelling pro-life professionals:

I am a first-year medical student in the beginning stages of deciding which specialty I would like to pursue. I am currently very interested in Ob/Gyn, but I am afraid of the relationship between this field and abortion.

By the way, I am 100 percent against abortion, and there is no way I would perform one. Moreover, there is no way I would tell a patient that abortion is an option under any circumstance, because I do not believe it is an option.

My concern is that I will start a [medical] residence [program] and would subsequently be required at some point to give a patient the option of abortion, which I would refuse. My fear is that taking this stand would cost me my residence position.

Now, if that is what it comes down to, I will be glad to take the stand for Jesus Christ and give up my position.

---

[1] Joyce, James MD, personal story submitted at www.Freedom2Care.org, May 7, 2009.
[2] Personal email to Christian Medical Association from a physician requesting anonymity, October 7, 2006.

However, I would really like to be able to avoid this situation and complete my residence so that I could go on and serve the Lord in that field. So I guess my question is, can an institution take action against a resident for taking this type of a stand against abortion? And are there any institutions in particular that would be understanding of my beliefs and not ask me to compromise them?[3]

Trevor's dilemma illustrates the harm of weakening conscience protections for healthcare professionals. Obstetricians are already becoming hard for patients for find, with scores of Ob-Gyn physicians leaving medicine due to soaring malpractice insurance premiums.[4]

To make matters worse, the national association of obstetricians, American College of Obstetrics and Gynecologists (ACOG), aggressively promotes abortion and fights to limit conscience rights. As a result of an environment of abortion-related intimidation and discrimination, fewer and fewer pro-life obstetricians remain in or choose the profession, worsening the national shortage of Ob-Gyn physicians.

### Bias begins early

While ACOG threatened to end the careers of graduate physicians, abortion advocates on medical school campuses enforced abortion bias to keep individuals from even beginning a medical career. A study of the medical school application process turned up examples of clear and unmitigated bias. The students who suffered the discrimination doubtless either never realized that their faith had disqualified them or knew of no recourse to fight the bias, as described in the following published account:

Dr. George Zenner and I looked at what actually happened in interview reports at an American medical school and at subsequent admission committee meetings where these reports and the applicants were discussed.

We found that, contrary to the impression given the Congress, religious questions, including ones related to abortion, were being asked of the applicants and discussed before the Admission Committee. The answers to these questions, although the interviewers denied

---

[3] Personal email from Trevor Kitchens to Christian Medical Association, April 22, 2008.
[4] See "Hospital's Efforts to Boost Patient Safety Pay Off," *US News & World Report*, June 12, 2014, http://health.usnews.com/health-news/articles/2014/06/12/hospitals-efforts-to-boost-patient-safety-pay-off, accessed June 19, 2014.

144

it in the questionnaire, were affecting judgments regarding whether the candidates were appropriate for medical school admission.

Our published study, by its nature anecdotal and not statistical, showed that the bias cut one way: against the so-called religious applicant."[5]

A once-aspiring health professional, "Michelle S.," related to me the following sad result of how discrimination squelched her dream:

I would be writing as a healthcare professional but was blackballed for objective reasons from nursing college, despite scoring 98 in clinicals. I was washed out after defending a fellow student who made a pro-life declaration during ethics class.[6]

Another health professional recounted to me the following incident that illustrates how medical students face discrimination for their faith-based ethical convictions:

Several years ago I was interviewing at my then dream school, a leading medical school on the west coast. The interview was going very well-until the topic turned to abortion.

One of the interviewers stated, "I see that you were involved with a Christian student organization in college. What would you do if your patient asked you to help her obtain an abortion?" The interviewers then proceeded to have me act out a scenario with two of the interviewers playing parts, one as the pregnant woman with an unwanted pregnancy, and the other as her pro-life boyfriend.

"Tell my girlfriend that an abortion is a sin!" the faux boyfriend exclaimed. I did my best to diffuse the tension as I encouraged the two to communicate with each other their points of view, without unduly taking sides or inserting my own opinion unless asked. The scenario went on for almost 10 minutes. When it became clear that I was not going to automatically support the woman's desire for an abortion, the scenario-and the interview-ended. I was not admitted to that school. I did obtain admission

---

[5] "Religious Discrimination in the Academy," by Albert E. Gunn, Esq., M.D. *Eutopia*, Vol. 2 No. 5: March/April 1998. This article references Gunn, A.E.; Zenner G.O. Jr.; "Religious Discrimination in the Selection of Medical Students: A Case Study" *Issues in Law and Medicine*; 11(4) Spring 1996, 363-378.

[6] Story submitted at www.Freedom2Care.org, March 20, 2009.

at another top school and have now graduated and
moved on.
But that experience impressed upon me the not-so-
subtle bias within the medical field against those
who hold a pro-life position, even those who are very
careful to respect the autonomy of their pro-choice
patients.[7]

### Communicating the message

Most proposed changes to federal regulations require a public comment period lasting several months, during which anyone can voice views on the proposed regulation. Visitors to the Freedom2Care website sent over 34,000 comments to HHS, urging the administration to keep the conscience-protecting regulation. We also educated members of Congress, visiting their offices with healthcare professionals who told stories of discrimination and explained why conscience rights were essential to protecting patient access.

We contracted Kellyanne Conway and her firm, The Polling Company, Inc., to conduct a nationwide survey of American attitudes on conscience issues. To report the results, we held a news conference at the National Press Club in Washington, DC. In the front of the press room, we arranged dozens of physicians in white lab coats to help make our point visually for the cameras from FOX News, CNN and other national media outlets.

We unveiled the results of our scientific telephone poll of the American public and of an online poll of 2,865 faith-based physicians. The polls revealed that:

- 88 percent of American adults said it is either "very" or "somewhat" important to them that they enjoy a similar set of morals as their doctors, nurses, and other healthcare providers.
- 87 percent of American adults said it is important to "make sure that healthcare professionals in America are not forced to participate in procedures and practices to which they have moral objections."
- 63 percent of American adults supported the existing conscience protection regulation and 62 percent opposed the Obama administration's proposal to get rid of it.
- 91 percent of faith-based physicians agreed with the statement, "I would rather stop practicing medicine altogether than be forced to violate my conscience."

---

[7] Story submitted at www.Freedom2Care.org, December 31, 2010.

We emphasized that at a time when our nation was focused on expanding healthcare access, forcing out of medicine those who hold to life-honoring standards would only serve to *cut off* access to millions of patients– particularly the poor without insurance and those in medically underserved areas. Such patients often depend upon faith-based institutions and professionals, who are motivated both to reach out to the needy and also to conscientiously practice medicine according to faith-based moral standards.

We could have focused our arguments at the news conference on biblical reasons explaining why abortion is wrong and why we must obey God and not man. Most Americans who believe the Bible likely would have agreed with us. But to impact public policy in a democratic republic as diverse as ours, we have to motivate not only those who share our worldview but also convince those who do not.

### Universal language: Self-interest, harms and benefits

We employed the universal language for communicating with those of a different worldview–*self-interest*. We translated biblical principles for public policy into terms of the harms and benefits that a policy will bring to individuals and society.

For example, restricting conscience rights ultimately *harms* patients, because if pro-life, faith-based professionals and institutions are forced to choose between participating in abortion or following moral standards, they will leave medicine. The loss of faith-based professionals and institutions will cause millions of poor patients to lose access to faith-based healthcare.

The *benefits* of upholding conscience rights, on the other hand, include (a) protecting access for patients who depend on faith-based professionals and institutions; (b) protecting the First Amendment religious liberty rights of healthcare professionals and by extension, all Americans; and (c) protecting the rights of patients who want pro-life physicians.

When I make the case for conscience rights with policy makers who may not share a pro-life conviction, I explain that wherever one stands on abortion, protecting conscience rights makes pragmatic sense as a way to protect healthcare access for patients. Of course, this argument may not dissuade hard-core abortion ideologues who hold a visceral, and often deeply personal, attachment to abortion. But a pragmatic argument based on evidence and sound reasoning can convince reasonable individuals, especially those in the political center.[8]

---

[8] To stay updated on current developments in the fight for conscience rights and religious liberty, visit www.Freedom2Care.org.

Persuading the far left, however, is another story. I presented a pragmatic case about conscience freedom and healthcare access during a White House meeting with President Obama's faith-based office director, Joshua DuBois. President Obama, however, ignored our arguments and the overwhelming number of public comments favoring the conscience-protecting regulation. He and his HHS officials literally gutted the regulation, leaving pro-life healthcare professionals as sitting ducks for abortion zealots on the hunt for those who oppose their ideology.

The conscience freedom in healthcare battle is far from over, however. A subsequent president can reinstate the conscience-protecting regulation, and Congress can pass new anti-discrimination laws.[9,10]

The public policy battle over religious freedom has expanded well beyond conscience rights in healthcare, in ways that impact millions of Americans.

### Assaulting religious hiring rights

After gutting conscience protections for healthcare professionals, the Obama Department of Justice (DOJ) continued to pursue headlong an apparent campaign to undermine religious freedom, through bureaucratic policies and court action.

In the case of *Hosanna-Tabor Evangelical Lutheran Church and School v. EEOC,* DOJ attorneys attempted to overturn decades of legal precedent and convince the Supreme Court to use the case of a fired private Christian school teacher to restrict faith-based organizations' hiring rights. An organization I highly respect and enjoy working with, the Becket Fund for Religious Liberty, argued the case before the court.[11]

The Supreme Court handed the Obama administration an embarrassing *unanimous* 9-0 loss. Even President Obama's own appointees to the Court

---

[9] For example, the U.S. House of Representatives passed the Protect Life Act in 2011, banning discrimination in healthcare, by a vote of 251-172. While the Democrat-controlled Senate refused to pass the bill, the debate provided a valuable educational opportunity to highlight the critical need to respect conscience rights and preserve the American freedoms built into our Constitution.

[10] Current conscience law for health professionals does not provide any avenue for victims of discrimination to seek justice in the courts. Besides that glaring gap, healthcare conscience law also only bans discrimination when it is tied to specific federal funding programs. That means that outside the technical boundaries of these often narrow laws, bias and discrimination can run rampant, wrecking careers and inflicting unjust damage on individuals. For a fuller explanation of conscience laws in healthcare, visit http://www.freedom2care.org/learn/.

[11] For a summary, see http://www.becketfund.org/hosannatabor/.

deemed the administration's position a radical contradiction of Constitutional religious liberties.

Chief Justice John Roberts noted in his opinion[12] for the majority,

The Establishment Clause[13] prevents the Government from appointing ministers, and the Free Exercise Clause[14] prevents it from interfering with the freedom of religious groups to select their own.

Observers declared the decision one of the most important religious freedom cases in the past half century, and rightly so, given the implications if the government had won.

As Chief Justice Roberts explained,

The members of a religious group put their faith in the hands of their ministers. Requiring a church to accept or retain an unwanted minister, or punishing a church for failing to do so, intrudes upon more than a mere employment decision. Such action interferes with the internal governance of the church, depriving the church of control over the selection of those who will personify its beliefs. By imposing an unwanted minister, the state infringes the Free Exercise Clause, which protects a religious group's right to shape its own faith and mission through its appointments.

Imagine if the government could step in to prevent the firing of a minister who preached in favor of the current administration's policies, or to mandate the firing of a minister who preached in opposition to the administration. The First Amendment protects both religious freedom and freedom of speech, and the two are inextricably linked.

## Using the bureaucracy to exclude the faith community

We have already reviewed how the Obama administration changed federal grants requirements on human trafficking, requiring participation in abortion, to exclude the faith community from grants to combat human trafficking. The administration also was using the same tactic, I discovered, to exclude the faith community from grants to fight AIDS.

---

[12] Supreme Court decision Jan. 11, 2012, *Hosanna-Tabor Evangelical Lutheran Church and School v. Equal Employment Opportunity Commission, et al.* http://www.supremecourt.gov/opinions/11pdf/10-553.pdf, accessed June 19, 2014.

[13] i.e., The First Amendment section, "Congress shall make no law respecting an *establishment* of religion...."

[14] i.e., The First Amendment section, "Congress shall make no law ... prohibiting the *free exercise* thereof...."

In a meeting with President Obama's AIDS ambassador, Dr. Eric Goosby, I raised the issue of conscience freedoms in healthcare. I explained that the same faith principles that motivate healthcare professionals to care for the poor and marginalized also requires them to practice according to ethical standards. The provision of faith-based healthcare hinges on conscience freedoms.

A representative of a Catholic organization followed up on my comments by noting that their organization had been shut out of competing for the vast majority of federal AIDS grants because of requirements to participate in condom distribution, in contradiction to Catholic teaching. The Catholic groups provide many other valuable services to AIDS patients, however, so being excluded from US grants programs ultimately penalized the patients who could benefit from their effective care.

Dr. Goosby's office worked with faith-based groups and US Agency for International Development (USAID) officials to develop a written policy[15] to address the problem and bring administration policy in line with the federal law that reauthorized the Presidents Emergency Plan for AIDS Relief (PEPFAR).[16] The new policy noted:

> ...organizations shall not be required to endorse or utilize a multisectoral or comprehensive approach to combating HIV/AIDS or to endorse, utilize, make a referral to, become integrated with, or otherwise participate in any program or activity to which the organization has a religious or moral objection. For example, for moral or religious reasons, some organizations choose not to provide condoms or other contraceptives.[17]

---

[15] USAID Acquisition & Assistance Policy Directive (AAPD) AAPD 12-04, http://www.usaid.gov/sites/default/files/documents/1868/aapd12_04.pdf accessed July 10, 2014.

[16] That law, the Tom Lantos and Henry J. Hyde United States Global Leadership Against HIV/AIDS, Tuberculosis, and Malaria Reauthorization Act of 2008, provided that "An organization, including a faith-based organization (1) shall not be required, as a condition of receiving such assistance—(A) to endorse or utilize a multisectoral or comprehensive approach to combating HIV/AIDS; or (B) to endorse, utilize, make a referral to, become integrated with, or otherwise participate in any program or activity to which the organization has a religious or moral objection; and (2) shall not be discriminated against in the solicitation or issuance of grants, contracts, or cooperative agreements under such provisions of law for refusing to meet any requirement described in paragraph (1)." Text from Sec. 301, Assistance to combat HIV/AIDS. Full text at https://beta.congress.gov/110/bills/hr5501/BILLS-110hr5501enr.pdf accessed July 10, 2014.

[17] USAID AAPD 12-04, p. 5.

In other words, bureaucrats could no longer insist that faith-based candidates for federal AIDS grants had to give up their First Amendment religious exercise rights and follow every jot and tittle of the administration's ideology. Pretty simple. It often does not require all that much accommodation by the government to work with and fund the faith community, thereby helping to extend the faith community's services to aid many more people than the government could otherwise reach.

### War on women or war on faith?

Unfortunately, the AIDS accommodation proved the exception rather than the rule, and the Obama administration continued a relentless drive to elevate its own secular ideology over religious freedom.

Mr. Obama's Secretary of the US Department of Health and Human Services (HHS), Kathleen Sebelius, announced in 2012 that her agency would use its new power under Obamacare to mandate the provision of free contraceptives and sterilization nationwide. Though couched in terms of healthcare and recommended by a panel of medical experts stacked with abortion advocates,[18] the mandate appeared to many as political in motivation. Providing every woman in the country with free stuff in an election-year could energize the president's lethargic base by highlighting a contrast with their ideological opponents–the faith community and especially the Catholic Church.

Apparently to the Obama administration, the *cost* of the huge new entitlement was not an object, despite dire economic pressures nationwide. The administration decided to simply foist the cost of the "free" contraceptives and sterilization surgeries onto American insurance companies. The administration at the same time insisted that insurance companies must not raise premiums to make up the difference. HHS suggested, with scant evidence, that the cost should be recouped by the fact that insurance companies would not have to pay for as many baby deliveries.[19]

---

[18] For a critique of the panel's composition, see Americans United for Life website posting, "The Con: HRSA guidelines and the Institute of Medicine," http://www.aul.org/the-con-hrsa-guidelines-and-the-institute-of-medicine/ accessed July 10, 2014.

[19] The government maintained, "Specifically, the Departments indicated their plans for a rulemaking to require issuers to offer group health insurance coverage without contraceptive coverage to such an organization (or its plan sponsor) and simultaneously to provide contraceptive coverage directly to the participants and beneficiaries covered under the organization's plan with no cost sharing. Under this approach, the Departments would require that, in this circumstance, there be no premium charge for the separate contraceptive coverage. Actuaries and experts have found that coverage of contraceptives is at least cost neutral, and

In other words, the United States government was deliberately implementing a policy that favored *preventing* birth over giving birth. While Europe and Russia scrambled to compensate for birth rates that had sunk lower than the replacement rate–a birth dearth that threatens a nation's economy and security[20]–the United States ignored the implications and embarked on a plan to prevent births.

### Throwing the Church under the bus

Besides the darkly unethical and dangerously naïve economic rationale behind the Obamacare contraceptives and sterilization mandate, the draconian policy violently trampled religious freedom.

The Catholic Church, for example, has long opposed the use of contraceptives, as taught in Pope Paul VI's decades-old encyclical *Humanae Vitae*. Protestants historically have taken a more lenient view of contraceptives in general, yet many pro-life Protestants unswervingly oppose contraceptives that can end the life of a developing human embryo–such as the drugs Ella and Plan B, which the FDA notes have the potential to end the life of a developing human embryo.[21]

The Obama administration cast aside such concerns, however, and required the provision of all contraceptives.

Realizing that religious employers objected to paying for products and services they deemed immoral, the Obama administration figured they would sweep that argument under the rug. The administration suggested that since insurance companies provided the benefit to employees, the employer would not be directly participating. Faith-based employers countered that the employer would still be providing the premiums to pay for the contraceptives even if the insurer did the paperwork. They maintained that such indirect participation in immoral acts is still an impermissible violation of faith values and conscience.

---

may save money, when taking into account all costs and benefits for the issuer." "Certain Preventive Services under the Affordable Care Act," https://www.federalregister.gov/articles/2012/03/21/2012-6689/certain-preventive-services-under-the-affordable-care-act, accessed June 19, 2014.

[20] Consider the impact, for example, on the Social Security system or the armed forces when the younger sector of the population declines.

[21]"Highlights of Prescribing Information," FDA publication, http://www.accessdata.fda.gov/drugsatfda_docs/label/2010/022474s000lbl.pdf accessed June 19, 2014. Food and Drug Administration, *FDA's Decision Regarding Plan B: Questions and Answers* (updated Apr. 30, 2009), http://www.fda.gov/cder/drug/infopage/planB/planBQandA.htm accessed July 9, 2014.

The administration, of course, had no intention of accommodating religious freedom if that freedom happened to counter its own ideology. The administration's ideology rested on the notion that abortion and contraception are the keys to empowering women to achieve success in the working world.

So the administration set its sights on compelling faith-based ministries, schools and colleges, health care institutions and virtually every religious organization except actual houses of worship to participate in contraception. Not even Mother Teresa would have been exempted under the administration's narrow exemption guidelines. Even Tyndale House Publishers, which publishes Bibles and Christian literature and funnels virtually all profits into a nonprofit foundation, was not considered religious enough for an exemption from the administration when the publisher objected to participating in contraceptives it deemed immoral.[22]

Besides enforcing its abortion ideology, the power play also enforced the administration's radical push to restrict religious freedom to merely freedom of *worship*. That position countered the First Amendment protection of the "free *exercise*" of religion–the right to exercise one's faith in daily life– including in ministry, in the public square and in the marketplace.

The administration showed little inclination, other than public relations gestures, to accommodate religious freedom concerns. Since some Catholic leaders and other Christians had supported the administration's campaign for universal health care, it seemed possible that the President and his advisors had miscalculated that the faith community simply would not fight him over religious freedom.

### Submit...or else

Calls for conscience-based exemptions from the government edict, however, fell on deaf ears in the administration. President Obama merely nodded in that direction, verbally promising a compromise, ever confident of his ability to convince the public with smooth rhetoric regardless of his actual policies. The ensuing written rule published by HHS a few weeks after that promise in fact changed nothing of substance. The harsh mandate remained intact, and the religious community suddenly faced the grim prospect of being forced to pay millions of dollars in fines for refusing to comply by the looming deadline.

---

"[22] HHS: Bible publisher not a 'religious employer,'" *The Washington Times*, Oct. 2, 2012. http://www.washingtontimes.com/news/2012/oct/2/hhs-bible-publisher-not-religious-employer/, accessed June 19, 2014.

The president's continued refusals to provide simple accommodations for religious objectors revealed that the Obama campaign actually *wanted* the fight with the faith community.

Catholics and Protestants united in protests nationwide, launched dozens of lawsuits against the government, and issued a flood of writings, speeches and meetings to educate the faithful about the threat to their First Amendment religious freedom. The Catholic Church, though long friendly to much of the Democrat agenda, launched a "Fortnight for Freedom" featuring community rallies focused on religious freedom in general and on the HHS mandate as a specific example of threats to such freedoms. Nationwide, clerics read notices in church services highlighting the injustice of the mandate, and thousands gathered in public demonstrations.

The Democratic National Convention, on the other hand, highlighted the contraceptives mandate and the "war on women" theme in an aggressive promotion of abortion rights.[23] In October 2012, *USA Today* observed[24] that "Obama has made women a key part of his political coalition, emphasizing issues ranging from abortion rights to pay equity to health coverage for contraception; this new Quinnipiac poll bolsters that strategy."

When the dust settled from the 2012 presidential election, Obama had won the Catholic vote 50 to 48 percent–just a few points lower than in 2008. While voters who reported attending church more than once a week opted for Romney over Obama by a margin of 63 to 36 percent, Obama won among people who never attend church, 62 to 34 percent.[25] Wedge politics–using highly divisive issues to energize a political base–had prevailed.

### *Illegal but politically effective*

After the 2012 election, the HHS Obamacare mandate still faced the raft of lawsuits by individuals, family businesses and faith-based institutions. The Beckett Fund for Religious Liberty and Alliance Defending Freedom led the legal fight, buttressed by many pro-life and faith-based groups that participated in supportive "friend of the court" briefs.[26]

---

[23] "Democrats charge Republicans with 'war on women' at convention," Reuters, Sep. 4, 2012. http://www.reuters.com/article/2012/09/05/us-usa-campaign-women-idUSBRE88401T20120905, accessed July 4, 2013.

[24] "Poll: Obama leads 49 percent-45 percent, thanks to women voters," *USA Today*, Oct. 2, 2012. http://www.usatoday.com/story/theoval/2012/10/02/poll-obama-leads-49-45-thanks-to-women-voters/1607817/, accessed June 19, 2014.

[25] Pew Forum, "How the Faithful Voted," November 11, 2012, http://iheartcox.com/2012/11/11/how-the-faithful-voted-pew-forum-on-religion-public-life/, accessed June 26, 2014.

[26] For examples of *amicus curiae* (friend of the court) briefs, see

On June 30, 2014, the Supreme Court announced its decisions in two of the first of those lawsuits–*Sebelius v. Hobby Lobby* and *Conestoga Wood v. Sebelius*. The Court struck down the mandate as a violation of the federal Religious Freedom Restoration Act. That law, passed several decades ago on a bipartisan basis, requires that the government, if it threatens religious freedom, must demonstrate a compelling interest to do so and must use the least compelling means of achieving that interest.

The controversial contraceptives mandate may have served its inflammatory political purpose, but hopefully the Supreme Court's ruling will have a more lasting impact, by shoring up religious freedom protections.[27]

### *Accelerating state antagonism*

The HHS Obamacare mandate is just one example of how our government is trending toward the suppression of Christian teaching, preaching and the exercise of Christian conscience.

Recent policy and court decisions are aggressively promoting the acceptance of homosexual practices that societies for the past two millennia have considered out of bounds. While many followers of Christ draw from Scripture the concept of marriage as solely between a man and a woman, secular governments for centuries also have advanced such conjugal marriage because of its benefits to children, the economy[28] and social stability.[29]

Unfortunately, the modern debate over marriage often has been marked by more passion than reason, with relationships and reputations suffering as a result. Some who name the Name of Christ unfortunately have violated the highest tenets of our faith by showing only disgust and not love for those who practice homosexuality. This fuels a public misperception that all opponents of same-sex marriage are hateful bigots.

Other believers do show love toward homosexuals yet remain unpracticed in presenting rational arguments for a secular audience in the

---

http://www.becketfund.org/legaldocshl/ accessed July 10, 2014.

[27] For my in-depth analysis of the decision, see "Highlights from US Supreme Court opinion in Burwell v. Hobby Lobby Stores, Inc.," Freedom2Care blog posting July 1, 2014, http://freedom2care.blogspot.com/2014/07/highlights-from-us-supreme-court.html accessed July 9, 2014.

[28] See, for example, Patrick Fagan, "The Wealth of Nations Depends on the Health of Families," Public Discourse, February 6, 2013, http://www.thepublicdiscourse.com/2013/02/7821/, accessed July 10, 2014.

[29] For a thorough discussion of these characteristics, see Sherif Girgis, Ryan T Anderson and Robert P George, *What Is Marriage? Man and Woman: A Defense* (New York: Encounter Books, 2012).

public square. They feel at a loss to cogently defend what they know is a cornerstone of biblical teaching—namely, that sex is reserved for the marriage of a man and a woman. So they just accept same-sex marriage even though it counters what they know true marriage to be.

Believers, however, need not take either a position of bigotry or of defeatism regarding marriage. We can communicate love and simultaneously advocate for the truth about marriage.

A public message advocating for conjugal marriage might sound something like this:

We love and respect those who practice homosexuality and support policies that protect their dignity and appropriate[30] equal protection under the law. But marriage remains a consensual, exclusive and lifelong commitment between one man and one woman, expressed in a physical union uniquely designed to produce and nurture children.

Removing these objective defining factors makes marriage meaningless. By uprooting and replacing the definition of marriage with a subjective notion based on emotional relationship, divorced from the natural and objective marital elements of physical union and procreation, no rational parameters remain that would exclude further redefinitions of "marriage" as between multiple partners, related persons, or even persons and non-persons.

An affirmation of the exclusivity of marriage as between one man and one woman does not preclude separate personal, societal or legal sanction of any other consensual relationship. The core debate hinges not on a moral evaluation of various types of relationships, but rather on the objective qualities that make marriage, marriage.

Even those who lovingly and reasonably communicate in public the rationale for valuing conjugal marriage, however, face an incredibly harsh and judgmental reaction from activists, the media, politicians and other segments of society. We technically may still live in a democracy, but the

---

[30] The word "appropriate" indicates that equal protection under the law means that while the law must be applied without unjust bias, that does not mean that every law must apply to everyone in exactly the same way. A law pertaining to pregnancy will not apply to everyone because by definition, the state of pregnancy can only apply to women. A law pertaining to American citizens, such as the guarantee of a trial by a jury of peers, does not apply to enemy combatants.

intolerance of divergent views often seems more akin to a totalitarian state that systematically erases ideological diversity.

The drive toward ideological conformity looks like this:

1.  First the culture makes a controversial practice socially *acceptable*.
2.  Then policy makers and the courts make the practice *legal*.
3.  Finally, the culture and the government join to *enforce* the practice—including punishing objectors.[31]

### *Goodbye, tolerance*

The same-sex marriage movement has followed this slope, moving from cultural *acceptability* to *legalization* to *enforcement* and punishment.

Cultural forces, led by savvy activists, the entertainment industry and academia, succeeded in a remarkably short time in making same-sex unions culturally *acceptable*. Then a handful of states legalized same-sex marriage. The Supreme Court in 2013 handed down two decisions[32] (one striking down a part of the federal Defense of Marriage Act, the other denying standing to a group defending California's vote defining marriage as between a man and a woman) largely favoring supporters of same-sex marriage.

Those actions provided *legal* sanction for same-sex marriage.

The final phase now is *enforcing* acceptance of same-sex marriage, including punishing objectors. This enforcement and punishment phase poses perhaps the most significant threat to American religious freedom and people of faith in modern times.

Ironically, the LGBT[33] community based its cultural campaign in large part on sympathy to suffering discrimination. Yet having won popular acceptance and legal sanction, many who once advocated for toleration now seem bent on a campaign of intolerance for all who hold divergent opinions and beliefs.

---

[31] For example, the women's movement and other cultural forces made abortion *acceptable*. The Supreme Court made it *legal* in its 1973 Roe v. Wade decision. The Obama administration *enforced* the practice and punished objectors through federal agency policies.
[32] In declaring unconstitutional a federal law upholding "traditional moral teaching" regarding marriage, the United States Supreme Court essentially declared all opponents of same-sex "marriage" to be hateful bigots. The court maintained that protecting conjugal marriage only "seeks to injure" non-heterosexual couples, to "impose a disadvantage, a separate status and so a stigma," to "impose inequality," "to degrade or demean" and "to disparage and to injure." *United States, petitioner v. Edith Schlain Windsor, in her capacity as executor of the Estate of Thea Clara Spyer, et al.,* Justice Kennedy's delivery of the majority opinion of the Court, June 26, 2013.
[33] LGBT = Lesbian, Gay, Bisexual, Transgender

My colleague Thomas Messner of the Heritage Foundation chronicles real-life examples that illustrate how this enforcement and punishment phase proceeds:

- Catholic Charities in Boston and Washington, D.C., have been forced to abandon their participation in providing adoption services because government mandates would have forced them to place children with homosexual couples in violation of Catholic social teaching.
- Boy Scouts of America has lost equal access to public facilities and programs because of its position on open homosexuality.
- A Christian student organization at a state university was denied official recognition because it required officers and voting members to adhere to traditional Christian teachings on sexuality.
- In New Mexico, a family-owned photography business declined to photograph a same-sex "commitment ceremony" because the owners' religious beliefs conflicted with the message communicated by the ceremony. The New Mexico Human Rights Commission prosecuted the small business under the state's sexual orientation nondiscrimination law and demanded that it pay thousands of dollars in costs.
- In the United Kingdom … the High Court has suggested that Christians with traditional views on sexual ethics are unsuitable as foster carers. In a statement available on YouTube, one of the Christian carers involved in this case explained that "all we were not willing to do was to tell a small child that the practice of homosexuality was a good thing."
- [A] student obtaining professional training in a counseling program at a public university in Michigan was expelled, she alleges, because she was not willing to affirm homosexual behavior as morally acceptable.
- A student enrolled in a counseling program at a public university in Georgia faced a similar hardship when, she alleges, she was told to change her beliefs about homosexuality and undergo a re-education plan or leave the program.[34]

---

[34] Messner, Thomas, "From Culture Wars to Conscience Wars: Emerging Threats to

The Supreme Court's same-sex "marriage" decision unfortunately laid the legal groundwork for lawsuits, firings, censure, denial of government funds, denial of student organization privileges, loss of professional license and privileges and other severe forms of bias and discrimination against adherents of conjugal marriage.

Messner lists a few of the potential areas ripe for punishment following the Supreme Court's same-sex "marriage" decision:

- Exemptions from taxation and tax deductions for charitable contributions;
- Adoption or foster care services receiving federal funds;
- Conditions attached to government contracts, programs, or approvals;
- Discrimination by public colleges and universities receiving federal funds; and
- The accreditation process for institutions and programs of higher education.[35]

The Obama administration began in 2014 to enforce its ideology regarding same-sex marriage with trademark inflexibility and atypical efficiency. The administration began inserting into federal grants notices and other official policies sweeping new requirements and definitions of marriage:

> A standard term and condition of award will be included in the final Notice of Award (NOA); all grant recipients will be subject to a term and condition that instructs grantees to recognize any same-sex marriage legally entered into in a U.S. jurisdiction that recognizes their marriage....[36]

While the new policies cited as their rationale a need to implement the Supreme Court's *Windsor* decision, the way federal agencies applied that viewpoint to grants appeared aimed at eliminating from the public square any groups that disagreed with the administration's ideology.

---

Conscience," Heritage Foundation Backgrounder, April 13, 2011. http://www.heritage.org/research/reports/2011/04/from-culture-wars-to-conscience-wars-emerging-threats-to-conscience, accessed June 19, 2014.

[35] For an examination of potential actions against conjugal marriage supporters to which the Court's decision in *Windsor* gives rise, see Thomas M. Messner, "Religious Freedom and Marriage in Federal Law," Heritage Backgrounder #2865, http://www.heritage.org/research/reports/2014/01/religious-freedom-and-marriage-in-federal-law, accessed June 26, 2014.

[36] HRSA Electronic Submission User Guide, p.8, http://www.hrsa.gov/grants/apply/userguide.pdf, accessed June 19, 2014.

Groups especially impacted by the requirement to recognize same-sex "marriages" include:

- Faith-based organizations that maintain fidelity to Judeo-Christian sexual norms in their policies and personnel practices.
- Sexual education programs that emphasize the benefits of saving sex for (traditional) marriage.
- Adoption agencies that recognize in their policies the benefit to children of having a father and mother.
- Health organizations that emphasize the health benefits of male-female monogamy.

## Eliminating opponents from the marketplace

The battle today for religious free speech goes well beyond government funding issues. An increasing number of American elite would banish religious views altogether from the public square of ideas. They want to ban apostles from the Areopagus.[37]

In April 2014, for example, pressure from within and outside his company prompted Mozilla co-founder Brendan Eich to resign. His crime? Public records revealed that he had made a political contribution to California's successful Prop 8 campaign to define marriage as between a man and a woman.

My colleague Ryan Anderson of the Heritage Foundation writes of the hypocrisy that ousted Eich:

Mozilla co-founder Brendan Eich has resigned as CEO after a week of public pressure stemming from a campaign contribution he made six years ago. Eich supported the wrong cause; he supported California's Proposition 8, the ballot initiative that defined marriage as the union of a man and a woman. For some who favor the redefinition of marriage, tolerance appears to have been a useful rhetorical device along the way to eliminating dissent.

Christian adoption agencies already have been forced out of serving children because they believe orphans deserve a mom and a dad. Forcing out these agencies doesn't help those orphans, and it doesn't help our society. We need as many adoption agencies as possible.

Other cases include a photographer, a baker, a florist, a bed-and-breakfast, a T-shirt company, a

---

[37] Acts 17:19.

student counselor, the Salvation Army, and more. In each of these instances, there were plenty of other businesses available that were willing to provide similar services. [38]

Many people in powerful positions in America today have decided that people of faith not only have no legitimate role to play in influencing government due to a misconstrued "separation of church and state," but also that people of faith, libeled as "anti-reason," have no role to play in science or education, where "they impose their values."

A *New York Times* editorial promoting embryo-destroying stem cell research, for example, lambasted "religious and social conservatives [who] are once again trying to impose their moral code on the rest of the nation and stand in the way of scientific progress."[39]

Such bias against Christians is hardly limited to newspapers' editorial pages. In what somehow passed for a news story, *Washington Post* reporter Rick Weiss opined that American religious conservatives and the terrorist Taliban hold parallel goals:

"In November, researchers announced that they had made the first human embryo clones, giving immediacy to warnings by religious conservatives and others that science is no longer serving the nation's moral will. At the same time, the United States was fighting a war to free a faraway nation from the grip of religious conservatives who were denounced for imposing their moral code on others."[40]

Undaunted by protests written by many of my colleagues and me about his injection of bias, Weiss instead amplified his prejudice:

I fear that the current upswing in fundamentalist religious thought in any number of religions here and abroad is, among other things, getting people too comfortable with the idea of believing things on faith instead of thinking for themselves.[41]

[38] Ryan T. Anderson, "Eich Is Out. So Is Tolerance," Heritage Foundry blog, April 3, 2014. http://blog.heritage.org/2014/04/03/eich-tolerance/, accessed April 5, 2014.
[39] "Loosening the Stem Cell Binds," New York Times, April 13, 2007. Accessed on the web http://www.nytimes.com/2007/04/13/opinion/13fri1.html?_r=0 September 21, 2013.
[40] "Bush Unveils Bioethics Council, *Washington Post,* January 17, 2002, page A21.
[41] "Stem Cell Research: The Next Step?" Washington Post, Transcript, May 20, 2005; 12:00 PM. http://www.washingtonpost.com/wp-dyn/content/discussion/2005/05/19/DI2005051901031.html, accessed June 26, 2014.

Weiss later took on an assignment with an even more influential outlet for his anti-Christian views–as President Obama's Communications Chief at the White House Office of Science and Technology Policy.

### *Persecution on the horizon*

Bias and discrimination invade the daily lives and ambitions of many individuals of faith. By blocking individuals of faith from access to education and careers, bias and discrimination can essentially ban faith from vast sectors of American life.

Laws alone cannot wipe out discrimination, and many common forms of discrimination against people of faith are not even covered by laws. In the days before civil rights legislation, much bias and discrimination against African Americans went unchecked, and many would contend that even half a century after the Civil Rights Act, much racial discrimination continues without redress.

If policies and trends that insist on ideological conformity over religious freedom continue, people of faith and their message will experience increased suppression, discrimination and punishment in the United States just as they have in many other countries and over many centuries. While we can take comfort in the companionship of such a "great cloud of witnesses" who have suffered for the faith,[42] we also must *fight* for religious freedom while we have the freedom to do so. We must fight not only to protect our own consciences but also to protect our children, our churches and our culture.

In the next section, we examine how Christians have viewed and engaged in government, serving as dual citizens of this world and the kingdom of heaven.

---

[42] Hebrews 12:1.

# PART FOUR:
## Government and faith

# Chapter 14:
# *Toward a Christian view of government*

*"For the one in authority is God's servant for your good."*
–Romans 13:4

We now move from specific public policy issues to examine more broadly a Christian perspective on government and faith. This section includes theological views of government, the role of Christians in government and religious freedom.

To launch our study, we review the inspired biblical teaching of the Apostle Paul and also the perspectives of leaders of the American Revolution, early Church leader Augustine, Dutch politician Abraham Kuyper and evangelical thinker Charles Colson.

### The Apostle Paul

The Apostle Paul presents a theological framework for understanding government that stresses its divine purpose and charges Christians to submit to its authority. The following subheadings highlight the key principles the apostle outlines in Romans 13:1-7:

### Submit to governmental authority because God has established it.

Let everyone be subject to the governing authorities, for there is no authority except that which God has established. The authorities that exist have been established by God. Consequently, whoever rebels against the authority is rebelling against what God has instituted, and those who do so will bring judgment on themselves.

### Government holds power to restrain evil and reward good.

For rulers hold no terror for those who do right, but for those who do wrong.

Do you want to be free from fear of the one in authority? Then do what is right and you will be commended. For the one in authority is God's servant for your good.
But if you do wrong, be afraid, for rulers do not bear the sword for no reason. They are God's servants, agents of wrath to bring punishment on the wrongdoer.
Therefore, it is necessary to submit to the authorities, not only because of possible punishment but also as a matter of conscience.

### Christians should give government its due.

This is also why you pay taxes, for the authorities are God's servants, who give their full time to governing. Give to everyone what you owe them: If you owe taxes, pay taxes; if revenue, then revenue; if respect, then respect; if honor, then honor.

The biblical book of Genesis portrays how, after the first created man and woman broke off our perfect and direct relationship with God, evil infected the world and our relationships with each other. As a result, God established government to prevent anarchistic violence and lethal disorder. Once having established order, the role of government is to promote peace and goodness to the extent that mortal man can accomplish.

It is important in studying Romans 13, as with all Scriptures, to draw conclusions from what it says rather than from what it does not say. We need to apply His Word with reason and in concert with the rest of Scripture. It may be especially tempting for those of us who see every word of Scripture as God-breathed to apply those words technically rather than holistically. In doing so, we risk neglecting the weighty overarching biblical principles of love, justice and mercy.

Paul is outlining to the Romans the ideal, divinely ordered purpose for government and our relationship to it. Therefore, he stresses obedience to authority without mentioning the clearly established cases of justified, even required, *disobedience* to authority.

Otherwise, this passage would condemn Moses for taking Pharaoh's slaves and leading Pharaoh's army into annihilation. Daniel and his fellow Jewish companions in captivity would have been criminals, not heroes of the faith, for refusing to eat the king's forbidden food or worship his idolatrous statue. And if submission to authority is absolute, how could Jesus rightly confront and condemn the hypocrisy of the ruling Pharisees and challenge their legalistic system?

So what exactly is the role of the Christian with respect to submitting to government authority? To gain insight into this question, we will consider what some might see as a violation of the biblical command to submit to authorities: the American Revolution.

### American Revolution leaders

In the era of the American Revolution, many pastors stood as not only the moral but also the intellectual leaders of their communities. Besides charting the path to heaven, their sermons also helped citizens sort out the immediate challenge they were facing here on earth: developing a biblical and rational response to the governmental abuses of the English crown.

Jonathan Mayhew, a brilliant New England minister, methodically interpreted and applied the principles of Romans 13 to the current situation faced by his parishioners as the Revolution brewed. Mayhew's sermon points, quoted below, included the following key principles:

- That the end of magistracy is the good of civil society, as such.
- That civil rulers, as such, are the ordinance and ministers of God; it being by His permission and providence that any bear rule and agreeable to His will that there should be some persons vested with authority in society, for the well-being of it.
- That the true ground and reason of our obligation to be subject to the higher powers is the usefulness of magistracy (when properly exercised) to human society and its subservience to the general welfare.
- [I]t will not follow that because civil government is, in general, a good institution and necessary to the peace and happiness of human society, therefore, there be no supposable cases in which resistance to it can be innocent.
- [T]he civil rulers whom the apostle here speaks of, and obedience to whom he presses upon Christians as a duty, are good rulers, such as are, in the exercise of their office and power, benefactors to society….
- [I]f the motive and argument for submission to government be taken from the apparent usefulness of civil authority, it follows that when no such good end can be answered by submission there remains no argument or motive to enforce it; and

167

if instead of this good end's being brought about
by submission, a contrary end is brought about and
the ruin and misery of society effected by it,
here is a plain and positive reason against
submission in all such cases.

- It would be stupid tameness and unaccountable
folly for whole nations to suffer one
unreasonable, ambitious, and cruel man to wanton
and riot in their misery. And, in such a case, it
would, of the two, be more rational to suppose
that they who did not resist than that they who
did would receive to themselves damnation….

- To conclude, let us all learn to be free and to be
loyal. Let us not profess ourselves vassals to the
lawless pleasure of any man on earth. But let us
remember, at the same time, government is sacred
and not to be trifled with.

- And while I am speaking of loyalty to our earthly
prince, suffer me just to put you in mind to be
loyal also to the Supreme Ruler of the universe,
"by whom kings reign and princes decree justice"
(Prov. 8:15).[1]

Mayhew saw Romans 13 as a prescription for good government, not as a proscription against changing governments. When governors refuse to serve God and His purposes and promote the good of the people, even abusing and killing people without cause, then the people themselves hold a duty to replace the government with one aligned with goodness.

## Democracy requires a virtuous people

Once the people replace a wicked government and establish another, they themselves must insure the goodness of the successor government–especially in a democratic republic such as the United States.

As the following quotations illustrate, political leaders of the American Revolution and crafters of the Constitution affirmed in no uncertain terms that apart from a virtuous and religious people, a democratic republic cannot long stand:

- Our Constitution was made only for a moral and
religious people.–**John Adams**[2]

---

[1] Jonathan Mayhew, " A Discourse Concerning Unlimited Submission and Non-Resistance to the Higher Powers,"1750.
[2] President John Adams to the Officers of the First Brigade of the Third Division of the Militia

- [T]he only foundation for a useful education in a republic is to be laid in Religion. Without this there can be no virtue, and without virtue there can be no liberty, and liberty is the object and life of all republican governments.-**Benjamin Rush**[3]
- Of all the dispositions and habits which lead to political prosperity, religion and morality are indispensable supports.-**George Washington**[4]
- Only a virtuous people are capable of freedom. As nations become corrupt and vicious, they have more need of masters.-**Benjamin Franklin**[5]

As French reformer Alexis de Tocqueville observed of the American experiment,

[R]eligion in America takes no direct part in the government of society, but it must be regarded as the first of their political institutions…. How is it possible that society should escape destruction if the moral tie is not strengthened in proportion as the political tie is relaxed? And what can be done with a people who are their own masters if they are not submissive to the Deity?[6]

### *Augustine*

Centuries before the American Revolution, a Christian statesman sought to interpret the overthrow of another long-standing government–the Roman Empire. The great Roman civilization had crumbled in the face of a barbarian invasion, its foundation rotted by political, military and economic failures, cultural degradation and moral degeneration.

Yet some Roman citizens insisted on blaming the demise of Rome on Christianity, the upstart religion that had supplanted the worship of gods long seen as the protectors of Rome. So from AD 413-426, Augustine of Hippo (AD 354–430) engaged his pen to counter the attack on Christianity, writing

---

of Massachusetts, 1798.

[3] Benjamin Rush, Of the Mode of Education Proper in a Republic, 1798 - Selected Writings 87–89, 92, 94–96; quoted at http://press-pubs.uchicago.edu/founders/documents/v1ch18s30.html, accessed June 7, 2014.

[4] George Washington, "Farewell Address," first published in the *Philadelphia Daily American Advertiser*, September 19, 1796. Washington wrote the address with the assistance of Alexander Hamilton and James Madison.

[5] Benjamin Franklin letter to Abbes Chalut and Arnaud, April 17, 1787.

[6] Alexis De Tocqueville, *Democracy in America*, translated by Henry Reeve, public domain book, Vol. 1, pp. 253-54.

what would become a theological classic and the only philosophy of history during the Middle Ages: *City of God*.

Like America's founders, Augustine stressed that a republican form of government depends for its success upon Christian morality and true justice:

> True justice has no existence save in that republic whose founder and ruler is Christ, if at least any choose to call this a republic; and indeed we cannot deny that it is the people's weal.[7]
>
> [T]there can be no people, and therefore no republic, where there is no justice.[8]

History professor Dr. Glen Sunshine provides a succinct summary[9] of the view of government Augustine expresses in *City of God*:

> Virtue is absent since the citizens of the [worldly City of Man] love themselves more than others, though good behavior may be enforced by social customs or by coercion by the state. In this environment, the state is necessary to restrain evil.
>
> The problem is, the government itself is part of the City of Man and is itself dominated by self-love. The state is more interested in self-aggrandizement and power than it is in promoting the good.
>
> At the same time, Augustine believed that government was instituted by God and is therefore potentially good. But because of original sin, in the City of Man government turns away from the good and therefore becomes evil—a necessary evil, in view of the need to restrain vice, but evil nonetheless.[10]

### Finding common ground between two kingdoms

As we have discussed, the divine purposes of government include providing order and promoting stability.[11] Yet Augustine also saw

---

[7] Augustine, *City of God* and *Christian Doctrine*, Philip Schaff, ed., Grand Rapids: Wm. B. Eerdmans, Kindle edition, location 1484.

[8] Ibid, location 14479.

[9] With Augustine's tome weighing in at just under a thousand pages written in fifth-century style, summaries such as Dr. Sunshine's provide a welcome timesaver for twenty-first-century readers. Another helpful summary is the Shepherd's Notes on Christian Classics, *Augustine's City of God*, Nashville: B&H Publishing, 1998.

[10] Glenn Sunshine, *The City of Man*, *Christian Worldview Journal*, The Chuck Colson Center for Christian Worldview web article, September 10, 2012, http://www.colsoncenter.org/the-center/columns/indepth/18421-the-city-of-man accessed May 17, 2014.

[11] Social and governmental stability also forms a foundation principle of political conservatism, as profoundly articulated by the British statesman, Sir Edmund Burke (1729-

government and governors as fallible and bent toward evil. As such, government too often strives for stability not in order to protect the people but to protect its own power.

While contrasting secular government's motivation toward stability with the kingdom of God's motivation toward true peace, Augustine nevertheless saw opportunity for cooperation between adherents of both kingdoms. As Dr. Sunshine explains,

> The City of Man always seeks stability, if for no other reason than to maintain its own power, and as a result it legislates at the level of the minimal standards needed to preserve society. The City of Man therefore emphasizes tolerance of differences (as long as they don't interfere with the government's power) in order to avoid conflict. For the City of Man, this passes for peace, albeit distorted by greed and selfishness.
>
> The City of God also seeks peace, though of a different and more profound sort. This means that the City of God and the City of Man can cooperate to some extent in promoting peace and stability within society.
>
> [B]oth Cities share an interest in promoting good behavior, and their work can complement each other: the magistrate's threat of violence may contribute to the growth of the City of God by encouraging penitence, while the City of God's emphasis on virtue can lead to the stability of the City of Man.
>
> Even further, the City of God can encourage the City of Man toward the good, though without taking on the responsibility for making laws, while the City of Man can promote good behavior through the courts and can defend society and provide stability to allow the City of God to flourish.
>
> Augustine's efforts to find common ground between the City of God and the City of Man provided an important theological justification for Christians to be involved in civil government: by promoting true goodness and virtue as a civil magistrate, the

---

1797). Since the wisdom of previous generations has produced a time-tested governmental structure, Burke contends, only the unwise would quickly and radically overthrow it, as occurred in revolutionary France (1789-1799). Burke's in-depth critique of the French Revolution, *Reflections on the Revolution in France* (1790), helped sway British sentiment against the radical, anti-Christian movement in France.

Christian can work to advance the interests of both Cities simultaneously. [12]

Augustine highlights a key theme of *Faith Steps:* Christians have an opportunity to *work through government to advance God's principles.*

While Christians in a secular society do not use government to spread the *words* of the Gospel, Christians can use government to spread the *principles* of the Gospel. To the extent that we can demonstrate that those principles are universal and yield beneficial results for every person regardless of faith, such views can prevail in the public square.

### Abraham Kuyper

The nineteenth-century Dutch scholar, theologian and political leader Abraham Kuyper embraced this view of Christians influencing government, teaching the seamless integration of our faith and political engagement. His famous "Stone Lectures," delivered in 1898 at Princeton and based largely on the teachings of Protestant reformer John Calvin, offer a theological foundation for the nature and necessity of government and our role in it:

It is therefore a political faith which may be summarily expressed in these three theses:
1. God only—and never any creature—is possessed of sovereign rights, in the destiny of the nations, because God alone created them, maintains them by His Almighty power, and rules them by His ordinances.
2. Sin has, in the realm of politics, broken down the direct government of God, and therefore the exercise of authority, for the purpose of government, has subsequently been invested in men, as a mechanical remedy.
3. In whatever form this authority may reveal itself, man never possesses power over his fellow-man in any other way than by an authority which descends upon him from the majesty of God. [13]

As a result of sin, Kuyper explains, God has provided government as an agency for our good.

Thus the word of Scripture stands: "By Me kings reign," or as the apostle has elsewhere declared: "The powers, that be, are ordained of God. Therefore he that resisteth the power, withstandeth the

---

[12] Sunshine, *The City of Man.*
[13] Kuyper, Abraham, *Lectures on Calvinism*, p. 77, Kindle location 1364, Grand Rapids, Eerdmans Publishing Co, 2000. Originally published 1931. These lectures were first delivered at Princeton University in 1898 under auspices of the L. P. Stone Foundation.

ordinance of God." The magistrate is an instrument of "common grace," to thwart all license and outrage and to shield the good against the evil.

But he is more. Besides all this he is instituted by God as His Servant, in order that he may preserve the glorious work of God, in the creation of humanity, from total destruction. Sin attacks God's handiwork, God's plan, God's justice, God's honor, as the supreme Artificer and Builder.

Thus God, ordaining the powers that be, in order that, through their instrumentality, He might maintain His justice against the strivings of sin, has given to the magistrate the terrible right of life and death.

Therefore all the powers that be, whether in empires or in republics, in cities or in states, rule "by the grace of God." For the same reason justice bears a holy character. And from the same motive every citizen is bound to obey, not only from dread of punishment, but for the sake of conscience.[14]

### *Government without God*

Kuyper condemns the underpinnings of the French Revolution and its atheistic, humanist agenda that fatally attempted to divorce government from God. He notes how, divorced from absolute truth and the divine foundation for justice and government, the resulting arbitrary law renders every citizen vulnerable to the whims of a powerful few.

Besides ruthless and rampant executions, the Jacobinic revolution also severed all ties to the God of the Scriptures and natural law. Having separated law from universal, objective principles, the French Revolution produced a government that ruthlessly wielded power over the people as an omnipotent, arbitrary tyrant.

Disconcertingly, Kuyper's analysis in 1898 of how the French Revolution severed law from Truth speaks to the trend we are witnessing in America today:

Thus all transcendent right in God, to which the oppressed lifted up his face, falls away. There is no other right, but the immanent right which is written down in the law. The law is right, not because its contents are in harmony with the eternal principles

---

[14] Kuyper, p. 74, Kindle location 1318.

of right, but because it is law. If on the morrow it fixes the very opposite, this also must be right. And the fruit of this deadening theory is, as a matter of course, that the consciousness of right is blunted, that all fixedness of right departs from our minds, and that all higher enthusiasm for right is extinguished. That which exists is good, because it exists; and it is no longer the will of God, of Him Who created us and knows us, but it becomes the ever-changing will of the State, which, having no one above itself, actually becomes God, and has to decide how our life and our existence shall be.[15]

## Charles Colson

The late Charles Colson, President Richard Nixon's former "hatchet man" who spent jail time for his role in the Watergate scandal, knew exactly what happens when government wields power in violation of transcendent law and truth. The Machiavellian, power-obsessed president he served flagrantly flouted the law for his own ends.[16]

Colson traces through the ages government's insatiable quest for power and its inevitable conflicts with the supremacy of God's kingdom:

The tension between the Kingdom of God and the kingdoms of man runs like an unbroken thread through the history of the past two thousand years. It began not long after Christ's birth. Herod feared Christ because He represented a Kingdom greater than his own. Jesus was later executed for this same reason.[17]

The Romans persecuted Christians not because they worshiped Christ– the Romans tolerated many gods–but because they refused to acknowledge Caesar as supreme. Governments often seek to eliminate competition. Colson explains the church-state conflict:

Both church and state assert standards and values in society; both seek authority; both compete for allegiance. As members of both the religious and the political spheres, the Christian is bound to face conflict.[18]

---

[15] Kuyper, Abraham, *Lectures on Calvinism* (p. 81). Eerdmans Publishing Co., Kindle Edition.
[16] Nixon resigned in disgrace after attempting to cover up his henchmen's bungled break-in at the Watergate offices of political opponents.
[17] Charles Colson and Ellen Santilli, *God and Government,* Grand Rapids: Zondervan, 1987, updated 2007. Kindle locations 2228 and 2237. Used by permission of Zondervan, www.zondervan.com.

Colson contends that despite this conflict, Christians remain duty-bound, as dual citizens of the Kingdom of God and the kingdoms of man, to participate in their own government. He reaches back to ancient philosophers who, even apart from biblical revelation, highlighted this universal principle:

"True law," wrote Cicero, "is right reason in agreement with Nature; it is of universal application and everlasting; it summons to duty by its commands, and averts from wrong-doing by its prohibitions."[19]

With this foundational understanding of the purpose and nature of government, in our next chapter we focus on government protection of the free exercise of religion.

---

[18] Colson, Kindle location 2224.

[19] Marcus Tullius Cicero, *Republic, The Laws*, 59 - 47 B.C., cited in Colson, Kindle location 4917.

# Chapter 15:
# *The "free exercise" of religion*

*So Paul stood in the midst of the Areopagus and said,*
*"Men of Athens, I observe that you are very religious in all respects."*
*–Acts 17:22*

On September 25, 1789, the First Congress of the United States proposed to the state legislatures 12 amendments to the Constitution. The amendments articulated what the original Constitution, which upon ratification by the ninth of the 13 states went into effect on June 21, 1788, had not clearly spelled out.

The states eventually adopted ten of the 12 proposed amendments, putting freedom of religion at the top of the list of five freedoms guaranteed in the First Amendment:

```
Congress shall make no law respecting an
establishment of religion, or prohibiting the free
exercise thereof; or abridging the freedom of speech,
or of the press; or the right of the people peaceably
to assemble, and to petition the Government for a
redress of grievances.
```

Notice the phrase that does not appear anywhere in the First Amendment to our Constitution: "separation of church and state."

The "separation" perspective originated in a letter to a religious group[1] by Thomas Jefferson. Jefferson, however, was not necessarily the most qualified interpreter of the First Amendment. When Congress developed the First Amendment, Jefferson actually was far away in France.

### Unreasonable extrapolation

Some activists today extrapolate from Jefferson's "separation of church and state" phrase a wholesale opposition to all religious influence in

---

[1] The phrase appeared in Jefferson's letter of reply of January 1, 1802, to an address of congratulations from the Danbury (Connecticut) Baptist Association.

government. This common application of the phrase runs counter not only to Jefferson's own demonstrated regard for religious influence in government but also to the views of the First Congress that passed and the states that ratified the First Amendment.

To fully understand Jefferson's actual views on the influence of religion within government, an examination of his daily practice proves instructive. As an article published by the US Library of Congress explains,

> It is no exaggeration to say that on Sundays in Washington during the administrations of Thomas Jefferson (1801-1809) and of James Madison (1809-1817) the state became the church. Within a year of his inauguration, Jefferson began attending church services in the House of Representatives.
> Madison followed Jefferson's example, although unlike Jefferson, who rode on horseback to church in the Capitol, Madison came in a coach. Worship services in the House-a practice that continued until after the Civil War-were acceptable to Jefferson because they were nondiscriminatory and voluntary.[2]

Let's look again at exactly what the First Amendment says about church and state:

> "Congress shall make no law respecting an establishment of religion, or prohibiting the free exercise thereof; or abridging the freedom of speech, or of the press; or the right of the people peaceably to assemble, and to petition the Government for a redress of grievances."

First, the amendment protects the free exercise of religion from government interference ("Congress shall make no law..."). Then the amendment continues seamlessly to also protect from government interference the free exercise of speech, press, assembly and petition. The goal in each section is identical–protecting the *freedom of the people to believe and express as they choose.*

To interpret the first part of this Amendment as somehow attempting to limit the expression of religion in government is to ignore the First Amendment's clear and consistent pattern, its parallel provisions:

- The people are free to practice their religion.
- The press is free to publish its views.
- The people are free to assemble.

---

[2] "Religion and the Founding of the American Republic," Library of Congress, http://www.loc.gov/exhibits/religion/rel06-2.html accessed Sep. 29, 2013.

- The people are free to petition the Government and demand justice.

From start to finish, the First Amendment *protects the freedom of the people, by limiting the reach of the government.* The United States Congress may not abridge–reduce, restrict, deprive–these five fundamental freedoms: religion, speech, press, assembly and petition.

Having just fought and won a war against tyranny, American leaders sought to keep the power of government in its place–serving and heeding the will of the people. The *last* thing on their minds was preventing the people from influencing their government.

Unfortunately, in the centuries subsequent to that first Congress, judges and lawyers have perverted the establishment clause ("respecting an *establishment* of religion") with concocted theories, to the point where its original language and the clear intent of its framers appears hardly recognizable.

By contrast to creative reconstruction of the First Amendment, an "originalist" view bases constitutional interpretation on the actual historical record of its framing. Such a view will show that the establishment clause protects religious freedom for the people by prohibiting the federal government (a) from passing a law elevating one denomination as the national religion to the exclusion of other denominations, and (b) from passing a law restricting the right of people to freely exercise their faith and conscience.

As Professor John Baker of the Catholic University Columbus School of Law explains,

The addition of the word "respecting" is significant. It prohibits Congress from legislating either to establish a national religion or to disestablish a state religion.

As Laurence Tribe has written, "[a] growing body of evidence suggests that the Framers principally intended the Establishment of Religion Clause to perform two functions: to protect state religious establishments from national displacement, and to prevent the national government from aiding some, but not all, religions."[3]

---

[3] Baker, John, *The Heritage Guide to the Constitution,* "Amendment I: Establishment of Religion," p. 6. http://www.fed-soc.org/publications/id.29/author.asp accessed Oct. 23, 2013.

## *Freedom to exercise faith*

What exactly does the First Amendment mean by protecting the freedom of the people to "exercise" their religion?

The process that led to the First Amendment's "free exercise" wording makes clear that exercising religion means not only to believe, but also to *act* on those beliefs, as one's conscience directs. *Acting* on our beliefs in the public arena–*exercising* our faith in our daily lives–is a wholly different matter than merely meditating on religious matters privately or even singing hymns within the four walls of a church.

The first draft by the House of Representatives of the text that eventually became the First Amendment proposed that "no religion shall be established by law, nor shall the equal *rights of conscience* be infringed" [emphasis added].

Notice the emphasis not merely on belief or worship, but on the exercise of *conscience*–living out of one's beliefs. The framers of the First Amendment did not view religious freedom as merely the freedom to believe. Who would need legal protection for that? No government can monitor its citizens' thoughts or personal worship.

Nor did the First Congress seek to prevent deep connections between government and religion. Incredible as it may sound to modern ears, in 1787, six of the original thirteen states still had established state churches.

Therefore, some members of the First Congress viewed the broad prohibition originally proposed by the House for the amendment, "no religion shall be established," as threatening states' rights regarding religion. On the advice of James Madison, the House finally settled on narrower, more specific language: "*Congress* shall make no law establishing religion, or prohibiting the free exercise thereof, nor shall the rights of Conscience be infringed" [emphasis added].

It's hard to imagine how Congress could have been clearer.

Professor Baker explains how, despite this clarity, over a century and a half later the Supreme Court began to twist the original intent of the framers:

> The modern view of the Establishment of Religion Clause began with *Everson v. Board of Education of Ewing* in 1947, where the Court initiated the current separationist approach to the Establishment of Religion Clause. On the way to reaching its decision, the Supreme Court held that the Due Process Clause[4] of

---

[4] "No state shall make or enforce any law which shall abridge the privileges or immunities of citizens of the United States; nor shall any state deprive any person of life, liberty, or property, without due process of law; nor deny to any person within its jurisdiction the equal protection

the Fourteenth Amendment applied the First
Amendment's proscriptions against establishment to
the states.[5]

Thus the courts took what the original framers of the First Amendment meant as a proscription that only applied to the federal Congress and expanded it to apply to all states. Courts also turned around the meaning of preventing government from restricting religion to instead forbidding any mixing whatsoever of faith and government.

The First Congress, by contrast, knew full well that governments such as the British government often had sought to extinguish the conscientious exercise of faith. Governments even had killed religious resisters perceived as challenging the power of the state.

Rulers tend to hate any opposition to their power. People of faith through the centuries have opposed myriad governmental policies: emperor worship, participation in wars, official state religious dogma, slavery, abortion and more. Governments did not kill the martyrs merely because they harbored private religious beliefs in their heads; they killed them because they dared to *exercise* those beliefs in the public square.

It is the *free exercise* of religion—not mere belief or worship—that requires protection from government power. The framers of the First Amendment rightly integrated the free exercise of religion with the free exercise of conscience.

In his *Memorial and Remonstrance*, James Madison, the primary author of the Constitution, explained it this way:

The Religion then of every man must be left to the
conviction and conscience of every man; and it is the
right of every man to exercise it as these may
dictate. This right is in its nature an unalienable
right.[6]

---

of the laws."

[5] Baker, p. 6. Prof. Baker continues, "Although there is vigorous debate as to whether the provisions of the Fourteenth Amendment 'incorporate,' or replicate, the guarantees of the Bill of Rights and fastens them on the states, most commentators opine that the Establishment of Religion Clause is the least likely candidate for incorporation. The Establishment of Religion Clause was designed as a protection of the states against the federal government. It seems anomalous to many scholars, even to some who support incorporation generally, that the Establishment of Religion Clause could be called an individual right for purposes of the Fourteenth Amendment."

[6] James Madison, "Memorial and Remonstrance against Religious Assessments," 1785. http://religiousfreedom.lib.virginia.edu/sacred/madison_m&r_1785.html, accessed June 14, 2014.

The same year the framers drafted the Constitution, 1787, Congress passed the landmark Northwest Ordinance. The Ordinance reflected the expectation of the vast majority of America's leaders that "Religion, morality, and knowledge, being necessary to good government and the happiness of mankind, schools and the means of education shall forever be encouraged." Virtually every American leader expected that people of faith would influence their government, and many considered religious influence essential to the survival of the Republic.

### *Religious freedom: a natural right*

The Declaration of Independence references the "separate and equal Station to which the Laws of Nature and of Nature's God entitle" all people.

In light of these natural laws, the founders contended, "We hold these Truths to be *self-evident*, that all Men are created equal, that they are endowed by their Creator with certain unalienable Rights, that among these are Life, Liberty and the Pursuit of Happiness."

Consider how our founders drew upon the "laws of nature" to defend religious freedom:

- "The error seems not sufficiently eradicated that the operations of the mind as well as the acts of the body are subject to the coercion of the laws. But our rulers can have authority over such natural rights only as we have submitted to them. The rights of conscience we never submitted, we could not submit. We are answerable for them to our God. The legitimate powers of government extend to such acts only as are injurious to others" –Thomas Jefferson.[7]
- "Because we have no government, armed with power, capable of contending with human passions, unbridled by morality and religion. Avarice, ambition, revenge and licentiousness would break the strongest cords of our Constitution, as a whale goes through a net. Our Constitution was made only for a moral and religious people. It is wholly inadequate to the government of any other" –John Adams.[8]
- "The Citizens of the United States of America have a right to applaud themselves for having given to mankind examples of an enlarged and liberal policy: a policy worthy of imitation. All possess alike liberty of conscience and immunities of citizenship. It is now no more that toleration is spoken of, as if it was by the indulgence of

---

[7] Thomas Jefferson: Notes on Virginia Q.XVII, 1782.
[8] John Adams, Letter to the Officers of the First Brigade of the Third Division of the Militia of Massachusetts, October 11, 1798.

one class of people, that another enjoyed the exercise of their inherent natural rights"–George Washington.[9]

- "I have lived, Sir, a long time and the longer I live, the more convincing proofs I see of this truth–that God governs in the affairs of men. And if a sparrow cannot fall to the ground without his notice, is it probable that an empire can rise without his aid?"–Benjamin Franklin.[10]

- "No provision in our Constitution ought to be dearer to man than that which protects the rights of conscience against the enterprises of the civil authority." –Thomas Jefferson.[11]

### *Americans unclear on religious freedom guarantees*

Much of the American public today, tragically and ominously, does not even seem cognizant of the Constitution's guarantee of the free exercise of religion. A poll by the Newseum's First Amendment Center revealed the following:

> Asked to name the five specific freedoms in the First Amendment, 59% of Americans could name freedom of speech, followed by 24% who could name freedom of religion, 14% freedom of the press, 11% the right to assemble, and 4% the right to petition. Thirty-six percent of Americans cannot name any of the rights guaranteed by the First Amendment.
> Americans were asked what they believed was the single most important freedom that citizens enjoy. The majority (47%) of people named freedom of speech as the most important freedom, followed by freedom of religion (10%); freedom of choice (7%); right to vote (5%); right to bear arms (5%); right to life, liberty and the pursuit of happiness (3%), and freedom of the press (1%).[12]

What this loss of knowledge and commitment means is that those of us who depend upon religious liberty to live out our faith without reprisal stand in danger of losing the support of the culture. From Pilgrims to Baptists to

---

[9] George Washington, letter to the Hebrew Congregation in Newport, Rhode Island, August 18, 1790.

[10] Benjamin Franklin, Constitutional Convention, June 1787.

[11] Thomas Jefferson to New London Methodists, 1809.

[12] "State of the First Amendment: 2013 - A Project Sponsored by the First Amendment Center," conducted May 2013. http://www.newseum.org/news/2013/07/state-of-the-first-amendment-2013.pdf, accessed September 21, 2013.

Catholics to Mormons, minority sects and denominations throughout the history of this land have depended upon the culture coming over to the side of religious liberty to put a halt to discrimination and violent persecution.

The current climate of growing governmental disregard for religious liberty, combined with declining religious affiliation, Constitutional ignorance and apathy, could degenerate quickly. If history is a guide, that degeneration will manifest itself in an onslaught of hostile state and federal laws and local ordinances, coercive financial penalties, loss of employment, imprisonment and even violence against churches and individual believers.

## *Americans fear decline in religious freedom*

Americans may not be well-versed in our heritage of religious freedom, but we are growing increasingly concerned about the loss of that freedom. A Barna / Clapham Group poll underscores our rising concerns:

> "Many Americans express significant angst over the state of religious freedom in the U.S. Slightly more than half of adults say they are very (29%) or somewhat (22%) concerned that religious freedom in the U.S. will become more restricted in the next five years."[13]

It remains unclear, however, whether the American Church, from pulpit to pew, is taking adequate steps to fortify the defense of religious freedom. Have you have lately, or ever, heard a sermon on religious freedom? Are any Christians in your area discussing governmental threats to conscience rights, free speech or other religious liberty concerns? Is your church prepared for legal action in the event of a conflict between church teaching or ministries and local, state or federal laws and regulations?

At the national level, the faith community needs strategic research on messaging to craft an effective case to make to the American public on religious freedom. Polling on concepts and wording, focus groups to gain man-on-the-street perspectives, and research on emotional motivation can help provide insight and direction.

Faith-based organizations cannot expect to win public policy battles by relying solely on legal and policy experts. We need to balance our staffs with effective, professional communicators informed by research.

We would also do well to develop seminars and curricula to educate key communities, including grade school and college students, business leaders,

---

[13] "Most Americans are Concerned about Restrictions in Religious Freedom," Barna Group, Jan. 18, 2013. http://www.barna.org/culture-articles/600-most-americans-are-concerned-about-restrictions-in-religious-freedom accessed Feb. 2, 2013.

health professionals, political leaders and others to reach the general public. We should make far greater use of culture-shaping tools including the arts and entertainment, books and magazines, newspaper Op-eds, and social media.

### Ready for battle?

This Scripture about the Lord's return also offers us wisdom for preparing for looming threats to our First Amendment free exercise of religion:

> Be dressed in readiness, and keep your lamps lit. Be like men who are waiting for their master when he returns from the wedding feast, so that they may immediately open the door to him when he comes and knocks.
> But be sure of this, that if the head of the house had known at what hour the thief was coming, he would not have allowed his house to be broken into.[14]

America's Constitution provides for the free exercise of religion and for the community of faith to fully engage and impact our government. But despite possessing this potential power, some suggest we should not use it.

In the next chapter, we tackle this question: Should followers of Christ actively engage in public policy or instead separate from the public square for the sake of spiritual purity? We address common objections to Christian involvement in politics and examine how public policy engagement can fulfill the Christian's mission on earth.

---

[14] Luke 12:35, 39.

# Chapter 16:
# *The role of Christians in government*

*"I wrote you in my letter not to associate with immoral people; I did not
at all mean with the immoral people of this world,
or with the covetous and swindlers, or with idolaters,
for then you would have to go out of the world."*
–I Corinthians 5:9

A member of a local church within the conservative branch of the
Mennonite community–the kind in which women sit on one side of
the church and men on the other–stops by our house periodically to deliver a
monthly Mennonite outreach publication. He is a kind, winsome fellow, and
I admire his outreach. It's not easy to reach out to modern American culture
when the women of your sect have to wear head coverings and the men
oppose military service. This church deserves credit for courage as well as
conviction.

### *"But God is sovereign; we don't need to engage in politics"*

In our conversations, I have come to appreciate the devotion and
sincerity of my Mennonite friend's persuasions. He knows that I am engaged
in government for a living (which I suspect seems to him the equivalent of a
tax collector in Jesus' day), and we've occasionally talked about political
engagement.

During one such conversation about politics, my friend explained that in
the view of his church, God has instituted governments, and their [only] duty
is to pray for and submit to them. I learned to my astonishment that my
friend and his fellow church members do not even vote. They simply trust, he
explained, in God's sovereignty.

This view is not an anomaly.

A leader in a Mennonite Church USA Delegate Assembly, in the interest
of pursuing peace with fellow Mennonites (who reportedly were engaging in

unseemly internecine squabbles over presidential candidates that year), echoed these sentiments when he offered the following proposal:

> Mennonites in the United States should commit themselves to a five-year sabbatical from affiliations with any political party. That is, we should publicly resolve to sit out the next presidential election and to consciously abstain from all literature, web-sites, organizations and lobbying efforts supported by groups partisan to the Democrats or the Republicans.[1]

Not all Mennonites agree with this strategy. At that same Assembly, another leader offered the following alternative perspective:

> Our [Confession of Faith in a Mennonite Perspective] says that we "witness by being ambassadors for Christ, calling the nations … to move toward justice, peace and compassion for all people" (Article 23). Just as with evangelism, our example alone is not enough. Words are also necessary.[2]

This same Mennonite leader proceeded to eloquently articulate additional reasons "why we as Christians do well to speak to government:"

- Because it's biblical. The Bible is filled with stories about people of faith who resisted unjust laws and called rulers to act more justly. In practice, North American Anabaptists have, for many years, spoken to government officials about issues like military conscription that directly impact our own congregations. So speaking to government is nothing new.
- We are Christians living amidst the world's lone economic and military superpower. And we live in a democracy where we have the opportunity to make our voice known. These two realities create a special responsibility for us.
- Because church has prophetic imagination. People of faith see possibilities that others cannot. Indeed, why would Christians want a public policy that is devoid of a moral voice?[3]

---

[1] "Speaking to government," J. Daryl Byler, Mennonite Church USA Delegate Assembly, July 6, 2005. http://www.mennoniteusa.org/resource-center/resources/statements-and-resolutions/speaking-to-government/, accessed July 27, 2013.

[2] Ibid.

[3] Ibid.

### Godless government

Imagine if all Christians dropped out of public policy and left the government with no Christian influence.

Actually, we don't need to imagine a government without Christian influence. The French Revolution provides an apt illustration of a government that excluded faith.

As Alexis de Tocqueville observes of the faith-purging agenda of the French Revolution,

> Passionate and persistent efforts were made to wean men away from the faith of their fathers…. Irreligion became an all-prevailing passion, fierce, intolerant and predatory.[4]

When Christians are forced from the public square, or when we deliberately choose to abstain from government participation, governing is left to those who do not follow God's principles. The results are not pretty. In the case of France, removing Christian influence and standards literally created a *government of the guillotine*.

### "But engagement in politics is 'worldly'"

Some believers through the ages, unlike the real-life Jesus they have sought to imitate, have reacted to the temptations and confusions of public life by retreating to a "spiritual" safe harbor, even to the point of living physically removed from the rest of civilization. Similarly, some sincere believers today have deserted the tempting and confusing public policy arena, retreating into the safer interiors of churches to devote themselves to more obviously spiritual pursuits such as Bible study, prayer and contemplation, venturing out only for overt evangelistic outreach.

Some might justify such a retreat from secular society by pointing to Paul's exhortation to the Colossians, "Set your mind on the things above, not on the things that are on earth."[5] Some may misinterpret this passage to mean that true spirituality requires blotting out considerations of the current world around us.

Yet Paul's own example suggests otherwise. The intrepid Apostle Paul vigorously engaged in the public square, hashing out competing philosophies with secular thinkers, challenging false teaching in the religious community and standing before political leaders to make a defense for the faith.

---

[4] Alexis de Tocqueville, *The Old Regime and the French Revolution*, translated by Stuart Gilbert (Garden City: Doubleday/Anchor Books, 1955), 149.
[5] Colossians 3:2.

Granted, life seems so much easier when our toughest decisions do not involve embryonic versus adult stem cell research but instead whether we should bring the spinach squares or tuna casserole to the church potluck. But surely church is not a mere way station in which to sing, pray and talk to ourselves while waiting for heaven–as if God were absentmindedly tardy in taking us home from our communities and nation in which we have no purpose. Evangelism surely must involve not only challenging others to a decision for Christ, but also genuinely and lovingly walking with them in the daily issues of life–including the many life issues that intersect with public policy.

### God became flesh

Rather than encouraging us to divorce from the world, the New Testament instead exhorts us to first align our minds and values with our Father in heaven and then to work out His principles and fulfill His will here on earth. If we can apprehend this truth, we will discover wonderful opportunities to help many individuals open their hearts and minds to the Good News.

God Himself demonstrated for us the integration of the eternal and the temporal, the spiritual and the physical. The invisible God, the glorious Spirit, manifested Himself as a mortal man and descended to earth. Jesus, fully God, for our sake became fully man.

This Jesus, the Divine sent to Earth, taught us to pray with one eye focused on heaven and the other on earth:

```
Our Father who is in heaven,
Hallowed be Your name.
Your kingdom come.
Your will be done,
On earth as it is in heaven....[6]
```

How do we carry out God's will "on earth as it is in heaven"? We believe on His Son, Jesus Christ.[7] We follow the principles of His Word.[8] And we help others to do the same.[9]

---

[6] Matthew 6:9-10, emphasis added.

[7] John 6:40: "For this is the will of My Father, that everyone who beholds the Son and believes in Him will have eternal life, and I Myself will raise him up on the last day."

[8] Luke 11:28: "But He said, 'On the contrary, blessed are those who hear the word of God and observe it.'"

[9] Matthew 5:19: "...whoever keeps and teaches them, he shall be called great in the kingdom of heaven."

We help others on an individual basis through counsel and teaching. We help others on a national basis by advocating for the integration of God's principles, which benefit everyone, into the governments He has established.

## *Showing that Christian faith works in the real world*

When we neglect the "earthly" public policy arena in favor of the "heavenly" evangelistic arena, we may unwittingly advance the notion that Christianity itself remains removed to a separate "spiritual" realm, separated from the world in which those we would reach actually live. People can come to view Christianity as a mere myth that cannot thrive or even survive in the "real world" of temptations, hostility and competition with other belief systems or philosophies.

Christian engagement in government and policy advocacy offers an opportunity to show skeptics that faith can work in the real world–even in the intensely challenging, often battering world of public policy. Christian principles such as teaching teens to save sex for marriage can not only survive head-to-head competition with the prevailing condom-centered approach; it can actually prove superior under rigorous testing.[10] Ethical and non-lethal adult stem cell research, as contrasted with embryo-destroying research, not only offers an ethical alternative; it also produces real cures for real patients.

The Christian faith is not so fragile as to fail in the face of the complexities and competitions of public policy. The Church's engagement in public policy provides us a tremendous opportunity to demonstrate how the Gospel of a relationship with Jesus Christ addresses not just personal belief and worship, but *all of life.*

Someone may argue that the Bible does not detail political solutions; it does not outline, for example, an ideal delivery system for healthcare. But it does offer highly relevant principles about compassion for the poor, individual responsibility and the perils of power–principles upon which to build political solutions to social problems. The Bible does not mention stem cell research, but God's Word teaches clearly about the sanctity of human life and the folly of a utilitarian ethical system. The Bible also teaches the

---

[10] A University of Pennsylvania School of Medicine study concluded, for example, that "an abstinence-only intervention for pre-teens was more successful in delaying the onset of sexual activity than a health-promotion control intervention." "Onset of Sexual Activity in Tweens Delayed By Theory-based Abstinence-only Program," U. of Penn. Medical School news release, Feb. 1, 2010, http://www.uphs.upenn.edu/news/news_releases/2010/02/theory-based-abstinence-education/, accessed July 19, 2014.

191

sanctity and value of marriage and the boundaries of human sexuality that make for healthy lives, social stability and sound government policy.

### *"But politics is corrupt, and our involvement will tarnish our reputation"*

Throughout history, politics certainly has provided ample evidence of its corruptive influence. So much so that some argue that followers of Christ should simply avoid all that mess and temptation in order to prevent even the appearance of corruption.

But surely the mere presence of temptation does not categorically preclude Christian participation. The Holy Spirit "impelled" Jesus to go into the wilderness where He would be tempted,[11] and the Lord spent 40 intense days and nights successfully resisting temptation. The followers of Christ possess the same power to resist and prevail over temptation.

Some insist that just associating with politics sullies the reputations of Christians. I see it the other way. How we conduct ourselves in the public square offers an opportunity to *enhance* the reputation of Christians. When our countrymen see that followers of Christ can actually function in the world of politics and still maintain integrity and charity, the contrast with cutthroat politics and corruption actually serves to highlight the power of faith.

Objections to participating in politics due to temptations and associations may arise in part from misunderstandings about Christian purity. The Apostle Paul addressed such misperceptions, explaining how Christians should live out their faith fully engaged in the world of unbelievers:

```
I wrote you in my letter not to associate with
immoral people; I did not at all mean with the
immoral people of this world, or with the covetous
and swindlers, or with idolaters, for then you would
have to go out of the world. But actually, I wrote to
you not to associate with any so-called brother if he
is an immoral person….[12]
```

God's call to holiness and purity no longer means physical segregation from non-believers, as the old Law had prescribed.[13] Rather than relying on

---

[11] Mark 1:12.

[12] I Corinthians 5:9.

[13] Joshua 23:6-7: "Be very firm, then, to keep and do all that is written in the book of the law of Moses, so that you may not turn aside from it to the right hand or to the left, so that you will not associate with these nations, these which remain among you, or mention the name of their gods...."

physical segregation to keep from sin and apostasy, we now submit our natural desires to the sanctifying, purifying power of the Holy Spirit:

[W]alk by the Spirit, and you will not carry out the desire of the flesh.[14]

Jesus prayed for us to the Father for the spiritual fortification to minister in the midst of worldly temptations:

I do not ask Thee to take them out of the world, but to keep them from the evil one. They are not of the world, even as I am not of the world. Sanctify them in the truth; Your word is truth. As You sent Me into the world, I also have sent them into the world.[15]

The Scriptures reassure us that we need not fear temptation as long as we walk with God:

No temptation has overtaken you but such as is common to man; and God is faithful, who will not allow you to be tempted beyond what you are able, but with the temptation will provide the way of escape also, so that you will be able to endure it.[16]

## We engage to help others

The story of the Good Samaritan offers still another, powerful answer to the question of why Christians would enter the messy, tempting world of public policy.

Jesus replied and said, "A man was going down from Jerusalem to Jericho, and fell among robbers, and they stripped him and beat him, and went away leaving him half dead. And by chance a priest was going down on that road, and when he saw him, he passed by on the other side. Likewise a Levite also, when he came to the place and saw him, passed by on the other side.

But a Samaritan, who was on a journey, came upon him; and when he saw him, he felt compassion, and came to him and bandaged up his wounds, pouring oil and wine on them; and he put him on his own beast, and brought him to an inn and took care of him.

On the next day he took out two denarii and gave them to the innkeeper and said, 'Take care of him; and

---

[14] Galatians 5:16.
[15] John 17:15-18.
[16] I Corinthians 10:13.

193

whatever more you spend, when I return I will repay
you. '
Which of these three do you think proved to be a
neighbor to the man who fell into the robbers'
hands?"
And he said, "The one who showed mercy toward him."
Then Jesus said to him, "Go and do the same."[17]

Jesus teaches us through this story to be willing to step out and take risks
in loving and caring for our neighbor. The priest and the Levite, by contrast,
kept to themselves, preferring sanctimony to the risk of being "corrupted"
with a despised Samaritan.

Individuals and societies lacking the protection of a Christian moral
foundation are like the defenseless man in the parable who was beaten by
robbers and left by the side of the road to die. A child or teenager without the
protection of abstinence strategies is vulnerable to the physical, emotional
and spiritual damages of sexual license. A society without the protection of
godly morals is vulnerable to the ravages of *anomie*–the total breakdown of
law, social norms and community.

Advocating for and implementing good public policy helps people. It's a
way to *love your neighbor*.

The faith God prescribes in His Word often expresses itself through
practical helps for others:

But someone may well say, "You have faith and I have
works; show me your faith without the works, and I
will show you my faith by my works."
You believe that God is one. You do well; the demons
also believe, and shudder.
But are you willing to recognize, you foolish fellow,
that faith without works is useless? Was not Abraham
our father justified by works when he offered up
Isaac his son on the altar?
You see that faith was working with his works, and as
a result of the works, faith was perfected....[18]

Practical works in the pursuit of justice and mercy fulfill the first two of
the three-pronged walk of the believer highlighted in the book of Micah:

And what does the Lord require of you but to do
justice, to love kindness, and to walk humbly with
your God?[19]

---

[17] Luke 10:30-37.
[18] James 2:18-22.
[19] Micah 6:8.

### *"But the New Testament Church did not engage in politics"*

A political separatist also may protest that Christians during the times of the writing of the New Testament apparently did not pursue politics, and that Scripture mentions few believers who held political power.

It is not convincing, however, to assume that simply because the Bible does not highlight something that therefore it never happened. We also must remember that the early Christians typically were either fleeing for their lives from persecutors or suffering daily discrimination and abuse by oppressive tyrants. A government that demanded emperor worship often viewed monotheists as a threat to be eradicated.

Yet as noted above, even in such a hostile political environment, Paul appealed to Roman government authorities for legal redress and took full advantage of opportunities for hearings with Roman rulers.[20]

### *"But we are supposed to focus on the 'Great Commission'"*

Still, it is not difficult to see how a dedicated Christian reading the New Testament stories that focus on preaching and evangelism might conclude that politics is not on the menu. Most Bible-honoring preachers and teachers stress our need to focus on what is known as Jesus' Great Commission:

> Go therefore and make disciples of all the nations, baptizing them in the name of the Father and the Son and the Holy Spirit, teaching them to observe all that I commanded you....[21]

Some understandably conclude from this message that the primary focus of followers of Christ is overt evangelism–i.e., preaching or stating the message of salvation and inviting a response. But this inchoate view actually limits evangelism to its final stage–inviting an individual to express repentance and profess faith in Christ–while neglecting the often lengthy process of observation, consideration and making moral decisions ("faith steps") that leads up to that ultimate profession of faith.

The latter part of Jesus' command, "teaching them to observe all that I commanded you," suggests that our evangelistic mission actually extends much wider than simply outlining the steps to salvation. To understand what the teaching part of our mission might encompass, we can look to the example of Jesus Himself.

Jesus didn't simply teach by outlining a neat and tidy few steps to salvation, followed by an altar call. As He preached to crowds comprised of

---

[20] See, for example, Acts 21:37-39 and 22:25-29 and chapters 25 and 26.
[21] Matthew 28:19.

both the devout and the doubting, Jesus taught *how to live life*. Through stories of prodigals, unjust judges, sowers, builders, farmers, unforgiving debtors, savvy stewards and treasures, He taught people how to live according to God's kingdom principles.

As people learned and practiced those kingdom principles, they learned what it means to know and follow God.

Likewise, I suspect that many of us who have made a decision to follow Christ first benefited from a good deal of Christian teaching, much of which was not focused specifically on salvation but on living the Christian life. Learning those principles provided an essential foundation for our commitment to follow Christ. This is certainly true of children raised by Christian parents. The children first learn all kinds of Christian principles–kindness, respect, compassion, love–before they actually make their own decision to follow Christ.

The principle of *Faith Steps* laid out in this book is based on just this premise: that receiving and learning God's principles is a step toward a commitment to follow Jesus Christ. As such, communicating God's principles in the public square is an essential act of evangelism.

## The "Great Omission"

Influencing public policy is a natural and integral part of the Great Commission, which is taking the Good News of salvation in Jesus Christ to our neighbors and our countrymen. If we engage with, counsel and encourage others on an individual basis to consider God's principles to lead them toward faith in Christ, we can do the same on a national basis. Christians have an opportunity through public policy to influence an entire nation toward God, by encouraging faith steps toward God's kingdom principles, plowing a path toward saving faith in the living God.

Neglecting this open door to lead our nation closer to God and encouraging receptivity to His principles–which ultimately can help our countrymen receive Christ Himself–is a "Great Omission." And we have no excuse for such neglect.

Unlike the early Christians, modern Americans enjoy full and free access to public policy makers and decisions. In today's democracy, "We the people" *are* the government.

I have enjoyed several private meetings with pastor and author Rick Warren, who has a wonderful way of communicating concepts clearly. He explains the role of Christians in a democratic republic:

Romans 13 tells us to submit to all authority. Who is the authority in the United States? We don't have a

196

king. In a democracy the people are the authority.
You are the authority. So there is not like somebody
up here saying, I'm making the laws and you've got to
submit to them.
In a democracy, the people are the authority and they
have the right to elect and to kick out [lawmakers]
and to do laws. And so this whole idea [of] sitting
back and being passive is not the way to go, not in a
democracy…. [22]

If "we the people" are the government, what a dereliction of duty we
commit when we fail to exercise our democratic prerogative.

We know that according to Scripture, the "natural man"–the individual
who has not received God's truth or Spirit–does not understand how to make
good laws in accordance with God's truth. But those who have received His
truth do understand. Because we do, we hold a God-given responsibility to
help guide government so that people can benefit from truth and goodness.

Apart from being conquered, captured or incarcerated, how can a
Christian justify abdicating such a divinely appointed opportunity and
responsibility? How can we decline the privilege of helping to provide a life-
respecting, honest and compassionate government that will benefit those who
have little connection to the Divine or understanding of His ways?

Abraham Kuyper, echoing John Calvin, offers us an apt warning:

In his Commentary on Samuel, Calvin therefore
admonishes such peoples: "And ye, O peoples, to whom
God gave the liberty to choose your own magistrates,
see to it, that ye do not forfeit this favor, by
electing to the positions of highest honor, rascals
and enemies of God."[23]
But with equal decision, Calvin asserts that God has
the sovereign power, in the way of His dispensing
Providence, to take from a people this most desirable
condition, or never to bestow it at all, when a
nation is unfit for it, or, by its sin, has utterly
forfeited the blessing.[24]

---

[22] Transcript: "Hobby Lobby and the Future of Religious Liberty," panel held June 9, 2014 at
the Southern Baptist Convention in Baltimore, Maryland. http://erlc.com/article/transcript-
hobby-lobby-and-the-future-of-religious-liberty, accessed June 12, 2014.
[23] Kuyper, Abraham (2009-08-08). *Lectures on Calvinism* (p. 76). Eerdmans Publishing Co.,
Kindle Edition.
[24] Ibid.

### *Reaching individuals, reaching nations*

So we *engage* the world while avoiding evil and immorality, empowered and protected by the indwelling Holy Spirit. We are not to pursue purity by disengaging with people and the world around us, but by drawing upon God's Holy Spirit, fully engaging with others to share the life and love He has given us.

Many Christian separatists exhibit evangelical fervor in engaging and influencing non-believers, on a personal level, toward Christ. The benefits of such devotion can be multiplied simply by extending such evangelical ardor to include influencing their countrymen through public policy.

### *Our dual citizenship*

Charles Colson summarizes the key principles of government that the Scriptures and church leaders from Augustine to the present have taught:

It is this first step of Christian citizenship in the Kingdom of God-knowledge and confidence in classical Christian truth-that enables the Christian to be a good citizen in the kingdoms of man.
On the one hand Scripture commands civil obedience-that individuals respect and live in subjection to governing authorities and pray for those in authority. On the other it commands that Christians maintain their ultimate allegiance to the Kingdom of God. If there is a conflict, they are to obey God, not man.
That may mean holding the state to moral account through civil disobedience. This dual citizenship requires a delicate balance. Christians who are faithful to Scripture should be patriots in the best sense of that word.[25]

Colson also explains how Christian citizens can turn their dual citizenship into a witness to God's outreaching love:

They are "the salvation of the commonwealth," said Augustine, for they fulfill the highest role of citizenship. Not because they are forced to or even choose to, not out of any chauvinistic motivations or allegiance to a political leader, but because they love and obey the King who is above all temporal leaders.

---

[25] Charles Colson and Ellen Santilli, *God and Government,* Grand Rapids: Zondervan, 1987, updated 2007. Kindle location 5233. Used by permission of Zondervan, www.zondervan.com.

Out of that love and obedience they live in
subjection to governing authorities, love their
neighbors, and promote justice. Since the state
cannot legislate love, Christian citizens bring a
humanizing element to civic life, helping to produce
the spirit by which people do good out of compassion,
not compulsion.[26]

When Christians engage in public policy, we do so not only to protect
our own rights but also to protect others, especially those who cannot speak
for themselves: the unborn, children, the infirm, the poor, the socially
marginalized. Public policies not only invite God's blessing or judgment on a
nation; to the extent to which they follow or violate God's design for our
lives, they also yield practical benefits or harms to the citizenry.

## *"Thy will be done"*

"Thy kingdom come, Thy will be done on earth as it is in heaven" means
that we will actively live out and advance God's principles here on earth.
There is no reason to believe this command applies only to doctrine and not
to practice, or only to individuals and not to nations, or only to our private
lives and not to our public lives.

The command, "Thy kingdom come, Thy will be done on earth as it is in
heaven" applies to all of life. And it is not an option but a foundation of the
Christian life.

If Christians insist on separatism and refuse to influence public policy,
Government will assuredly impose anti-Christian values. As I explained to
my separatist Mennonite neighbor during our conversation about public
policy engagement, the Obama administration was at that very time pursuing
policies that would severely hinder Christian organizations–like the one my
friend worked for–from hiring individuals according to faith principles.

What sense does it make for Christian parents to refuse the opportunity
to influence the communities in which their children play, the schools they
attend, and the government that holds the power to take children away from
their parents? Or can we conceivably hold to the sanctity of life for our own
children and yet not try to influence a neighbor, our community, or our
nation to hold to the sanctity of life–at a time when over one million
developing babies are losing their lives in this country every year?

Son of man, I have appointed you a watchman to the
house of Israel; whenever you hear a word from My
mouth, warn them from Me. When I say to the wicked,

---

[26]Colson, Kindle location 5241.

"You will surely die," and you do not warn him or speak out to warn the wicked from his wicked way that he may live, that wicked man shall die in his iniquity, but his blood I will require at your hand.[27]

## Called as ambassadors

When Paul stepped outside the synagogue, meandered through the marketplace of Athens and mounted the podium to address the skeptical Greeks debating in the Areopagus, he demonstrated how believers can use every avenue available–church, mission field and public arena–to spread His kingdom.

Paul often communicated Christian principles in a rational, systematic fashion that a skeptical secular audience would respect and appreciate. In Paul's address at the Areopagus–a center of Greek philosophical, religious and political debate–he entreats his skeptical audience by laying out a rational case for Christ, beginning with the dominant viewpoint of the prevailing culture.[28] Likewise, the apostle laid out a systematic and earnest defense to Festus in the auditorium of King Agrippa. The effective defense would have set him free had he not invoked a Roman citizen's rights to appeal to the Emperor.[29]

God may call some to serve as ambassadors in the marketplace and the public policy arena in this way, just as He calls some to serve in the pastorate or the mission field. He designs each of us with unique gifts and attributes to fulfill His purposes. Artificially segregating "spiritual and sacred" from "earthly and secular" endeavors can cause us to deny our divine design and miss our mission. Instead, we should embrace His design, remain open to His calling and employ our gifts for His heavenly purposes here on earth.

Eric Liddell, the Christian Olympic runner profiled in the movie, "Chariots of Fire," offers us insight into the seamlessness of the physical and the spiritual missions God has given us:

"I believe God made me for a purpose, but he also made me fast. And when I run, I feel His pleasure."[30]

I attended seminary intent on discerning and preparing for God's calling, which I assumed would lead me to one of two destinations–the pastorate or the mission field. But a combination of practical considerations and

---

[27] Ezekiel 3:17-18.

[28] Acts 17:22.

[29] Acts 26.

[30] *Chariots of Fire*, film, 1981. For this and more quotes from the film, see http://www.imdb.com/title/tt0082158/quotes, accessed July 19, 2014.

convictions challenged me to reassess that presumption, and I came to understand that He was calling me to neither. I sensed a leading instead to stay in the USA and use whatever gifts and interests He had given me, according to His intentional design, to advance His kingdom.

Over a decade after seminary, I sensed a deep and strong conviction that God was calling me to Washington, DC to work in public policy. As soon as I arrived in Washington, He immediately began to open doors and opportunities that far exceeded the influence of the small nonprofit I represented. I saw that and subsequent opportunities as confirmation of His calling.

### Vocational and avocational service

My own experience illustrates how God equips, calls and positions His soldiers, according to His master plan, at different posts. He appoints some to serve vocationally in the Church, some on the mission field and some in the public arena. Yet all fulfill the same ambassadorial mission:

Now all these things are from God, who reconciled us to Himself through Christ and gave us the ministry of reconciliation, namely, that God was in Christ reconciling the world to Himself, not counting their trespasses against them, and He has committed to us the word of reconciliation.

Therefore, we are ambassadors for Christ, as though God were making an appeal through us; we beg you on behalf of Christ, be reconciled to God.[31]

While He calls some individuals to serve on a vocational basis, we all can serve as laypersons in in each of these arenas. We can serve as lay leaders our local church, as lay missionaries to immigrants in the USA and on short-term missions overseas, and as citizen advocates for kingdom principles in the public arena.

Once we determine to engage in the world as ambassadors for Christ and to help others benefit from the principles of God's kingdom, we need to prepare to translate our commitment into reality. In our next section, we take a look at leading and responding in the public policy arena:

- what it's like to engage in controversy while remaining *Christ-like*;
- how to effectively *communicate* with a secular audience;
- why we must lead by *example*, and;
- how we can stay *encouraged* to persevere in the battle.

---

[31] II Corinthians 5:18-20.

# Chapter 17:
# *Christ-like in controversy*

*"...and you shall be My witnesses both in Jerusalem, and in all Judea
and Samaria, and even to the remotest part of the earth."*
–Acts 1:8

As we embark on the mission of helping others move in the direction of God's kingdom, a word is in order about how we go about our mission. Our King sends us out as sheep in the midst of wolves,[1] commanding us to love our enemies[2] and to count persecution as a blessing.[3]

## Feel the heat

If you haven't yet experienced ostracism or persecution because of your faith, just strike up a conversation with a neighbor tomorrow and explain your commitment to the idea of reserving sex as between a married man and woman. Then stand around the work water cooler at lunch time and hold forth on why researchers and the government should not invest in embryo-destroying stem cell research that scientists claim will heal diseases. Top off your day on the bus ride home by explaining to the person next to you why you don't want the government to pay for the abortions of poor women.

You might notice that not everyone agrees with your Christian principles.

Gallup polling reports that 73 percent of Americans aged 18-34 think it's fine to have "sex between an unmarried man and woman."[4] Fifty-five percent of Americans favor legalized same-sex marriage,[5] contrasted with "seven in 10 weekly church attenders opposed to same-sex marriage."[6] Over 58 percent

---

[1] Matthew 10:16.

[2] Matthew 5:43-44.

[3] Matthew 5:10.

[4] "Older Americans' Moral Attitudes Changing," Gallup, Inc. June 3, 2013. Web accessed Nov. 8, 2013 at http://www.gallup.com/poll/162881/older-americans-moral-attitudes-changing.aspx.

[5] "Same-Sex Marriage Support Reaches New High at 55%," Gallup, Inc., May 21, 2014. http://www.gallup.com/poll/169640/sex-marriage-support-reaches-new-high.aspx?utm_source=SAME_SEX_RELATIONS&utm_medium=topic&utm_campaign=tiles accessed April 19, 2015.

of Americans aged 18-34 support "medical research using stem cells from human embryos."[7]

The news is somewhat better on abortion; Gallup reveals that "48% of Americans call themselves pro-life and 45% pro-choice."[8] But try convincing a fired-up feminist and you'll feel the heat.

### Confronting unavoidable conflict

In light of these contrasts of secular and Christian values, it is tempting to simply seek peace and neutral common ground rather than stirring up the conflict that seems inevitable in politics. Some in the faith community for this reason eschew or even condemn public policy participation.

As appealing as that peace-loving, consensus-building perspective may seem, we have to sync passages about seeking peace with the biblical example of John the Baptist confronting the ruling Pharisees as a "brood of vipers"[9] or challenging Herod regarding his unlawful marriage.[10]

We note also the words of the Prince of Peace, who said:
```
Do not think that I came to bring peace on the earth;
I did not come to bring peace, but a sword. For I
came to set a man against his father, and a daughter
against her mother, and a daughter-in-law against her
mother-in-law; and a man's enemies will be the
members of his household.[11]
```

Such conflicts result not only from one person professing Christ while the other does not; they arise from *following Christ* in daily life. Most people will not care that we worship Christ; what bothers them is that we strive to live out our faith according to His Word. So conflicts arise not so much over matters of doctrine but over matters of practice such as sexual ethics, end-of-life issues, beginning-of-life issues and the like–the individual decisions that find their parallel in the public policy arena.

---

[6] "Religion Big Factor for Americans against Same-Sex Marriage," Gallup, Inc., December 5, 2012. http://www.gallup.com/poll/159089/religion-major-factor-americans-opposed-sex-marriage.aspx accessed Nov. 8, 2013.
[7] "Older Americans' Moral Attitudes Changing," Gallup, Inc. June 3, 2013. Web accessed Nov. 8, 2013 at http://www.gallup.com/poll/162881/older-americans-moral-attitudes-changing.aspx.
[8] "Americans Misjudge U.S. Abortion Views," Gallup, Inc., May 15, 2013. Web accessed Nov. 8, 2013 at http://www.gallup.com/poll/162548/americans-misjudge-abortion-views.aspx.
[9] Matthew 3:7.
[10] Matthew 14:4.
[11] Matthew 10:34.

So the conflicts and alienation in public policy simply mirror the conflicts and alienation we find in our everyday Christian life. The only way to avoid such conflicts and alienation is to compromise on the principles, and that is not an option for true followers of Christ.

Why would we deny the One who loves us so much that He died for us–even while we had been set against Him–in order to curry the favor of people who hate us if we simply disagree with them?

The preceding passages remind us that the presence of conflict and alienation is not in and of itself a reason to disengage from public policy. Even committed spouses find that some conversation topics may lead to conflict, but those topics still need to be addressed in order to maintain or restore a healthy relationship.

In the political realm, much conflict and alienation arises unavoidably from conflicting worldviews and moral choices. Apart from greater engagement of Christians in venues of cultural change and a life-changing revival of Christian faith and values, America seems poised to descend with breathtaking velocity into a worldview entirely opposed to biblical moral principles.

### Friendly fire

The harshest criticisms of Christians in public policy sometimes come not from political opponents but from fellow believers. Christians who have worked hard to build bridges to nonbelievers through charm and charity can view Christians in politics as loud-mouthed hillbillies wrecking their carefully crafted image as modern and sophisticated followers of Christ.

Some within the Church adamantly insist that the Church should avoid stances on controversial public policy issues, since that will turn people off to the Church. I agree with their diagnosis but not their prescription. Engaging in public policy issues most assuredly *will* turn some people off to the Church–for the same reasons that they also take offense at preaching on any counter-culture biblical topic. But the potential for offense is not a valid reason to avoid topics in the Church.

An abortion rights activist will be turned off by a sermon illuminating the sanctity of life expressed in how we are "fearfully and wonderfully made."[12] A dyed-in-the-wool capitalist will not like hearing an exhortation "to divide your bread with the hungry and bring the homeless poor into the house."[13] A gay rights activist will not appreciate hearing that "from the

---

[12] Psalm 139:14.
[13] Isaiah 58:7.

205

beginning of creation, God made them male and female. For this reason a man shall leave his father and mother, and the two shall become one flesh."[14]

So would we prohibit our preachers from teaching on personal and moral issues such as marriage, the sanctity of life and helping the poor? If not, then why would we prohibit our preachers from broaching topics such as abortion, same-sex marriage and welfare policy?

Public policy issues are simply personal and moral issues addressed in the context of government.

The past few decades have witnessed a growing awareness among churches of the need to deemphasize certain superficial forms and traditions that tend to keep the uninitiated out of church. We want anyone to feel comfortable coming to church, for example, even if they do not own or wear a suit. Some feel that a less formal service will prove more inviting than a more formal and liturgical service that may seem foreign or intimidating to the uninitiated.

While revising our *customs*, however, we need to avoid overreacting and deemphasizing Christian *principles* simply because they are not popular. Jesus is *Lord*–not a product for marketing.

## Faith and offense

Our faith is full of offense. Some people despise the Christian faith not only for what it teaches about God but also for what it teaches about right and wrong.

People take offense at Jesus Himself.[15] Scripture explains that the very idea of God dying to pay the penalty for sin and redeem sinners by His grace is "to Jews a stumbling block and to Gentiles foolishness."

Still others take offense at Christian moral principles. John the Baptist lost his head for chastising Herod about his unlawful marriage.[16] A mob offended by Christian teaching against idol worship nearly lynched the Apostle Paul and his companions. Saints throughout the ages and up to this very day have suffered loss of property, livelihood and their very lives for taking moral stands in accordance with Scripture but counter to culture.

Christians in our own nation have given their lives for standing up to oppose slavery and to fight for civil rights. The offense they caused by speaking out on the public policy issues of the day proved so great that opponents beat their pastors and burned their churches to the ground.

---

[14] Mark 10:6-8.
[15] Matthew 13:57 and 11:6; Mark 6:3; Luke 7:23.
[16] Mark 6:17-28.

Would we prefer that these had kept silent on public policy issues for the sake of avoiding offense in the popular culture?

"Oh, do not oppose slavery; you will offend the slave owners."

"Please keep silent on civil rights, or you will offend the racists."

If we think that the Christian faith means keeping peace at any price, accommodating the culture, appeasing our opponents, we are quite mistaken.

As Jesus said when He described the interpersonal conflicts that would result from following Him,

> He who loves father or mother more than Me is not worthy of Me; and he who loves son or daughter more than Me is not worthy of Me. And he who does not take his cross and follow after Me is not worthy of Me.

If we are to follow Christ, we have no option but to stand for His words and principles—*especially* in the midst of a society headed in the opposite direction.

> If anyone wishes to come after Me, he must deny himself, and take up his cross and follow Me. For whoever wishes to save his life will lose it, but whoever loses his life for My sake and the gospel's will save it.
>
> For what does it profit a man to gain the whole world, and forfeit his soul? For what will a man give in exchange for his soul?
>
> For whoever is ashamed of Me and My words in this adulterous and sinful generation, the Son of Man will also be ashamed of him when He comes in the glory of His Father with the holy angels.[17]

## The price of peace at any cost

Christians who attempt to maintain a neutral peace by avoiding controversial issues will find it increasingly impossible in these times to do so. Do not expect militant opponents of the Christian faith and values to content themselves with achieving cultural acceptance of their ideology or even changes in law.

They aim to force *submission* to their ideology.

Followers of Christ will find no middle ground, no peace with such activists—only a clear choice of either countering the ideology or sacrificing their faith.

In such an environment, Jesus warns us not to sacrifice our moral distinctive in a vain pursuit of harmony:

---

[17] Mark 8:34-38.

207

Blessed are you when men hate you, and ostracize you,
and insult you, and scorn your name as evil, for the
sake of the Son of Man. Be glad in that day and leap
for joy, for behold, your reward is great in heaven.
For in the same way their fathers used to treat the
prophets.
Woe to you when all men speak well of you, for their
fathers used to treat the false prophets in the same
way. [18]
If the world hates you, you know that it has hated Me
before it hated you. [19]

Many will oppose you and your message when you articulate biblical
principles for public policy, just as many with whom you share the Good
News of salvation in Christ will oppose you and your message. That's
because the source of your message and the source of their antagonism in
both ventures is the same—Jesus Christ.

His Word is the dividing sword of the world.

Just as with overt evangelism, engaging in public policy is not for the
faint-hearted. Be prepared to experience insults, libel, mocking and
ostracism.

For this reason, Jesus and the Apostle John remind us,
In the world you have tribulation, but take courage;
I have overcome the world. [20]
If you were of the world, the world would love its
own; but because you are not of the world, but I
chose you out of the world, therefore the world hates
you. [21]
...this is the victory that has overcome the world—our
faith. [22]

### Rejecting our message or our conduct?

We can rejoice when we experience persecution because others reject
our Christian *message*. But we should grieve, however, when others reject
our un-Christian *conduct*.

The book *UnChristian* presents important research data that can help
Christians see our faults and misconceptions that apparently are much more

---

[18] Luke 6:22-23, 25.
[19] John 15:18.
[20] John 16:33.
[21] John 15:19.
[22] I John 5:4.

obvious to those around us. The data is especially helpful in better understanding the perceptions of younger Americans, who are the focus of the book.

Through their polling with The Barna Group, authors David Kinnaman and Gabe Lyons discovered that younger Americans see Christians as anti-homosexual, judgmental, hypocritical, too involved in politics and out of touch with reality.[23] They conclude that to this generation, "Modern-day Christianity no longer seems Christian."[24]

Clarifying the objection to political involvement, Kinnaman and Lyons note,

> Many outsiders clarified that they believe Christians have a right (even an obligation) to pursue political involvement, but they disagree with our methods and our attitudes.[25]

Assuredly some Christians in politics have turned off observers within and outside the church by a lack of grace and humility. It is too easy when standing for God's principles to come across as–or even actually be– judgmental, proud and belligerent. Our self-righteousness can too easily obscure God's righteousness.

When we come across as merely angry, intolerant and ignorant, we betray the grace, acceptance and wisdom that Jesus demonstrated. We portray a Christ totally different than the real Jesus Christ who washed others' feet, dined with sinners and demonstrated love and forgiveness to His mortal enemies.

We cannot change what the Bible says about moral issues, but we can certainly change destructive attitudes of pride and judgmentalism.

We need to address moral issues like sex outside marriage while conveying humility and love for those who have chosen that path–just as we ourselves had chosen sinful, selfish paths before God graciously opened our eyes.

It's not easy when engaged in the culture wars to remember that the goal is not just to win a policy battle but to *love others*–including our political opponents. Just imagine the message we send when we demonstrate love to political opponents in a culture that seeks to humiliate, intimidate and destroy political opponents.

---

[23] Kinnaman, David and Lyons, Gabe, *UnChristian*, Grand Rapids, MI: Baker Books, 2007, p. 28.
[24] Kinnaman, p. 29.
[25] Kinnaman, p. 168.

## Who links politics with heaven?

Unfortunately, it's easy to read the book *UnChristian* and conclude what the authors seem to suggest, that Christians should be less involved in politics because their involvement turns off non-believers. The authors also suggest, without offering any convincing evidence, that many Christians rely too heavily on politics.

While that is perhaps possible, I personally don't know any believers with whom I work in Washington who think that legislation will bring heaven on earth. They simply work in the public policy arena to express their faith values and to help others.

Why would anyone in the pro-life movement equate politics with anything even close to salvation? We have lost political battles more times than we can count, especially at the federal level during the Clinton and Obama administrations. We would have to be either deluded or masochistic to rely too heavily on politics.

Yet despite setbacks, pro-life activists remain firmly devoted to winning the battles in which we engage because we know they matter. The battles matter both in terms of life and death and in terms of moving people closer to or further away from God. This does not mean we "rely too heavily on political influence," as authors and Kinnaman and Lyons warn, but simply that we engage in our work heartily, in dependence on God.

> Whatever you do, do your work heartily, as for the Lord rather than for men, knowing that from the Lord you will receive the reward of the inheritance. It is the Lord Christ whom you serve.[26]

Kinnaman and Lyons urge us to focus less on politics and more on culture. That's an unfortunately dichotomized proposition, since both are crucial to our mission and to the direction of our nation. While politics is often downstream from culture, culture also takes cues from politics. The law is a teacher, public officials set an example, and public policy influences behavior.

## Fitting our message to target and audience

Some may think that a Christian in the public square must always use kind and gentle words and never express anger or speak ill of others. Such an insistence fails to distinguish that the Bible does not condemn all anger[27] and

---

[26] Colossians 3:23-24.

[27] "Be angry, and yet do not sin; do not let the sun go down on your anger, and do not give the devil an opportunity" - Ephesians 4:26-27.

neglects that Jesus, John the Baptist and others roundly and angrily condemned evil leaders who misled and exploited the people.

Jesus did not gently and quietly reason with the vendors in the Temple who profaned His Father's house.[28]

Followers of Christ must not mince words or shrink back from exposing leaders as malevolent whose policies pose great harm to others and especially to those who cannot defend themselves. In such cases, we can follow the examples of Jesus and John the Baptist.[29]

Aside from exposing corrupted leaders and others irreconcilably antagonistic to truth, however, we will typically take a gentler approach. To win over an undecided and open-minded audience, we do well to follow the exhortation of Augustine, the master rhetorician. Augustine challenged Christians to communicate effectively and persuasively, employing both stories and reason:

> It is the duty, then, of the interpreter and teacher of Holy Scripture, the defender of the true faith and the opponent of error, both to teach what is right and to refute what is wrong, and in the performance of this task to conciliate the hostile, to rouse the careless, and to tell the ignorant both what is occurring at present and what is probable in the future.
>
> But once that his hearers are friendly, attentive, and ready to learn, whether he has found them so, or has himself made them so, the remaining objects are to be carried out in whatever way the case requires. If the hearers need teaching, the matter treated of must be made fully known by means of narrative. On the other hand, to clear up points that are doubtful requires reasoning and the exhibition of proof.[30]

Augustine likely drew heavily upon the rhetorical teachings of the ancient Greeks, who advanced three main keys to the art of persuasion:

1. *ethos* - appeals to the credibility of the speaker
2. *logos* - appeals to evidence and reason
3. *pathos* - appeals to emotion

For purposes of persuading others on public policy issues, these three elements translate as follows:

---

[28] John 2:13-17.

[29] See, for example, Matthew 23:13-36, in which Jesus roundly criticizes and condemns the Pharisees.

[30] Augustine, *City of God* and *Christian Doctrine*, Philip Schaff, ed., Grand Rapids: Wm. B. Eerdmans, Kindle edition, location 19874.

211

1.  Act and speak like a Christian–loving, compassionate and honest.
2.  Make a reasonable case built on logic, evidence and testimonials.
3.  Motivate others with stories and emotion.

### *Minimizing casualties while staying in the battle*

While recognizing and addressing our faults, we must not expect that we or our fellow Christians under fire in the heat of cultural battle will always react perfectly. Think of the last time you had a heated argument with a friend or a spouse. Even if you were in the right on the issue, did you say everything perfectly?

Battles are not neat and tidy, and we can't hide from the battle altogether just because we might not engage perfectly.

It is possible, in fact likely, that even with the most diplomatic and careful approach, we still may not reach those who oppose our engagement. Some simply detest the values we represent. But we can certainly endeavor to attract more individuals outside the church, and to keep more believers within the church, by expressing godly principles wisely and winsomely.

We cannot control the disdain of those who have closed their mind to Christian things. We can control how we think and act. Jesus commands us to love our enemies. For those of us who were undeniably hostile and obnoxious before we met Christ, we of all people should remember to exercise patience and grace with others.

We cannot, we must not retreat. The battle requires courage as well as character, and most of all, God's power:

```
"Behold, I send you out as sheep in the midst of
wolves; so be shrewd as serpents and innocent as
doves. But beware of men, for they will hand you over
to the courts and scourge you in their synagogues;
and you will even be brought before governors and
kings for My sake, as a testimony to them and to the
Gentiles.
"But when they hand you over, do not worry about how
or what you are to say; for it will be given you in
that hour what you are to say. For it is not you who
speak, but it is the Spirit of your Father who speaks
in you."31
```

---

31 Matthew 10:16-20.

# Chapter 18:
# *Reaching a secular culture*

*Pure and undefiled religion in the sight of our God and Father is this:*
*to visit orphans and widows in their distress,*
*and to keep oneself unstained by the world.*
–James 1:27

In the second scene of the third act of Shakespeare's Henry the Eighth, the king confronts the arrogant, ambitious and manipulative Cardinal Wolsey. The church leader had plotted with the Pope to oppose the king's desire to marry Anne Boleyn, assumed an ambassadorial post without the king's authorization and amassed an immense personal fortune on the backs of his own countrymen.

Until this point in the drama, as a trusted advisor appointed by the king's father, the Cardinal had endeavored through his counsel to manipulate Henry VIII to do Wolsey's bidding.

The king enters the room, and, unbeknownst to Cardinal Wolsey, is holding papers that reveal Wolsey's disloyal communications with the Pope. The papers also contain irrefutable evidence of the Cardinal's unseemly accumulation of wealth and properties.

The Cardinal, oblivious to his "outing," flatters the king as usual, spouting flowery praise alongside assertions of loyalty.

To which the king replies,
```
'T is well said again,
And 't is a kind of good deed to say well:
And yet words are no deeds.
```
The king peered past the curtain of Wolsey's vain words and saw his corrupt deeds. He abruptly ended the Cardinal's career and tarred him with disgrace.

### Words are no deeds

A jarring survey[1] by the Pew Research Center reveals that the United States is quickly shifting away from a religious majority, as more Americans disdain any religious affiliation and view the Church askance.

While the survey report noted that "the United States remains a highly religious country–particularly by comparison with other advanced industrial democracies" such as Britain, France, Germany or Spain, religion in America appears to have stagnated. As the Pew report observed, "[Mark Chaves of Duke University] recently summarized trends in American religion by asserting that 'no traditional religious belief or practice has increased in recent decades.'"

In fact, in the United States today, one in five adults now claim no religious affiliation whatsoever–and they are not looking for any affiliation:

`"One-fifth of the U.S. public - and a third of adults under 30 - are religiously unaffiliated today, the highest percentages ever in Pew Research Center polling."`

The decline is so rapid, Pew reports, that in the last five years alone, "the unaffiliated have increased from just over 15 percent to just under 20 percent of all U.S. adults." The startling rise of the "nones"–individuals with no religious affiliation–follows a long-term trend first emerging in the 1990's.

Who is dropping out from religious affiliation?

1. *Young*: "A third of adults under 30 have no religious affiliation...."
2. *Whites*: "When it comes to race, however, the recent change has been concentrated in one group: whites."
3. *Men*: "Among the unaffiliated as a whole, 56 percent are men and 44 percent are women."
4. *Unmarried*: "Religiously unaffiliated Americans are more likely than U.S. adults as a whole to be living with a partner or never married."
5. *Grads*: "Unaffiliated college graduates claiming no religious affiliation rose seven points in just five years–now at 22 percent."

What do these "nones" think and value?

1. *Disaffected with the Church:* "Overwhelmingly, they think that religious organizations are too concerned with money and power, too focused on rules and too involved in politics."
2. *Resisting Church's moral influence*: "The religiously unaffiliated population is less convinced that religious institutions help protect morality...."

---

[1] Pew Research Center, "'Nones' on the Rise," October 9, 2012.
www.pewforum.org/Unaffiliated/nones-on-the-rise.aspx, accessed Nov. 10, 2012.

3.  *Skeptical about the Church's social problem-solving*: Just 45 percent of the unaffiliated say that churches and other houses of worship contribute either some or a great deal to solving social problems, compared to seven-in-ten of those *with* a religious affiliation.
4.  *Watching the works of the Church:* "[A] majority agree that religious organizations have positive effects on society, such as bringing people together and playing an important role in helping the poor and needy."
5.  *Self-defined spiritually:* "[T]hose who describe their religion as 'nothing in particular' – say they believe in God or a universal spirit. Thirty-seven percent say they are spiritual but not religious."
6.  *Earth-bound:* "…less likely than other religious groups to think about the meaning and purpose of life," but "no less likely than the public overall to say they often feel a connection with nature and the earth."
7.  *Liberal:* "…about twice as likely to describe themselves as political liberals than as conservatives, and solid majorities support legal abortion (72 percent) and same-sex marriage (73 percent)."

If the views of these unaffiliated Americans toward the Church could be described in a sentence, it might be the same message that Henry the Eighth gave Cardinal Woolsey: "Words are no deeds."

### Backing up talk with deeds

As the Pew survey highlights, now one in five Americans claims no religious affiliation whatsoever. We need to learn to connect with them in new ways, primarily to invite them into the kingdom of God and secondarily to retain religious liberty in our nation.

Polling shows that these disaffected observers of the Church may have tired of our words but remain open to our deeds. We can take encouragement from the Pew survey's conclusion that "a majority agree that religious organizations have positive effects on society, such as bringing people together and playing an important role in helping the poor and needy."

Since the religiously unaffiliated still value the good works of the Church, we should highlight faith-based social programs such as aiding the poor, feeding the hungry, caring for the sick and ministering to the outcasts. In public policy, we need to demonstrate how harming religious freedom ultimately harms the needy individuals served by faith-based social programs.

### Sharing our faith through medicine

I wrote a cover story for *World* magazine in 1999, entitled, "No Cure for the Fall," in which I traced historical highlights of the Church's involvement in caring for the sick. In the Middle Ages, for example:

```
...the church powerfully exerted its moral influence
upon medicine. It fostered the development of medical
science during the Middle Ages, helped establish many
university medical schools and hospitals, and at
times assumed the role of physical and spiritual
healer. The Benedictine order of monks, for example,
stressed the study of medicine and provided health
care for lepers and the poor.
As late as the 12th century, monastic clinics
provided the only means of health care available to
many communities.[2]
```

In the summer of 2014, the world witnessed similar sacrificial love when medical missionaries contracted the Ebola virus while serving infected patients in West Africa. Dr. Kent Brantly, a Christian physician serving with Samaritan's Purse, a relief agency I formerly worked for, exemplified the selflessness that marked the service of these faith-motivated healthcare professionals.

While undergoing treatment back in the States for Ebola, Dr. Brantly wrote the following:

```
One thing I have learned is that following God often
leads us to unexpected places. When Ebola spread into
Liberia, my usual hospital work turned more and more
toward treating the increasing number of Ebola
patients. I held the hands of countless individuals
as this terrible disease took their lives away from
them. I witnessed the horror firsthand, and I can
still remember every face and name.
When I started feeling ill on that Wednesday morning,
I immediately isolated myself until the test
confirmed my diagnosis three days later. When the
result was positive, I remember a deep sense of peace
that was beyond all understanding. God was reminding
me of what He had taught me years ago, that He will
give me everything I need to be faithful to Him.[3]
```

---

[2] Imbody, Jonathan, "No Cure for the Fall," *World*, July 31, 1999.
http://www.worldmag.com/issue/1999/07/31/ web accessed June 12, 2013.
[3] Statement by Kent Brantly, MD, made available through Samaritan's Purse at
http://www.samaritanspurse.org/article/dr-kent-brantly-statement/ accessed August 29, 2014.

Even as Dr. Brantly recovered from his near-death experience with Ebola, other faith-based groups continued to demonstrate Christian love in action, as they recruited and sent healthcare professionals to aid Africans in battling the Ebola virus.

As *USA Today* reported,

```
[T]he epidemic has done little to dissuade others
from embarking on the rigorous, often dangerous
missions. Groups like Dallas-based Faith in Action
Initiatives, New York-based Doctors Without Borders
USA and the Christian Medical & Dental Association,
known as CMDA, all report a steady stream of doctors,
nurses and medical workers still willing to go off to
places like Cameroon, Ethiopia, Haiti and other
developing nations.⁴
```

## *Sharing our faith through social justice*

Though a public school student might not learn it today, American Christians have helped lead the fight against tyranny, slavery and racism. Hospitals and clinics established and still run by Christians today reach the poor and medically underserved who otherwise might not receive any care at all. Christian shelters protect the homeless and victims of domestic violence and human trafficking. Christian adoption agencies find loving families for orphans and unwanted babies, and Christian pregnancy centers care for mothers in need.

A battalion of Christian organizations including the Salvation Army, Samaritan's Purse, World Vision, Catholic Relief Services and many other faith-based organizations currently stand in the gap by providing vital social services to millions of needy individuals. If these Christian ministries suddenly disappeared from the American landscape, the government could not afford to replace them, and our country would degenerate into a mean and violent battle for survival of the fittest.

Many American Christians today and throughout the ages have taken to heart biblical admonitions to not merely talk about faith but also to put faith into action. Faith-based organizations represent the tip of the iceberg of the Church's ministry, as God uses countless individual Christians to quietly share Christ's love in practical and profound ways.

---

⁴ "Ebola outbreak doesn't deter medical missions," *USA Today*, August 7, 2014.

## Sharing our faith through AIDS action

Many with a stereotypical view of the Church might be surprised to learn how many Christian organizations and individuals work with and for homosexuals, fighting HIV and AIDS.

One such follower of Christ who has been putting his faith into action for decades is my friend Shepherd Smith. Along with his wife Anita, Shepherd essentially launched the evangelical response to AIDS. Shepherd explained to me how he got engaged in the fight against AIDS in the 1980's–a time when few knew of the scourge and even fewer had determined to fight it.

After accepting Christ into my life as an adult, I did something pretty foolish.

In prayer I told God that I had truly changed in every way possible in order to follow Christ. However, I shared with the Lord that I found homosexuality of such great concern that I would rather not have to deal with it in any way.

That was 1982. Fast forward three years. My wife Anita and I were consultants to nonprofit organizations. My father, a physician with a public health degree, started talking to my wife Anita and me about how this new disease AIDS would spread unchecked–unless we employed traditional medical/public health measures such as early diagnosis and voluntary and confidential partner notification.

My father urged Anita and me to start a not-for-profit organization to address HIV/AIDS as a public health issue rather than as a civil rights issue, as was the case in 1985. We agreed, and we formed Americans for a Sound AIDS/HIV Policy (ASAP). Unfortunately, we were unable to find anyone to run the organization. So, believing this was what God had called us to do with our lives, we closed down our consulting business and ran the organization ourselves.

ASAP largely achieved its policy goals by the early 1990s. We changed the name to the Children's AIDS Fund because of the extensive work we were doing with children and families at the time.

The Children's AIDS Fund is probably the only AIDS organization in the world formed without its founders knowing anyone living with or dying from AIDS when it was started. I believe strongly that this fact has

given us an objective outlook and has contributed
greatly to how we deal with the pandemic today.
We have sought to be open to all who are ill and have
learned to love the individual, regardless of what
sin or circumstance has put that individual in harm's
way in acquiring HIV. In our policy pursuits in
various legislatures, we have sought to find
bipartisan agreement while never compromising our
personal faith or principles.
For years this issue was dominated by homosexual men,
many of whom we have come to know quite well and love
as individuals and as children of God. But that
domination is changing with the global epidemic now
affecting more women worldwide than men.
We would hope to have conducted our lives in such a
way that we have been true ambassadors for Christ,
and that others, seeing our compassion and good
works, have been led closer to God.

## *Communicating harms and benefits*

Besides highlighting good works, how can followers of Christ
communicate on public policy issues with the increasing number of
Americans outside the Church?

Because the religiously unaffiliated may not view Scripture as
authoritative, quoting biblical passages is probably not the wisest way to
begin a conversation. People of faith can, however, explain key principles
like religious freedom in universally understood terms of pragmatic natural
consequences–harms and benefits.

For example, the experience of many Germans who lived through the
Nazi regime demonstrates how quickly we can all lose religious freedom
when we allow the government to violate one group's freedom. After
liberation from a concentration camp in 1945 by the Allies, Martin
Niemoller, a prominent Protestant pastor, helped write the "Stuttgart
Confession" to acknowledge the failure of many clergy to act to prevent Nazi
horrors.

Here is how Niemoller expressed his regret:

First they came for the Jews. I was silent. I was not
a Jew. Then they came for the Communists. I was
silent. I was not a Communist. Then they came for the
trade unionists. I was silent. I was not a trade
unionist. Then they came for me. There was no one
left to speak for me.[5]

If the government can arbitrarily trample the rights of one group of citizens, none of our rights remains safe.

If today an ideologically driven administration comes for Catholics over contraception, tomorrow they can come for homeschoolers over sex education. If one administration can trample the rights of the faith community, another administration can come for environmentalists, for homosexuals, for peace activists, for anyone who dares oppose the government's edicts.

Americans need to regain the understanding, once common, that everyone benefits when protecting religious freedom for others.

As Thomas Jefferson advised,

It behooves every man who values liberty of conscience for himself, to resist invasions of it in the case of others; or their case may, by change of circumstances, become his own.[6]

The Constitution's protection against the government "prohibiting the free exercise" of religion also prevents "an establishment of religion," thus protecting faith adherents and non-adherents alike. Opposing abortion is considered conservative, while opposing the death penalty is considered liberal. Yet the right of conscience-guided physicians to decline to participate in abortion mirrors the right of conscience-guided physicians to decline to participate in the death penalty.

Conscience freedoms know no boundaries of right and left; they protect all from ideological coercion.

### Proving God and His principles

Protecting the freedom to exercise faith and conscience and to speak about religious principles, however, is just the first step in engaging our neighbors and our nation. The next step is allowing people to consider faith principles and test them out in real life.

God's principles work in nations and also in individual lives. As non-religious or nominally religious people consider how effectively faith principles practically work in public policy and in their individual lives, they likely will become more receptive to the spiritual message behind those principles.

---

[5] Niemoller, Martin, quoted in *Historical Dictionary of the Holocaust,* Jack R. Fischel, Scarecrow Press, 2010, p. 184. Fischel notes that the quote appears on the wall of the US Holocaust Museum.

[6] Thomas Jefferson (1743 - 1826), Letters to Benjamin Rush, April 21, 1803.

In the biblical days of the true prophet Elijah, prophets of the peculiarly enticing false god Baal had convinced many people to forsake biblical principles and to turn from God to idolatry. The courageous prophet Elijah gathered together all of Israel and 850 false prophets in one place.

> Elijah came near to all the people and said, "How long will you hesitate between two opinions? If the Lord is God, follow Him; but if Baal, follow him."[7]

Then Elijah proposed a real-world experiment–a battle of gods and worldviews.

> "Now let them give us two oxen; and let them choose one ox for themselves and cut it up, and place it on the wood, but put no fire under it; and I will prepare the other ox and lay it on the wood, and I will not put a fire under it.
> "Then you call on the name of your god, and I will call on the name of the Lord, and the God who answers by fire, He is God."
> And all the people said, "That is a good idea."[8]

Elijah put his full faith and trust in the one living, powerful, true God–the God who created the universe and laid down principles by which every living being could thrive. Elijah also knew that God delighted in those who tested, who proved His principles and His power.

> Then the fire of the Lord fell and consumed the burnt offering and the wood and the stones and the dust, and licked up the water that was in the trench.
> When all the people saw it, they fell on their faces; and they said, "The Lord, He is God; the Lord, He is God."[9]

Put God's principles before the people and let them test those principles. He will prove Himself.

## Live like Jesus

Disappointing elections and discouraging polls have provided a wake-up call to the faith community: Influence our culture or lose it.

It is time to build bridges to others beyond our choir. We have before us an opportunity for soul-searching and for developing a more authentic Christian witness.

---

[7] I Kings 18:21.
[8] I Kings 18:23-24.
[9] I Kings 18:38-39.

We can't make people believe, but we can make belief more attractive while minimizing stumbling blocks. That means personally demonstrating authentic Christian character. Showing integrity, not hypocrisy. Reaching out with acceptance instead of judgment. Offering a loving community to counter alienation.

In short, our works must back up our words. We need to *live* like Jesus, not just talk like Him.

As Jesus taught us,

```
Let your light shine before men in such a way that
they may see your good works, and glorify your Father
who is in heaven.¹⁰
```

### *Authentic Christian character*

While demonstrating the values of our faith through good works, we also need to demonstrate authentic Christian character.

The watching world wants to see integrity–not hypocrisy. As Christians we can become so intent on presenting a "good witness" that we can't seem to bring ourselves to admitting our faults and failures. Yet that's exactly the kind of authenticity that many outside the Church are waiting to see. And it's the mark of a Christian.

A person who is not accessing or aware of God's grace and forgiveness to cover personal failures, by contrast, may find it extremely difficult to confess failure. Many have learned painfully that admitting failure sometimes brings on harsh punishment, disdain or degradation.

How amazing, then, when such a person sees a Christian not only admit failure but also rest in God's amazing grace of forgiveness!

Besides integrity, the watching world also wants to see acceptance–not judgment. Judging others poses a tough temptation for those of us focused on justice and righteousness. Yet somehow we need to find a way, while still retaining our moral standards and faithfulness to God's teachings in His Word, to reach out with grace, understanding and love to individuals who are violating God's principles.

After listing a litany of sins deserving judgment, the Apostle Paul inserts a blunt reminder that we will do well to remember: "Such were some of you...."¹¹

Apart from grace and the mercy of forgiveness in Christ, we, too once stood condemned as enemies of God. Even after salvation from judgment by

---

[10] Matthew 5:16.
[11] I Corinthians 6:11.

putting our faith in Christ, which one of us can say that we have gone a single day without violating God's principles? Have we always loved God with all our heart, soul, mind and strength? Have we always loved our neighbor as ourselves? If we who know Christ sin despite clearly understanding His principles, how can we judge others who sin in comparative ignorance of God's commands?

Once we realize our own commonality with individuals who are still attempting to live outside God's grace, we can begin to reach out with genuine empathy, compassion and acceptance.

So as we endeavor to help individuals and our nation take faith steps toward God by articulating His principles, let's remember that *how* we present our message–through personal integrity and gracious acceptance–is integral to the message itself. We cannot for long advance godly values while living ungodly lives. God has a way of exposing our hypocrisy, as do our ideological opponents.

### Winsome and truthful

Let us commit ourselves anew to communicating winsomely and truthfully, with Christ's love and courage. When we speak the truth in humility and love, as those who also deeply need God's grace, we may occasionally experience the favor that our Lord did:

And all were speaking well of Him, and wondering at the gracious words which were falling from His lips.[12]

While appreciating this occasional favor with our hearers, we also do well to remember that just moments after the people spoke so well of Jesus, the same crowd indignantly dragged him to the edge of a cliff, ready to throw him off. So we determine to speak truth courageously regardless the reception. We can share the perspective of the apostles Peter and John, who though threatened by antagonistic rulers refused to back down from their God-given message:

But Peter and John answered and said to them, "Whether it is right in the sight of God to give heed to you rather than to God, you be the judge; for we cannot stop speaking about what we have seen and heard."[13]

As we live genuinely Christian lives and communicate with grace and courage, with full reliance on God's power, we can help move our nation

---

[12] Luke 4:22.
[13] Acts 4:19-20.

toward the good and God, help keep minds open and hearts softened, and help lay a foundation for a sweeping spiritual reformation.

# Chapter 19:
# *Is America too far gone?*

*"And who knows whether you have not attained royalty
for such a time as this?"*
−Esther 4:14

As Americans of faith survey our cultural condition today, we cannot help but flirt with despair. From abortion to assisted suicide to embryo-destructive research, so many choose death instead of life. Laws increasingly promote what God labels as lawlessness. Men, women and even children commit breathtakingly cold-hearted crimes.

Such evidence reminds us of what Jesus described as the "beginning of birth pangs" before the "end of the age"−a time marked by the loosening of moral restraints and selfishness:

> Because lawlessness is increased, most people's love will grow cold.[1]

Paul's words to the Galatians apply all too well to Americans, as he warns of the "deeds of the flesh"−the observable evidences of people set against God and His kingdom principles:

> Now the deeds of the flesh are evident, which are: immorality, impurity, sensuality, idolatry, sorcery, enmities, strife, jealousy, outbursts of anger, disputes, dissensions, factions, envying, drunkenness, carousing, and things like these….[2]

All this disturbing evidence leads to an inescapable question: *"Is America too far gone?"*

History offers illustrations of nations and empires, such as the Roman Empire, that eventually crumbled under the weight of its moral decay. But history also offers a few instances of nations and empires that addressed the roots of societal decay, by uprooting moral degradation through spiritual, cultural and legal reform.

---

[1] Matthew 24:12.
[2] Galatians 5:19.

### Eighteenth century England: A similarly sordid cultural landscape

Eighteenth century England around the time of the American Revolution appeared strikingly similar to modern-day America.

The elite mocked religion. Religious superficiality rather than vibrant faith predominated. Most of the wealthy felt no obligation to help others, only to indulge themselves in luxury and frivolity.

The British economy depended heavily on the exploitation of slaves and children, and few seemed to care a whit about the human misery and deaths that produced the sugar for their tea.

Eric Metaxas, in *Amazing Grace*, his outstanding biography of William Wilberforce (1805-1873), describes the wretched cultural landscape the abolitionist faced following his conversion to Christianity. He describes how "religion's retreat" for over a century had yielded a brutal, selfish and exploitative country whose populace found entertainment in public hangings and burnings and reveled in the rampant prostitution of young girls.

All of these things were swimming around in Wilberforce's mind as he began to think and pray about how his newfound faith would express itself in his life and work.[3]

God's work, through William Wilberforce and his Christian colleagues, in turning around the desperate depravity of eighteenth-century England, offers us an encouraging case study of faith-initiated, widespread cultural revolution that transformed a nation in decay.

### "For such a time as this"

In the midst of this era of depravity and despair, evangelical preachers such as George Whitfield and John and Charles Wesley had begun to lead a spiritual awakening and revival in Britain and America. God's Spirit was on the move in the British Empire, and He was calling men and women to grand missions at home and abroad.

Besides leading an Anglican church, converted slave ship captain and hymn writer John Newton (1725-1807) also played a pivotal role in the public policy arena, in the decades-long fight against British slavery. William Wilberforce as a boy had become acquainted with Newton, who had served as his pastor for a time. But Wilberforce had later abandoned the

---

[3] Metaxas, Eric, *Amazing Grace: William Wilberforce and the Heroic Campaign to End Slavery*. San Francisco: Harper, 2007, p. 76.

Christian faith and embraced the life of the privileged, wasting his life away with drinking, gambling and partying.

Newton, an Anglican pastor, preached about what he saw and experienced as captain of slave ships. Newton had written a highly influential and widely distributed tract, "Thoughts upon the African Slave Trade." Through such eyewitness testimonies, of both slave traders and slaves, the horrible reality of the slave trade would begin to dawn on and awaken the consciences of the British people.

Newton's spiritual testimony, expressed in "Faith's Review and Expectation"–now the classic hymn "Amazing Grace," mirrored hope for a nation finally beginning to recognize its grievous sin:

```
Amazing Grace, how sweet the sound,
That saved a wretch like me.
I once was lost but now am found,
Was blind, but now, I see.
```

After experiencing his "great change" from decadence to discipleship, the young Wilberforce, now a Member of Parliament, sought the Anglican pastor's counsel about a vexing matter. Should he abandon the "secular" world of politics and pursue church ministry?

Newton had loved Wilberforce as a boy and had seen great promise in him, though for years that promise had seemed vain. Now seeing the Parliamentarian appear in his humble chapel, Newton told Wilberforce that he always confidently had hoped that God would bring Wilberforce to him once again.

The movie of Wilberforce and the abolition of the slave trade in Britain, *Amazing Grace*, presents a scene in which Wilberforce vents his vexation to the old seaman turned pastor, now sixty. Newton responds to Wilberforce's dilemma with directness:

```
Are you contemplating a life of solitude? People like
you too much to let you live a life of solitude. And
besides, Wilber, you have work to do.
Do it. Blow their dirty, filthy ships out of the
water.[4]
```

Newton saw a seamless spiritual and political calling on Wilberforce:

```
Maintain your friendship with [Prime Minister] Pitt,
continue in Parliament. Who knows that but for such a
time as this God has brought you into public life and
has a purpose for you.[5]
```

---

[4] This scene is available for viewing, along with other video clips, at http://www.amazinggracemovie.com. Accessed Nov. 29, 2013.

[5] "William Wilberforce," BBC web page,

Newton later reiterated this advice in a letter in which he summarized his counsel to the young statesman:

It is hoped and believed that the Lord has raised you up for the good of His church and for the good of the nation.

Even Wilberforce's good friend William Pitt, the politically focused Prime Minister who had expressed reservations about Wilberforce's conversion, advised him to exercise his newfound faith by pursuing legislation:

Surely the principles as well as the practice of Christianity are simple and lead not to meditation only, but to action.

As Wilberforce prayed one day, God laid on his heart a special message and mission, recorded in his diary entry of October 28, 1787:

God almighty has set before me two great objects: the suppression of the slave trade and the reformation of manners.

By "reformation of manners," Wilberforce referred to a society-wide transformation of the internalized moral principles and values that guide how people behave toward their fellow man. Nobles and other wealthy British allowed scant concern for the poor and downtrodden, reasoning perversely that God Himself sovereignly had destined such wretches to misery. Many of the poor lived in physical, psychological and spiritual squalor, with women and children faring worst in a heartless society where only the fittest survived.

Wilberforce emerged from seeking God and the counsel of others fully convinced of an unambiguous, providential mission. His ministry in the public square would provide the foundation from which to launch the campaign to reform moral sensibilities and abolish slavery. He embarked with fresh vigor on that mission, determined to use his divinely bequeathed talents, popularity and strategic skills to advance the Kingdom of God through both public policy and cultural transformation.

### Transforming the culture

William Wilberforce and his colleagues[6] in the cause of abolition embarked upon this mission with a brilliant strategy that instructs us today.

---

http://www.bbc.co.uk/religion/religions/christianity/people/williamwilberforce_1.shtml accessed Nov. 27, 2013.
[6] Wilberforce's colleagues were primarily evangelical Anglicans and included writers, ministers and evangelists, financiers, a mathematician, a brewer and other societal leaders.

While pursuing legal change through Parliament, they simultaneously pursued cultural and personal change through the arts, music, literature and other channels of cultural influence.

As my friends Bill Wichterman and Mark Rodgers explain,

Indeed, many of our policy objectives will only be achieved by a prior work or concurrent change in the cultural norms that shape the political realm. Legislation is never created in a vacuum, but in a "cultural context" in which people's beliefs and worldviews have largely already been shaped at a foundational level.

In short, the culture, both broadly and narrowly defined, is upstream from politics. Politics is more about reflecting the beliefs forged in other, more powerful "gatekeeping" institutions.

Wilberforce's two Great Objects [abolishing slavery and reforming "manners"] reflected this understanding. As a Member of Parliament, he sought to change the laws of the nation. But he leveraged his work in the political sphere by seeking to renew the culture of his times, to shape hearts and minds through other institutions, both as a means to an end and an end in itself.

The success of his efforts are a model for us as we seek to fashion just laws and renew American culture. Examining how Wilberforce changed England will help guide today's reformers in their efforts to create a better society.[7]

## A strategy on all fronts

Wilberforce's Christian colleagues, many of whom formed a group that became known as the "Clapham Sect," formed an incredibly talented and broad team of cultural change agents. These included poet William Cowper (1731-1800), writer Hannah More (1745-1833), musician Granville Sharp (1735-1813,) potter Josiah Wedgwood (1730-1795) and a former slave turned author, Olaudah Equiano (1745-1797).

Cowper stirred the hearts of English readers with anti-slavery poems like "The Negro's Complaint" (1793):

Is there, as ye sometimes tell us,

---

[7] Wichterman, William and Rodgers, Mark, "Making Goodness Fashionable," p. 202 in *Creating the Better Hour: Lessons from William Wilberforce*, ed. Chuck Stetson. Macon, GA: Stroud and Hall, 2007.

```
Is there one who reigns on high?
Has he bid you buy and sell us,
Speaking from his throne the sky?
Ask him, if your knotted scourges,
Matches, blood-extorting screws
Are the means that duty urges
Agents of his will to use?[8]
```

Wilberforce also developed a social marketing technique called "launchers"–sayings or objects designed to stir conversations and consideration of the issues. Potter Josiah Wedgwood provided one of the most famous and effective of these "launchers."

Wedgwood, credited with establishing the first pottery factory and mass marketing techniques such as direct mail and money-back guarantees, used science to develop a unique glaze that set Wedgwood pottery heads above the rest.[9] Wedgwood used his popular products and considerable creativity to stoke the public policy fight to end slavery.

Wedgwood's company designed a cameo of a black man, shackled hand and foot, kneeling and raising his hands and head upward, with a caption below that read simply, "Am I not a man and a brother?"[10] Wedgwood reproduced and donated hundreds of the black-on-white image to an anti-slavery society for distribution throughout society. Meanwhile, the image penetrated the world of fashion, as women began wearing it on bracelets and hairpins, while men used clay tobacco pipes engraved with the image.

### Challenging spiritual complacency and hypocrisy

Literary great Hannah More wrote penny tracts that even the poor could afford, such as "Thoughts on the Manners of the Great to General Society." She tore into the smug religious nominalism and hypocrisy that permeated British society, inoculated its citizens against true religion and allowed the slave trade to flourish in a nation supposedly committed to Christian principles:

```
When an acute and keen-eyed infidel measures your
lives with the rule by which you profess to walk, he
finds so little analogy between them, the copy is so
```

---

[8] Cowper, William, "The Poems of William Cowper." A reproduction of Cowper's works is available for purchase at http://www.amazon.com/dp/158960119X/ref=rdr_ext_tmb. Accessed Nov. 22, 2013.

[9] Wedgwood bequeathed to his family both a love for science and his company's wealth, which enabled his grandson to enjoy much leisure time instead of working–time which the young man, Charles Darwin, used to develop a theory of evolution.

[10] To view this image, see http://www.pbs.org/wgbh/aia/part2/2h67b.html.

unlike the pattern, that this inconsistency of yours
is the pass through which his most dangerous attack
is made.
He hears of a spiritual and self-denying religion; he
reads the beatitudes; he observes that the grand
artillery of the Gospel is planted against pride and
sensuality.
He then turns from the transcript of this perfect
original to the lives which pretend to be fashioned
by it.
There he sees, with triumphant derision, that pride,
self-love, luxury, self-sufficiency, unbounded
personal expense, and an inordinate appetite for
pleasure, are reputable vices in the eyes of many of
those who acknowledge the truth of the Christian
doctrines.[11]

More challenged her countrymen to match their walk to their talk:
Let us, then, be consistent, and we shall never be
contemptible, even in the eyes of our enemies. Let
not the unbeliever say that we have one set of
opinions for our theory, and another for our
practice; that to the vulgar-
> We show the rough and thorny way to heav'n,
> While we the primrose path of dalliance tread.
If there be a model which we profess to admire, let
us square our lives by it. …[I]f the Bible be in
truth the Word of God, as we profess to believe, we
need look no further for a consummate pattern.
"If the Lord be God, let us follow Him": if Christ be
a sacrifice for sin, let Him be also to us the
example of an holy life.[12]

More also encouraged female education and helped establish Sunday
School in places like Blagdon in Somerset, a notorious mining village whose
inhabitants were described as "ignorant, profane and vicious beyond belief."[13]

---

[11] More, Hannah, *Thoughts on the Manners of the Great*, included in *Profession and Practice*, Henry Craik, ed., 1916. Vol. IV. http://www.bartleby.com/209/908.html accessed Nov. 23, 2013.

[12] More, Hannah, *Thoughts on the Manners of the Great*, included in *Profession and Practice*, Henry Craik, ed., 1916. Vol. IV. http://www.bartleby.com/209/908.html accessed Nov. 26, 2013.

[13] Roberts, Making English Morals: Voluntary Association and Moral Reform in England, 1787-1886. 64. Mark Smith and Stephen Taylor (editors), Evangelicalism in the Church of England C.1790-C.1890: A Miscellany (Woodbridge, Suffolk: The Boydell Press, 2004), 10, 11. Cited by Dr. Stuart Piggin in "Public Lecture on William Wilberforce and his Impact on

More realized that anti-slavery laws alone could not transform Britain. True change required personal transformation nationwide, as the British people learned to move beyond the shallow rhetoric of nominal religion and truly align their lives with the principles of the living God.

## Leveraging the courts for justice

Granville Sharp and his family held concerts in their home, and he published one of the first anti-slavery tracts. To defend slaves through the legal system, Sharp studied law but found that few in England, including judges, saw slaves as meriting justice or possessing natural rights.

Sharp's knowledge of English law and individual rights finally bore fruit, as he advised lawyers in *Somerset v. Stewart*, a 1772 case defending a captured slave. That case produced a landmark judgment that not only extended to a slave the right of *habeas corpus* (providing a person under arrest with access to the courts for review of his case) but also helped establish the breakthrough recognition that English law did not uphold slavery. As one of the attorneys in the case had argued, "the air of England is too pure to be breathed by a slave."[14]

William Cowper enshrined that sentiment in a highly popular poem, "The Time-Piece":

```
I had much rather be myself the slave,
And wear the bonds, than fasten them on him.
We have no slaves at home-Then why abroad?
And they themselves once ferried o'er the wave,
That parts us, are emancipate and loos'd.
Slaves cannot breathe in England; if their lungs
Receive our air, that moment they are free;
They touch our country, and their shackles fall.
That's noble, and bespeaks a nation proud
And jealous of the blessing. Spread it then,
And let it circulate through ev'ry vein
Of all your empire; that, where Britain's power
Is felt, mankind may feel her mercy too.[15]
```

Australia." http://www.marketplaceconnections.com/archive/PDF/Wilberforce.pdf accessed Nov. 22, 2013.

[14] Wiecek, Sources of Antislavery Constitutionalism, 21. Cited in Powers, Emma L., "The Newsworthy Somerset Case: Repercussions in Virginia," article on The Colonial Williamsburg website. http://research.history.org/Historical_Research/Research_Themes/ThemeEnslave/Somerset.cfm#n13 accessed Oct. 9, 2014.

[15] Cowper, William, "The Task." http://www.amazon.com/The-task-William-Cowper/dp/1175842109 accessed Oct. 9, 2014.

## Preaching public policy

Evangelist and social reformer John Wesley wrote a popular tract, "Thoughts on Slavery," in which he laid bare the personal corruption and the eternal consequences of trading in men:

Now must not the reasonable and humane nature of those who order these dreadful tortures, as well as those who execute them, be changed into devilish, who can thus put their fellow creatures to such extravagant, such exquisite torment?
And for what? Often, even for that which their tormentors themselves would have done if in their situation. If thro' the exertion of barbarous and unjust laws, the natural attendant on slavery, these our hapless fellow men are doomed to die, yet in their deaths, let it at least be remembered that they are men.
We hear with horror and detestation of some such execution in the inquisitions and under some tyrannic governments; but these inhumanities are certainly contrary to the genius and disposition of the British nation, and quite abhorrent of its laws, which do not allow of tortures either in punishment, or to extort confessions.
How Britons can so readily admit of a change in their disposition and sentiments, as to practice in America what they abhor and detested in Britain, can be accounted for on no other principle, but as being the natural effect of slave-keeping, which as the celebrated Montesquieu observes, "insensibly accustoms those who are in the practice of it, to want all moral virtues, to become haughty, hasty, hard-hearted, passionate, voluptuous and cruel."
The evil attendant on the condition of the poor slaves will end with their lives, and the merciful father of the family of mankind will doubtless look on their deep affliction, and where their hearts are thereby humbled, requite them good in another state of existence for their sufferings in this: but with respect to their lordly oppressors, this horrible abuse of their fellow men, will doubtless extend its baneful influence even into the regions of eternity.[16]

---

[16] Wesley, John, *Thoughts upon Slavery*, Electronic Edition, p. 25. This work is the property of the University of North Carolina at Chapel Hill. It may be used freely by individuals for

A former slave published an autobiographical account, *The Interesting Narrative of the Life of Olaudah Equiano, or Gustavus Vassa, the African,* that appealed to the better nature and conscience of his British readers. He introduces his work with a gentle entreaty:

> Permit me, with the greatest deference and respect, to lay at your feet the following genuine narrative; the chief design of which is to excite in your august assemblies a sense of compassion for the miseries which the slave trade has entailed on my unfortunate countrymen.
>
> By the horrors of that trade was I first torn away from all the tender connections that were naturally dear to my heart; but these, through the mysterious ways of Providence, I ought to regard as infinitely more than compensated by the introduction I have thence obtained to the knowledge of the Christian religion, and of a nation which, by its liberal sentiments, its humanity, the glorious freedom of its government, and its proficiency in arts and sciences, has exalted the dignity of human nature.
>
> May the God of heaven inspire your hearts with peculiar benevolence on that important day when the question of abolition is to be discussed, when thousands, in consequence of your determination, are to look for happiness or misery![17]

British readers devoured tens of thousands of Olaudah Equiano's immensely popular autobiography. One cannot help but marvel at the gracious tone and winsome approach of this slave who suffered the lash and loss of loved ones at the hands of the British.

This gracious and forgiving approach of many within the abolition movement not only served to win many converts to the side of abolition but also demonstrated the true Christianity about which they wrote.

### Real Christianity

Wilberforce wrote a plain-speaking yet winsomely expressed volume on living a genuine Christian faith, *A Practical View of the Prevailing Religious System of Professed Christians, in the Higher and Middle Classes in This*

---

research, teaching and personal use as long as this statement of availability is included in the text. http://docsouth.unc.edu/church/wesley/wesley.html accessed November 26, 2013.

[17] Equiano, Olaudah *The Interesting Narrative of the Life of Olaudah Equiano, or Gustavus Vassa, the African,* preface. Public domain: http://www.amazon.com/Interesting-Narrative-Olaudah-Equiano-Gustavus-ebook/dp/B00849XAN8 accessed November 26, 2013.

*Country, Contrasted with Real Christianity* (popularly abbreviated as *Real Christianity*) that flew off bookstore shelves. Wilberforce's humble, sometimes rambling but piercingly forthright writing struck at the heart of religious hypocrisy and pretention and poured out water for souls thirsting for revival.

*Real Christianity* exposed and contrasted the nominal faith that had permeated and inoculated British society with the true, vibrant and demanding Christian faith. Keenly perceiving a truth that still applies to our times, Wilberforce recognized that the recipe for reaching a decadent society was not accommodation or compromise but a bold and courageous contrast of devout and uncompromising Christianity.

Wilberforce warned his fellow believers against vainly pursuing a strategy of appeasement in the name of evangelism:

```
Some well-meaning people have thought that by joining
in the customs and practices of those who lack faith,
they would soften the prejudices people sometimes
feel against religion; by doing this, these people
have mistakenly hoped to counteract the reputation
that religion has for being austere and gloomy. They
hoped to win it a more pleasant reputation, thinking
that this would help them to have an opportunity to
explain their faith to others.
The damage that may be done through this approach is
too great to be described. At any rate, it is a
policy that is particularly unsuitable to our
thoughtless and dissipated era, especially when we
have already sunk to the depths that we have.
In circumstances like these, the best course of
action is to boldly point out the differences between
the adherents of "God and Ba'al." The expediency of
this action is confirmed by another consideration-
that when people are aware that they are faced with
the challenge, their spirits rise to the necessary
level; they make up their minds to bear hardship and
brave danger, to persevere in spite of fatigue and
opposition.
On the other hand, if they regard an event as being
easy and ordinary, they are apt to fall asleep over
their work and fail to accomplish much of anything at
all. Working from this characteristic of human
nature, then, we should boldly draw the line of
demarcation between the friends of faith and its
enemies; the separation between the two should be
clear and obvious.[18]
```

As a prominent Member of Parliament, Wilberforce recognized that the law is a teacher of right and wrong and a tool for restraining evil. He did not hesitate to prescribe the infusion of Christian principles into the laws of the land.

> Christianity raises a civilization's morals higher than they were ever to be found in the pagan world. Christianity has always and everywhere improved a society's character as it also spread comfort, particularly to the poor and the weak (those whom from the beginning Christianity has cared for most).[19] Nor should we only concern ourselves with our personal conduct, though this line of action will always be the most effective for people of authority and influence to promote the cause of goodness. But we should also encourage virtue in all our interactions with others, and at the same time express our disapproval of sin.
> We should help enforce the laws that our forefathers' wisdom put in place to guard us against the worst moral infractions. We should support and take part in any plans that are formed for the advancement of morality. Above all else, we must work to instruct and improve the next generation.[20]

Yet just as he had experienced personally the beguiling nature of vice and the wretched inability to attain moral excellence, Wilberforce knew that a nation no more than individuals could pretend successfully to Christian virtues. He knew that eventually the true inner sinful nature would win, and that vice would triumph over pretense.

> But all this will be a fruitless effort if we do not bring back the prevalence of evangelical Christianity. We cannot hope to sustain, much less revive, our nation's fainting morality without the support of a sincere and a living faith.
> We cannot change morals from the outside in; we need an internal living principle that works from the inside and out. Otherwise, we may succeed for a while

---

[18] Wilberforce, William, *A Practical View of the Prevailing Religious System of Professed Christians, in the Higher and Middle Classes in This Country, Contrasted with Real Christianity*, originally published in 1797 and updated and abridged by Ellyn Sanna, Uhrichsville, OH: Barbour Publishing, 1999, p. 252. Used by permission of Barbour Publishing, Inc.

[19] Ibid, 31.

[20] Ibid, 253.

forcing society's morals to take the shape we wanted, but they will soon relax back to their natural shape. That is why anyone who is serious about our country's welfare should make every effort to revive the Christianity of our better days.[21]

## Changing laws

While pursuing spiritual and cultural change, Wilberforce and his companions recognized that laws guide a nation, teaching people right and wrong, punishing evil and rewarding good.

As the Apostle Paul explained to the Romans in his treatise on the proper function of government,

For rulers are not a cause of fear for good behavior, but for evil. Do you want to have no fear of authority? Do what is good and you will have praise from the same; for it is a minister of God to you for good.
But if you do what is evil, be afraid; for it does not bear the sword for nothing; for it is a minister of God, an avenger who brings wrath on the one who practices evil.
Therefore it is necessary to be in subjection, not only because of wrath, but also for conscience' sake.[22]

Charles Colson explains the need for Christian principles to penetrate the law, through the influence of followers of Christ:

If the real benefits of the Judeo-Christian ethic and influence in secular society were understood, it would be anxiously sought out, even by those who *repudiate* the Christian faith. The influence of the kingdom of God in the public arena is good for society as a whole.[23]
The kingdom of God provides unique moral imperatives that can cause men and women to rise above their natural egoism to serve the greater good.[24]
[T]he fact that God reigns can be manifest through political means, whenever the citizens of the Kingdom

---

[21] Ibid, pp. 252-253.
[22] Romans 13:3-5.
[23] Charles Colson and Ellen Santilli, *God and Government,* Grand Rapids: Zondervan, 1987, updated 2007. Kindle location 4982. Used by permission of Zondervan, www.zondervan.com.
[24] Ibid, location 5006.

of God bring His light to bear on the institutions of
the kingdoms of man.[25]

As a prominent Member of Parliament, Wilberforce seized every
opportunity to speak out and lobby for the end of the slave trade. He gained a
seat in Parliament in 1780 and during 1785 experienced a new life in Christ.
Wilberforce likely had no inkling at the outset that his abolition mission from
God would take over two decades to win a major legislative victory and
nearly five decades to see Parliament pass the law that finally ended slavery.[26]

### Multi-pronged legislative strategy

A successful legislative campaign typically involves (a) a coalition of
influential and determined legislators; (b) public policy activists and
messengers unified in the goal of passing the bill; (c) skillfully written
legislation that highlights the rationale for the legislation while anticipating,
minimizing and neutralizing objections; (d) well-documented evidence and
testimony; and (e) stirring human interest stories that drive the point home
with emotional, motivating impact.

Wilberforce was a popular and charismatic Member of Parliament,
regarded as one of its finest orators. Yet he and his popularity alone could
not carry the herculean fight to change the law on slavery, which formed the
foundation of a huge segment of England's economy and the lynchpin of its
colonial enterprise.

In May 1787, Wilberforce joined his friends William Pitt and William
Grenville under an oak tree for a history-changing strategy session. That day,
they decided to launch the legislative drive to abolish slavery. Providentially,
both his companions under the oak tree that day would eventually rise to the
rank of Prime Minister and help lead the cause.

The abolition movement earned bipartisan support, including that of the
aptly named Charles Fox, a canny liberal legislator, licentious womanizer
and arch-rival of Pitt when the latter served as Prime Minister. Conservative
statesman Edmund Burke, who famously warned, "All that is needed for the
triumph of evil is for good men to do nothing," also supported the abolition
movement.

Still, support for the movement ebbed and flowed. Sometimes other
issues such as the war with France separated abolition allies, and sometimes

---

[25] Ibid, location 7986.
[26] The passage of the Slave Trade Act of 1807 abolished the trade of slaves in the British
Empire, and the passage of the Slavery Abolition Act of 1833 effectively abolished slavery
altogether in the British Empire.

239

pragmatic considerations of Britain's economic interests proved overpowering.

Pitt sympathized with the anti-slavery movement and generally proved a valuable ally. But Pitt also highly regarded political caution and the pragmatism of power, which at times conflicted with the zeal and determination of the politically independent Wilberforce. When Wilberforce reluctantly but on principle opposed Pitt regarding the war with France, it cost Wilberforce not only the benefit of unity with his powerful ally but also the favor of the king, who in retaliation dropped his support for abolition and turned decidedly against the movement.

## Not for the faint-hearted

The long abolition battle would play out in a series of significant and demoralizing losses, occasionally interspaced with an encouraging step forward. John Wesley's letter, written just a few days before he died, to Wilberforce would prove prophetic:

Unless the divine power has raised you up to be as Athanasius[27] contra mundum [against the world], I see not how you can go through your glorious enterprise in opposing that execrable villainy which is the scandal of religion, of England, and of human nature. Unless God has raised you up for this very thing, you will be worn out by the opposition of men and devils. But if God be for you, who can be against you? Are all of them together stronger than God? Oh be not weary of well doing![28]

Before a crucial vote on abolition in 1791, Wilberforce addressed his colleagues in Parliament with a stirring speech:

Whatever may be its success, I attach my happiness to their cause and shall never relinquish it. Supported as I have been, indeed, such a desertion would be most despicable. I have already gained for the wretched Africans the recognition of their claim to the rank of human beings, and I doubt not but the Parliament of Great Britain will no longer withhold from them the rights of human nature![29]

---

[27] Athanasius of Alexandria (c. 296-393), who served as a leading bishop and theologian in Egypt, spent 17 years in five exiles ordered by four emperors during his fight to defend the orthodox Christian doctrine of the unity of the Godhead from the false teachings of Arianism.
[28] Wesley, John, quoted in "William Wilberforce," BBC website
http://www.bbc.co.uk/religion/religions/christianity/people/williamwilberforce_1.shtml
accessed December 1, 2014.

The bill lost, 88-163. A year later, a second motion for abolition lost again, 87-234. Defeat after defeat after defeat continued for another 15 years.

### Evidence and strategy

Wilberforce studied the massive evidence about the slave trade assembled by abolitionist Thomas Clarkson and his anti-slavery activists. The evidence included documented details of the horrors on the ships that transported slaves, eyewitness accounts of beatings and inhumanities inflicted on the slaves, and an accounting of the massive numbers of slaves who died of disease and malnutrition or were murdered when thrown overboard during the journey to slave markets.

Wilberforce and his companions collected the carefully documented evidence, which he presented to a committee of the Privy Council during 1788. The promising effort failed, however, when key witnesses changed their testimony, apparently due to threats and bribes.

The abolitionists adopted a strategy of incrementalism that acknowledged the political improbability of immediately abolishing slavery and adopted as a crucial first step the ending of the slave trade. An incrementalist strategy can peel off opponents and provide skittish but sympathetic moderates with political cover, all the while building support and momentum toward the ultimate goal. The abolitionists reasoned that securing the end of the slave trade would provide a tipping point after which slavery itself would become vulnerable to abolition.

That strategy led to Parliament first passing a bill in 1806 that banned the slave trade with enemy France. The new ban drastically shrank the volume of British slave trading, severely weakening the industry.

The ascension to power of an abolitionist Prime Minister, William Grenville (along with Wilberforce and Pitt, one of the three aforementioned "oak-tree" strategists of 1787), coupled with the wholesale addition to Parliament of 100 Irish members, most of whom opposed slavery, also proved opportune.

In 1807, Parliament passed a bill banning the *slave trade* everywhere.

### Denouement

That 1807 law, however, did not lead to the end of *slavery* altogether, as the abolitionists had hoped. It would not be until 1833 that Parliament would pass the landmark legislation that put a final end to slavery in Great Britain.

---

[29] Wilberforce, William, speech to Parliament April 19, 1791.

By 1833, William Wilberforce had been retired from Parliament for eight years, devoting his time to continuing the cultural drive against slavery and also to other social reforms, such as founding the Society for the Prevention of Cruelty to Animals (SPCA). Despite having gained passage of the bill to end the slave trade, the earnest and humble legislator seemed to take little consolation in his hard-earned victories.

In a letter to a friend, he wrote:

> I am filled with the deepest compunction from the consciousness of my having made so poor a use of the talents committed to my stewardship. The heart knows its own bitterness.
> We alone know ourselves the opportunities we have enjoyed, and the comparative use we have made of time…. To your friendly ear … I breathe out my secret sorrows. I always spoke and voted according to the dictates of my conscience, for the public and not for my own private interest….
> Yet I am but too conscious of numerous and great sins of omission, many opportunities of doing good whether not at all or very inadequately improved.[30]

On July 26, 1833, Wilberforce learned that the House of Commons had passed the bill to abolish slavery in the British Empire; it would become effective within a month. He had at last witnessed the achievement of the first of the two "Great Objects" God had given him to pursue nearly 46 years earlier.

Three days later, William Wilberforce died.

The government suspended all public business for Wilberforce's funeral. Enormous crowds watching the stately funeral procession and scores of British leaders and royalty paid tribute to Wilberforce, ultimately laying their great statesman to rest in Westminster Abbey with great pomp and honor.

That event highlighted the popularity that Wilberforce and the values of his moral reform movement had earned among the British people. Mocking had turned to admiration. The people deeply mourned and honored the man who, by contrasting the evils of slavery with the compassion of Christ, had helped open their eyes to the contest between good and evil and the opportunity to take God's side in the battle.

This public display of affection and approbation illustrated the achievement of Wilberforce's second Great Object–the transformation of British moral sensibilities. The sensitizing of the British conscience and the

---

[30] Wilberforce, William, quoted in *Life of William Wilberforce*, Vol. 5, by R.I. Wilberforce and S. Wilberforce, London: John Murray, 1839, p. 230.

consequent transformation of its "Vanity Fair" culture of selfish indulgence and cold-heartedness helped form the foundation for the Elizabethan Era and its great works of social reform and cultural renewal.

Revival marked the early decades of the nineteenth century in England, and the Methodist movement in particular reached into every level of British society, rich and poor, young and old. Some historians credit the spiritual and moral revival of this period with saving England from violent uprisings and revolutions. As leaders and society at large better understood and more fervently embraced the social implications of Christian teachings, social reform through public policy flourished.

Noting that economic disparity and desperation had portended revolutions in both England and France, French historian and philosopher Élie Halévy contrasted England's reformations with the Jacobinic terror and tyranny that followed the French revolution. He succinctly summarized the divergence:

"Methodism was the antidote to Jacobinism."[31]

When the new slavery abolition law officially took effect, every slave freed that day–indeed, the entire British Empire–owed a debt to the humble Christian who had lived by the conviction that faith must translate into action. Wilberforce's joint public policy and culture-changing mission, ordained and empowered by God, had exposed hypocrisy and revitalized a nominally religious people while also rescuing thousands of human beings from misery and death.

The abolition and cultural reformation movement doubtless also delivered the British Empire from the same fate that had befallen the morally decadent and heartless Roman Empire. God used a small band of committed Christians, from pulpit to public square, to transform an entire empire through a great repentance, a turning from hypocrisy and inhumanity to real faith and compassion.

Whether America follows a similar path of repentance and reformation or descends to disintegration depends on Christians like you and me.

---

[31] Halévy, Élie, *History of the English People in the Nineteenth Century*, Vol. 1, 1913. Cited by Walsh, J. D. (1975). "Elie Halévy and the Birth of Methodism," Transactions of the Royal Historical Society, Fifth Series, Vol. 25, pp. 1-20.

# Chapter 20:
# *Our challenge and opportunity*

*"Therefore, we are ambassadors for Christ,*
*as though God were making an appeal through us;*
*we beg you on behalf of Christ, be reconciled to God."*
–II Corinthians 5:20

What would an American movement look like that aimed to turn our nation from apostasy and toward God and His principles?

Before we can launch such a movement, we must first humble ourselves, repent and pray for forgiveness and spiritual revival.[1] Once aligned with God and His purposes, we can reach out to our countrymen and pursue national transformation with three vital and integrated components:

1. *Personal character.*
2. *Cultural engagement.*
3. *Law.*

## Personal character

As ambassadors of Christ, we must represent Him well, by living and loving as He did when He walked among us.

A few personal questions illustrate what that means:

- Do I sympathetically care for and sacrificially serve others?
- Do I gently speak the truth in love?
- Do I associate with the lowly, help the poor and defend the vulnerable?
- Do I readily and candidly admit my shortcomings?

---

[1] "If ... My people who are called by My name humble themselves and pray and seek My face and turn from their wicked ways, then I will hear from heaven, will forgive their sin and will heal their land" –II Chronicles 7:13-14.

244

- Do I show grace and compassion to those who've wandered far from God?

Many of these qualities that Jesus so perfectly demonstrated caused anyone at all receptive to God to love Him. Even His enemies–those threatened by His truth and authority–could not prosecute Jesus on the basis of His character.

### Caring for others

In particular, we cannot underestimate the quality of caring for others. People instinctively know whether or not we care about them, and that makes all the difference.

A saying attributed to President Theodore Roosevelt puts it succinctly: "No one cares how much you know, until they know how much you care." If people perceive that we do not truly care about them and their welfare, while they may still respect our good deeds and even our passion for what we believe, they will not let us near their hearts.

Cold hearts do not warm hearts. And the heart is where God meets us.

If I … have not love, I am a noisy gong or a clanging cymbal.[2]

The secular philosopher Jean Jacques Rousseau attacked Christians in public policy on these grounds–that they simply did not care.

Christianity as a religion is entirely spiritual, occupied solely with heavenly things; the country of the Christian is not of this world. He does his duty, indeed, but does it with profound indifference to the good or ill success of his cares.

Provided he has nothing to reproach himself with, it matters little to him whether things go well or ill here on earth. If the State is prosperous, he hardly dares to share in the public happiness, for fear he may grow proud of his country's glory; if the State is languishing, he blesses the hand of God that is hard upon His people.[3]

We must engage in public policy not merely out of duty but enthusiastically as a means of *helping people*.

For example, we must recognize that it matters not only that healthcare policy respects Christian conscience, but also that it extends healing and hope to the *poor* and *vulnerable*. We must show that we support adult stem

---

[2] I Corinthians 13:1.

[3] Rousseau, Jean Jacques, *The Social Contract or Principles of Political Right,* Book IV, Chapter VIII. http://www.bartleby.com/168/408.html accessed Dec. 26, 2013.

cell research not only because it respects the life of the early human embryo but also because it provides the fastest path to cures and therapies for *those who suffer* from disease. We must show that we advocate sexual risk avoidance education not only because it comports with Judeo-Christian sexual mores but also because it enables *children and teens* to affirm their worth and pursue their dreams. We must explain that protecting religious freedom protects the free exercise of thought and speech not just for people of faith but for *all* Americans.

## Cultural engagement

Because law typically follows culture rather than the other way around, we cannot effectively implement ideas and ideals in public policy unless those ideas and ideals have permeated the culture and the public mind.

While the evangelical political movement helped elect Presidents Carter, Reagan and both Bushes, more recent elections suggest that evangelical political influence is declining. A political movement cannot sustain itself apart from a parallel cultural movement.

Even a large number of Christians cannot politically dominate a secular, multicultural country. Unless we learn how to *persuade* effectively those outside the Church to join the ranks, we will see the life-affirming, compassionate and proven principles we value fade from public policy.

That means our task is to engage the popular culture with a message that resonates not only with believers, but with seekers and skeptics as well. We can't expect to win friends by simply lambasting the culture, but if we can tease out the good from the evil and demonstrate how the culture is harming or helping people, we may at least gain some listeners.

Engaging the culture means entering the culture, participating in the culture, understanding the culture. Entertainment, the arts, literature, education, philosophy, science, media—we should engage in every avenue that imparts values to our culture. We must venture into our equivalents of the Areopagus, where the Apostle Paul delivered his Mars Hill address[4] to thinkers, skeptics and no doubt some eventual believers.

## Venturing outside the Church

We have to venture outside our safe churches, read books besides the Bible and interact with people who think outside Christian orthodoxy. We

---

[4] Acts 17:16-33.

can do so with the assurance that God and His truth can readily withstand all the threats that any culture, philosophy or person might pose.

Some pastors and Christian teachers have studied the culture and are equipping their congregations to analyze and address prevailing ideologies, literature, movies, music, science and art. They recognize that while God has called them personally to church ministry, He also has sent their congregants to use their God-given talents in the *agora*—the marketplace.

Many church members hold careers that profoundly impact the culture. They can reach individuals who might never set foot inside a church but will respond to someone who lives in their world, understands their perspective, and shows genuine concern for their personal welfare.

### Resisting the deceptive safety of separatism

On the other hand, some church leaders have studied intensively theological and devotional topics but never really have ventured outside the seminary curriculum to study the arts or popular culture. They may even pride themselves in this fact.

I used to pat myself on the back for not watching television, until I realized that I often had no idea what people were talking about regarding the popular culture. How could I engage with them if I had no knowledge of their reference points?

Given this narrow perspective, such pastors and teachers may focus all their attention on guiding congregants to church ministries and missions while neglecting the value of ambassadorial artists, writers and filmmakers. Given a choice between "spiritual" or "secular" occupations, this focus implies, the truly devout will always choose the "spiritual."

Church leaders with a separatist mindset may also leave a distinct impression that pursuing careers in the culture-engaging arena is either too morally risky or a hopeless cause. One can sympathize with such concerns. Aggressive secularism in education, literature, the arts and entertainment has eroded Christian values drastically. Lamentably, some Church leaders have reacted not by equipping their congregations to critically understand the culture and defend their faith but by simply adopting an anti-intellectual, anti-science, anti-arts stance.

If we adopt such a stance, pretty soon we are known not by what we support but by what we oppose. Rather than being known for caring for and reaching out to others, we are known simply for divorcing the rest of society.
[I]f I deliver up my body to be burned, but have not love, I gain nothing.[5]

Given this unfortunate loss of cultural impact through Christian self-segregation, it is not surprising that we face a cultural landscape increasingly bereft of and hostile to Christian influence. Besides leading individuals away from God, this cultural antagonism shuts out faith values from public policy. As a result, laws more and more mirror godlessness rather than godly principles, and evil spreads without restraint.

The "safe" and "spiritual" path of separatism turns out to be the most dangerous and deadly path of all.

Unless we radically expand and enhance our efforts to engage the culture, we stand to lose both the culture and the law, regardless of constitutional guarantees. The Courts have thoroughly demonstrated how easily they can reinterpret the paper protections of the Constitution and remold its principles to accommodate shifts in the culture.

### *Imagine this*

The task of understanding, engaging and influencing the culture remains immensely challenging but not insurmountable.

Think about some of the most profound changes in American history—the eighteenth-century American Revolution, the nineteenth-century abolition of slavery, and the twentieth century civil rights movement. Just as William Wilberforce and his Clapham colleagues did in England, each American movement drew upon culture-changing channels such as literature, religion, music and the arts as well as the news media, social networking and political protest and discourse.

Thomas Paine's secular "Common Sense" polemic for a political revolution and Jonathan Mayhew's stirring sermons convinced once-loyal subjects of the Crown to reclaim their rights from tyrannical King George. Harriet Beecher Stowe's *Uncle Tom's Cabin* helped fuel the work of a network of abolitionists, most prominently Evangelical Protestants, who awakened their countrymen's consciences. Freedom Rides, movies like "To Kill a Mockingbird" and public events such as Martin Luther King, Jr.'s "I Have a Dream" speech built pressure for civil rights.

In each case, a profound shift in the public's perspective opened the door to political action. The law–the US Constitution, the Fourteenth Amendment and the Civil Rights Act of 1964–followed the culture. Without a cultural movement, legal progress would have been unattainable. Without the law, the cultural movement would have been vain.

---

[5] 1 Corinthians 13:3.

## Building a culture bridge

But if people of faith have lost touch with the culture by cloistering ourselves inside the Church, how do we even start to reengage?

First, we can adjust our perspective on cultural contributions–art, literature, music, entertainment and the like–that are not expressly Christian.

When my wife Amy and I first began to homeschool our children, we took pains to shield them from many books and movies that did not spring from a Christian viewpoint. Understandably, we wanted them to learn truth first, and this approach is particularly appropriate for young children.

I value homeschooling for the ability it affords to customize educational approaches to individual children, to integrate academic learning with real-life experiences and to build faith and family values. In retrospect, however, my wife Amy and I wish we had made more room for critical thinking in our homeschooling approach with our older children. Rather than simply censoring or condemning much non-Christian literature, art and entertainment as missing the mark, we wish we had helped our older children more to critically examine materials and ideas, to help them discern elements of truth and error, beauty and corruption, helpfulness and harmfulness.

In fact, Amy now heads a private Christian school, Lorien Wood in Vienna, Virginia, that employs such an approach.

As the school's website explains,

The Redemptive Education model recognizes that "all truth is God's truth" and finds valuable content from both "sacred" and "secular" materials and sources.[6]

Rather than evaluating literature, music, art and other culture-shaping works as simply either "godly and good" or "secular and bad," the Redemptive Education approach aims to help students identify those qualities in the works that reflect God's principles and those qualities that stand at odds with God's principles.

As a practical example, students at Lorien Wood study the Romantic period of literature, which emphasized the individual, the physical senses, emotions, imagination and nature. Students begin with a biblical understanding that God created us as emotional and imaginative beings, placed us in the midst of a glorious natural creation and assigned us inestimable value. Romantic literature might *accord* with biblical principles when it highlights natural beauty, creative freedom or human innovation. Romantic literature might *conflict* with biblical principles when it portrays

---

[6] Lorien Wood School website, http://www.lorienwood.org/about-us/redemptiveeducation.cfm accessed online Dec. 26, 2013.

human beings as supreme, or elevates nature as god or rejects rational thought. Finally, Lorien Wood educators challenge students to consider how the study of Romantic literature might equip them to better understand and participate in God's redemptive work.

If Christians approach the popular culture in like fashion, we will not quickly dismiss a work of art, music or literature because it is not sacred or has elements not in accord with Scripture. Instead we will seek to understand critically where the work *syncs* with God's principles and where it *diverges*. We come to realize that rather than merely posing a threat to our faith, cultural works may also pose opportunities–for us to develop personally and also to build bridges with others.

The result of this open and analytical perspective is that Christians become less fearful, less judgmental, more discerning and more conversant about culture. By examining and interacting with the culture that most people swim in daily, we expand our own horizons and better understand how others us think and develop moral values.

Sharing culture forms a bridge.

### *Hope on the horizon*

Thankfully, a good number of Christian colleges and universities have recognized the value of preparing students not only for church and mission ministries but also for careers in the arts, entertainment, writing and other culture-impacting arenas. Meanwhile, the explosion of social media has democratized access to the public, which means that Christians enjoy opportunities to impact large numbers of people even without major funding. Indy films mean aspiring directors no longer need MGM's millions to make a movie.

As mentioned in the chapter on human trafficking, my friends Dr. Bill and Laurie Bolthouse, a Christian physician and his wife, traveled with their family to Cambodia on a medical mission. They had no idea of the amazing, culture-impacting journey on which that mission would take them.

The website for the film *Trade of Innocents* tells the story:

In 2007, Bill and Laurie Bolthouse found themselves and their three daughters, Meredith, age 10, Madison, 10, and Molly, 8, in Phnom Penh, Cambodia. Bill, a family physician, volunteered to go there for a Denver based not-for-profit organization sending specialty surgical teams to Cambodia.
During their stay, Laurie took their daughters to the beach for a vacation, and while there they hosted a dinner for an anti-trafficking team and seven young

girls who had recently been rescued from a brothel.
The evening was momentous for the family as the
Bolthouse girls came away from it deeply touched and
angry that such an atrocity as sex slavery of
children exists.
Their bedtime prayer that night was "God, where are
you and what are you going to do?"
The answer to that prayer came a few months later
when writer/director Christopher Bessette went to
Phnom Penh to film this same organization for a
Canadian TV show. His direct experiences and the
things he learned led to the vision for the movie. In
November 2009, through nothing less than a miraculous
dream, the Bolthouses and Mr. Bessette finally
connected on the possibility of making a movie. Their
shared goal was not only to making a compelling film
on a difficult subject but also to raise awareness
and move people to action. And so "Trade of
Innocents" was born.[7]

The movie that the Bolthouses produced and Bessette directed starred
actors Dermot Mulroney and Academy Award Winner Mira Sorvino, who
played an American couple who had lost their own child and later in life had
a chance to protect a girl from human traffickers. *Trade of Innocents* stands
as a prime example of Christians using the arts to influence culture, and the
film is motivating viewers worldwide to take action to address the plight of
human trafficking victims.

Similar creative ventures in the arts, literature, social media and yet-to-be
introduced new avenues for cultural influence offer Christians opportunities
to regain lost ground and reengage in the culture. Perhaps you, your children
or your friends possess God-given interests and talents just waiting to be
employed in such ways. Take the risk, invest in the preparation and dive into
the arena armed with God's courage, the aroma of the Holy Spirit and the
love of Christ.

## Law

If a culture is heading in a certain direction, public policy can accelerate
that momentum. The law serves as teacher, and many people shift their view
of right and wrong based on what is declared legal.

---

[7] "Trade of Innocents" website http://www.tradeofinnocents.com.au/about.html accessed
October 11, 2014.

The law is also powerful and, backed by government force or threat, holds the potential to prevent misguided sectors of society from engaging in wrongdoing. Such a mob-defeating legal process may take decades, as demonstrated by the deeply resisted anti-segregation efforts in the South. Nevertheless, even in the face of opposing culture, laws can protect a minority from the majority and the weak and vulnerable from the powerful and exploitative.

As Romans 13:3-4 makes clear, governments retain power under God for the purpose of enforcing justice and righteousness. The proper function of government is to restrain evil, through threat or use of force, and to establish good, through the rule of law.

History has shown, however, that without checks on power and constant vigilance, rulers tend to turn into tyrants and ruthless governments can exploit, abuse and even kill their own people.

So rather than leaving the power of government in the hands of the ruthless, the godless and the heartless, we must fight without rest for justice, righteousness and compassion. Rather than divorcing the biblical mandates to pursue justice and to make disciples, we must *rejoin* them and carry out our complete responsibility as followers of Christ.

### Laying the circuitry for spiritual life

We spread the Good News *and* help the poor. We make disciples *and* bring healing to the sick. We set spiritual prisoners free *and* rescue the victims of human trafficking, religious persecution and domestic violence.

Simultaneously pursuing evangelism and good works hardly represents a strange new approach to faith; it is the imitation of Christ.

This is the heart of the concept of *faith steps*–that by leading by example and encouraging individuals and societies to take steps toward God, we pave the way for individuals to receive the Good News of salvation in Jesus Christ. By demonstrating our love through policies that reach out to and help others, we light the way to the God who is reaching out to us in love for a relationship through His Son.

As we pursue justice and God's principles in law and public policy, we are *laying the circuitry for spiritual life.*

Through the revelation of His character and principles through nature and conscience, God invites us to take faith steps. Those faith steps, perhaps at first taken unaware of God's Word, form a trail that leads to the explicit Gospel, to a relationship with God through Jesus Christ.

To facilitate this process, we adopt a biblical worldview that encompasses public policy and determine to courageously encounter our culture with kingdom principles. We seek to serve as ambassadors of Jesus Christ in love, winsomely and encouragingly engaging our friends and neighbors.

Recognizing that we must portray the character of Christ while advancing godly values, we lead with good deeds, which helps others accept our words. We realize that in taking on this ministry as Christ did, we have no guarantee of earthly success, only of persecution and challenges that test our faith and our will to persevere.

If we do persevere, if we do remain faithful, if we do imitate Christ in His service and in His sufferings, then we stand to reap great reward–most notably the company in heaven of those whom we have helped find the way.

# Index

## A

abolition, 24, 130, 134, 139, 242, 244, 250, 254, 255, 256, 257, 259, 264
abortion, iii, 7, 26, 65, 66, 67, 97, 99, 100, 101, 102, 103, 104, 107, 110, 111, 112, 113, 114, 135, 136, 137, 138, 139, 153, 154, 155, 156, 157, 158, 160, 162, 164, 165, 168, 196, 218, 219, 220, 230, 235, 240
Abraham, 16, 43, 44, 62, 64, 70, 179, 186, 187, 188, 208, 211, 212
accreditation, 171
Adams, John, 183, 197
adoption, 171, 172
AIDS/HIV, 5, 11, 12, 21, 89, 116, 131, 133, 135, 136, 160, 161, 162, 233, 234
Akin, Todd, 111, 113
Allen, Claude, ii, 1, 10, 131, 132
American Center for Law and Justice, 135
American College of Obstetrics and Gynecologists, 114, 154, 155
Anderson, Ryan T., 121, 122, 173
Aristotle, 25
assisted suicide, iii, 7, 9, 78, 84, 85, 240
Athanasius of Alexandria, 255
Augustine, 179, 184, 185, 186, 212, 213, 225, 226
autonomy, 19, 21, 23, 24, 26, 27, 84, 156
Avdyeitch, Martuin, 47, 48, 49, 53

## B

Baker, John, 193
Barna Group, 199, 223
Barrows, Jeff, 3
Barrows, Jeffrey, 11, 139
Beckett Fund, 166

benefits, 12, 69, 71, 73, 74, 78, 82, 84, 85, 120, 124, 125, 126, 158, 163, 167, 172, 212, 213, 234, 235, 253
Bessette, Christopher, 267, 268
Bolthouse, William and Laurie, 142, 267
Bomberger, Ryan, 112, 113
Bottum, Joseph, 121, 122
Bowman, Matt, ii
Boy Scouts, 170
Brannon, Ashley, ii
Brantly, Kent, 231, 232
British Empire, 241, 254, 258, 259
Brownback, Sam, 79
Burke, Denise, 102
Bush, President George W., 1, 2, 3, 9, 10, 11, 118, 131, 133, 134, 141
Butler, Rhett, ii

## C

Calvin, John, 186, 211, 212
Capitol Hill Pregnancy Center, 114
Care Net, 113
Carlson-Thies, Stanley, ii
Carter, Jimmy, 62
Casey, Sam, ii
Catholic Charities, 169
Catholic Relief Services, 233
Cheshire, William, 107
Christensen, Autumn, ii
Christian Medical Association, 4, 9, 134, 139, 142, 153, 154
Christiansen, David, ii
Civil Rights Act, 10, 174, 265
Clapham sect, 199, 245, 264
cloning, 115, 116, 118, 119, 120, 124, 125
Colby, Kim, ii
Colson, Charles, 7, 179, 185, 189, 212, 213, 253, 254
Concerned Women for America, 134

condom, 6, 23, 88, 89, 90, 91, 136, 161, 205

conscience, iii, 30, 31, 32, 33, 34, 42, 73, 108, 110, 151, 152, 154, 156, 157, 158, 159, 161, 164, 165, 167, 171, 180, 188, 193, 194, 196, 197, 199, 235, 236, 250, 253, 258, 262, 269

consequences, 22, 23, 27, 30, 34, 57, 58, 59, 60, 68, 69, 71, 72, 73, 74, 86, 95, 125, 126, 235, 249

Constitution, 17, 25, 26, 27, 63, 64, 65, 67, 79, 100, 101, 151, 159, 183, 191, 194, 196, 197, 198, 200, 235, 264, 265

*contra mundum*, 256

contraceptives, 93, 99, 162, 163, 164, 165, 166

Conway, Kellyanne, 157

Cowper, William, 245, 248

creation, 16, 18, 30, 31, 32, 33, 74, 105, 187, 220, 266

Crick, Francis, 123

culture, ii, 6, 7, 8, 9, 12, 14, 15, 16, 17, 31, 32, 34, 42, 65, 67, 85, 88, 108, 113, 115, 168, 171, 174, 198, 199, 201, 214, 219, 221, 224, 225, 228, 237, 244, 245, 258, 259, 262, 263, 264, 265, 266, 267, 268, 269

## D

Darwinism, 26, 31

daughter test, 24, 25

Declaration of Independence, 17, 63, 64, 100, 196

discrimination, 155, 171

DNA, 30, 118, 119, 123, 124

Doerflinger, Richard, ii

Doherty, Katie, ii

Donovan, Chuck, ii

*Dred Scott*, 64, 65, 109, 110

DuBois, Joshua, 158

Dybul, Mark, 12, 131

Dylan, Bob, 17

## E

Elijah, prophet, 50, 236, 237

embryo, 30, 106, 107, 116, 117, 118, 120, 124, 125, 163, 173, 205, 217, 240, 262

Episcopal Church, 133

equal rights, 68, 194

Equiano, Olaudah, 245, 250

establishment clause, 63, 193

Establishment Clause, 160

Estrada, Will, ii

euthanasia, 78, 79, 80, 81, 82, 83, 84, 85

Evangelical Lutheran Church in America, 143, 144

evangelism, 202, 204, 209, 210, 222, 251, 269

Everett, Carol, 100, 101

## F

faith-based, 6, 7, 12, 13, 19, 27, 84, 139, 147, 148, 155, 157, 158, 159, 161, 162, 164, 166, 231, 232, 233

Family Research Council, 112, 134, 152

Farley, Melissa, 22, 23

FDA, 89, 90, 163

First Amendment, 134, 135, 151, 158, 160, 162, 164, 165, 191, 192, 193, 194, 195, 196, 198, 200

Focus on the Family, 12, 134

Ford, Leslie, ii

Forgette, Jeannine, 39

Fourteenth Amendment, 65, 109, 195, 265

Fox, Charles, 255

France, 185, 192, 203, 229, 255, 257, 259

Franklin, Benjamin, 183, 197

free exercise of religion, 63, 151, 160, 164, 190, 191, 192, 193, 194, 195, 196, 198, 200, 235, 262

French, 183, 185, 188, 203, 259

## G

Gallup polling, 18, 120, 217, 218
Garcia, Joxel, ii
Gerberding, Julie, 12, 13, 132
Gerson, Michael, 2, 132
Goeglein, Tim, ii
Goosby, Eric, 161
Gosnell, Kermit, 102, 103
grants, 5, 6, 93, 120, 122, 135, 137, 138, 139, 171
Great Commission, 3, 14, 209, 210
Grossu, Arina, ii

## H

Harder, Cherie, ii
harm, iii, 6, 11, 23, 24, 68, 69, 71, 73, 74, 84, 88, 130, 144, 154, 225, 234
harm reduction, 6, 23, 24, 130
Hawkins, Matthew, ii
Hayley, Katherine, ii
Heartbeat International, 113, 114
Heritage Foundation, 169, 170, 172
Hill, Kent, 12
*Hobby Lobby* case, 166, 211
Homeland Security, Dept. of, 133, 136, 137, 144, 148
homosexual, 12, 167, 170, 223, 234
*Hosanna-Tabor* case, 159
Hoss. *See* Hostetler, Ron
Hoss (Hostetler, Ron), 40, 41
Hostetler, Ron, 40
Huber, Valerie, ii
Hughes, Donna M., 134
Hurlbut, William, 124, 125

## I

Imbody, Amy, ii, 265
intelligent design, 30
International Justice Mission, 143

## J

Jacobinism, 259
Jefferson, Thomas, 64, 191, 192, 197, 198, 235
John the Baptist, 33, 105, 218, 220, 225
Johnson, Douglas, ii
Joyce, James, 152

## K

Kelly, Mike, 139
King, Alveda, 113
King, Martin Luther Jr., 113, 265
kingdom of God, 54, 55, 56, 58, 185, 230, 253, 254
Kinnaman, David, 223, 224, 225
Kitchens, Trevor, 153, 154
Koop, C. Everett, 131
Kuyper, Abraham, 16, 179, 186, 187, 188, 211, 212

## L

Lahl, Jennifer, 120
Lanza, Robert, 119
Lederer, Laura, ii, 4, 130, 146
Levatino, Anthony, 103, 104
LGBT, 169
Lincoln, Abraham, 59, 64
Lisa Thompson, ii, 20
Live Action, 101
Lorien Wood school, 265, 266
Lyons, Gabe, 223, 224, 225

## M

Madison, James, 183, 192, 195, 196, 267
Magna Carta, 151
Mahaney, C.J., 13
Maki, Natalie, ii
Manetto, Nick, ii

marriage, 21, 22, 24, 32, 66, 73, 80, 88, 94, 98, 143, 167, 168, 169, 171, 172, 205, 206, 217, 218, 220, 224, 230

Mars Hill address, 262

Marshall, Jennifer, ii

Marshner, Connie, ii

Martin, David, 40, 41

Mattox, Casey, ii

Mayhew, Jonathan, 181, 182, 264

McConchie, Dan, 102

McCormack, Lauren, ii

McCorvey, Norma, 101

McFarland, Steve, ii

McIlhaney, Joe, 3

Mennonite, 38, 40, 201, 202, 214

Messner, Thomas, 169, 170, 171

Metaxas, Eric, 241

Michelman, Kate, 99

Monahan-Mancini, Jeanne, ii

More, Hannah, 245, 246

Moses, 10, 33, 69, 70, 72, 73, 78, 106, 180, 207

Moses, Michael, ii

Mourdock, Richard, 111, 112

**N**

Napolitano, Janet, 136

Nathan, Debbie, 21

National Association of Evangelicals, 134

National Institute of Family & Life Advocates, 114

Netherlands, 78, 79, 82, 83

Newton, John, 241

Niemoller, Martin, 235

Nixon, Richard, 7, 189

nones - religiously non-affiliated, 229

**O**

Obama, Barack, 11, 66, 93, 102, 135, 136, 137, 138, 151, 152, 157, 158, 159, 160, 161, 162, 164, 165, 166, 169, 171, 174, 214, 224

Obamacare, 66, 137, 162, 163, 166, 167

O'Dea, Mike, ii

originalist view, 26, 193

**P**

Paine, Thomas, 264

Paprocki, Anna, 102

Pearcey, Nancy, 15, 16

Penn State, 8, 13, 38, 40

Pew Research, 166, 229, 230

Pitt, William, 243, 255, 257

Planned Parenthood, 100, 101, 133

Plato, 25

Pledge of Allegiance, 65

polling, 18, 120, 157, 165, 166, 198, 199, 217, 218

Pope Paul VI, 163

pornography, 20, 67, 128, 136, 142, 144

pregnancy centers, 100, 113, 135, 232

Prentice, David, ii

President's Council on Bioethics, 118, 124, 125

prostitution, 4, 5, 11, 21, 22, 23, 24, 67, 128, 133, 134, 135, 136, 142, 241

**R**

Randolph, Raymond, 135

rape, 21, 22, 23, 111, 112, 113

Reagan, Ronald, 122

Redemptive Education, 265, 266

Reiter, Erica, ii

Reitsema, Henk, 83, 84

Religious freedom, 64, 196

revelation, iii, 26, 31, 32, 33, 34, 41, 43, 60, 82, 84, 91, 123, 189, 269

right to life, 65, 68, 100, 109, 198

Roberts, John, 159

Rodgers, Mark, 244

*Roe v Wade*, 66, 99, 100, 101, 108, 109, 110, 111, 169

Roman Empire, 184, 240, 259

Roosevelt, Theodore, 261

Rousseau, Jean Jacques, 261

rule of law, 25, 26, 63, 68, 69, 268

Rush, Sarah, 39

Ryan Anderson, 172

# S

salvation, 43, 134, 143, 148, 173, 232

Salvation Army, 134, 143, 148, 173, 232

Samaritan Women, 143

Samaritan's Purse, 9, 231, 232

Saunders, Bill, 102

Scalia, Antonin, 26, 135

Scanlan, Teresa, 94

Schaeffer, Francis, 33

Schleppenbach, Jacqueline Halbig, ii

Schmidt, Jean, 101

SCNT. *See* cloning

Sebelius, Kathleen, 137, 162, 166

self-interest, 69, 70, 73, 74, 158

separation of Church and state, 3

sex, 1, 4, 5, 6, 11, 20, 21, 22, 23, 24, 32, 66, 73, 86, 87, 88, 89, 90, 91, 92, 93, 94, 95, 97, 101, 127, 128, 130, 133, 134, 135, 136, 140, 143, 144, 167, 169, 170, 171, 172, 205, 217, 218, 220, 224, 230, 235, 267

Sexual risk avoidance, 86

Sharp, Granville, 245, 248

slavery, 1, 11, 22, 64, 65, 67, 68, 127, 128, 137, 139, 140, 196, 221, 232, 242, 244, 245, 246, 247, 248, 249, 254, 255, 256, 257, 258, 259, 264, 267

slaves, 3, 21, 64, 121, 180, 241, 242, 248, 249, 254, 256

Smith, Anita, ii

Smith, Mailee, 102

Smith, Shepherd, ii, 184, 233

somatic cell nuclear transfer. *See* cloning

*Somerset v. Stewart* case, 248

Sorvino, Mira, 142, 143, 268

Southern Baptist, 134, 211

Steiger, Bill, 12

stem cells, iii, 116, 117, 119, 120, 121, 122, 124, 125, 126, 173, 204, 205, 206, 217, 262

Stevens, David, 8

students, 71, 86, 88, 135, 153, 155, 156, 170, 171, 173, 232

Sunshine, Glen, 184

Supreme Court, 10, 26, 64, 99, 101, 108, 109, 135, 151, 159, 166, 168, 169, 171, 172, 195

# T

testimony, 79, 84, 86, 93, 94, 99, 103, 104, 227, 242, 254, 257

Tocqueville, Alexis de, 183, 203

*Today's Christian Doctor*, 107, 108

Tolstoy, Leo, 47

Torre, Sarah, ii

*Trade of Innocents* film, 143, 267, 268

trafficking, human, iii, 1, 3, 4, 5, 10, 11, 12, 13, 20, 21, 22, 23, 24, 25, 27, 101, 127, 128, 129, 130, 131, 132, 133, 134, 135, 136, 137, 138, 139, 140, 141, 142, 143, 144, 145, 146, 147, 160, 232, 267, 268, 269

Transport for Christ, 143

Triple S Network, 143

Tryfiates, P. George, ii

# U

ultrasound, 107, 108

*UnChristian* book, 223, 224

United Nations, 142

US Conf. Catholic Bishops, 138

## V

Ventimiglia, Vince Jr., ii
virtue, 17, 59, 68, 183, 186, 252

## W

Walberg, Tim, 139
Walsh, Brian, ii
Washington, George, 68, 183, 197
Watson, James, 123
Wedgwood, Josiah, 245, 246
Weiss, Rick, 173
Wesley, John / Charles, 117, 241, 248, 249, 255, 256
White House, 1, 5, 6, 7, 10, 11, 12, 13, 130, 131, 132, 134, 141, 152, 158, 174
Whitfield, George, 241
Wichterman, Bill, ii, 244, 245
Wilberforce, William, 7, 139, 241, 242, 243, 244, 245, 247, 251, 252, 253, 254, 255, 256, 257, 258, 259, 264

*Windsor* case, 169, 171, 172
Wolsey, Cardinal, 228
World Hope International, 134, 143
*World* magazine, 231
World Relief, 134, 143
World Vision, 232
worldview, 2, 7, 14, 15, 16, 17, 18, 19, 20, 21, 22, 23, 24, 25, 26, 27, 65, 67, 133, 157, 158, 219, 269
Wright, Wendy, ii

## Y

Yoest, Jack and Charmaine, ii

## Z

Zaccheus, 44, 57
Zylicz, Zbigniew, 79

Made in the USA
Middletown, DE
25 October 2015